THE SUCCESSFUL
MARKETING PLAN

THE SUCCESSFUL MARKETING PLAN

A Disciplined and Comprehensive Approach

ROMAN G. HIEBING, JR.

SCOTT W. COOPER

NTC Business Books
a division of *NTC Publishing Group* • Lincolnwood, Illinois USA

1994 Printing

Published by NTC Business Books, a division of NTC Publishing Group.
© 1990 by NTC Publishing Group, 4255 West Touhy Avenue,
Lincolnwood (Chicago), Illinois 60646-1975 U.S.A.

Library of Congress Catalog Card Number: 89-62907

4 5 6 7 8 9 VP 9 8 7

FOREWORD

I know the authors of this book well. They've worked on projects for my brands, and I've guest lectured for their business school classes at the University of Wisconsin. So I speak from firsthand experience when I say readers of this book will get the real thing: Straight from the shoulder, Straight from real business life, This is how you do it! What Scott and Roman show you how to do in this book is exactly what they do for their own clients. Every day. And it works. This book gives you the information base, the insights, and the methodology to write a solid marketing plan that, properly executed, will get results.

I've been exposed to many marketing plans in my own career which includes running my own small business, managing multimillion dollar Kimberly-Clark and Procter & Gamble brands, and a stint managing retail, package goods, and franchise accounts for one of the country's largest advertising agencies. And, this book is the best all-around marketing planning tool I've seen, because it speaks to the needs of both the entrepreneur and the director of a traditional, structured marketing department.

But the best part of this book is its practical yet comprehensive approach. It doesn't just talk about what your marketing plan should include, it literally takes you by the hand and walks you through it, step-by-step. It takes what can seem an overwhelmingly complex process and breaks the task into manageable parts, providing an easy-to-follow path to completion of your successful marketing plan.

I believe that with this book as a guide any intelligent, persevering person—regardless of experience level—can write an effective marketing plan. Even with over 20 years of marketing planning experience behind me, this book gave me ideas for innovative but executable marketing methods.

Paul Geisler
Group President
Kimberly-Clark Corporation

PREFACE

Reasons and Goals for This Book

There is a growing emphasis on marketing planning in both the private and public sectors and an increasing number of books that discuss marketing planning. That not withstanding, it is our belief that a growing need exists for one definitive source that explains clearly, simply, and pragmatically *how to* prepare a marketing plan in a *disciplined* and *comprehensive* manner; a source that can be used as a planning guide by the inexperienced marketer and as a reference piece on planning by the experienced marketer.

While this *how to* on marketing planning is not meant to be a scholarly piece (although we believe in academia and teach part time in the School of Business at the University of Wisconsin), it is meant to be an easy to use, actionable resource from which to write a marketing plan that really does work. A marketing plan developed using principles in this book works because the disciplined planning process is based on proven marketing principles and many years of actual experience. We believe in the book's marketing methodology not just because we are the authors of the book but because we use the same planning methods every day to help market our clients' products and services, in our consulting firm, and in our own personal entrepreneurial endeavors. And it works because this approach forces us to do it the right way. You will find as we have, if you do it by this book, your marketing plan with the proper execution will dramatically increase the level of success for your product or service.

While the vast majority of what is presented in this book is based on hard factual data, we've included personal experiences, observations, and opinions. For these we take full responsibility. Likewise, any errors are our own.

Acknowledgments

From Both of Us

We would first like to thank all those wonderful people not specifically mentioned here who had a hand in making this book a reality. A big thank you to our fellow staff members at The Hiebing Group, particularly our partners, for their support and understanding as we ran a business with them along with writing a book. A special thank you to the clerical staff for word processing this piece more times than anyone cares to remember.

Individually, we would like to acknowledge the following staff members for their support as we wrote this book:

- Michael Rothschild, one of our original partners, for first putting us together with Harry Briggs (then with Crain Books/NTC Business Books), for warning us what a devouring task authoring a book really is, for editing major portions of this book, and for giving us the opportunity to draw upon his advertising and marketing communications books as we developed ours.

- Our partners, Sheila Dorton, Mike Kelly, and Marion Michaels who helped make this book more interesting and understandable to read; Dick Kallstrom and Bob Martin for providing concept ideas for the cover; and Michael Pratzel's valuable insights regarding market research.

- Sandy Weisberger and Michael Tobin for reading portions of this book and providing valuable insights.

- Former students Am Curet and Jim Andrews who, after paying their dues getting real world experience in the big Chicago advertising agencies, returned to Madison, Wisconsin to become part of our staff and provided considerable input as we prepared this book.

Also, we don't want to forget staff members no longer with us who might not be totally aware of their valuable input for this book. Thank you Doug McCoy now with Chiat/Day in San Francisco and Mike Gramling, formerly of J. Walter Thompson and Tatham-Laird & Kudner in Chicago—who is enviably traveling the country, possibly the world. Not professing to being the greatest writers in the world, we greatly appreciate the assistance from Barbara Walsh, Liz Cooper, and Doris Hill in editing our work, making it easier to read, and helping keep it to a manageable number of pages.

We would like to thank the following practitioners for taking time from their busy schedules to read the first manuscript and give valuable feedback in the preparation of subsequent manuscript drafts and of the finished product. Their varied experiences with different types and sizes of organizations especially helped make this book a practical resource for everyone with an interest in, or need for marketing planning methods.

Kevin Blodgett, Marketing Director, Famous Footwear

Jim Bradley, Jr., President, Home Savings and Loan

R. S. Fountaine, Vice President Market Research, Kimberly-Clark Corporation

Paul Geisler, Vice President, Kimberly-Clark Corporation

Richard Goedjen, Partner, Brat und Brau Restaurants

Michael Kern, Director Media Services, Kentucky Fried Chicken Corporation

John F. Kuypers, Vice President Marketing, W. T. Rogers Company

Donald Piepenburg, Director of Corporate Communications, Wisconsin Power & Light

Erik Risman, President, Étage, a Specialty Retailing Company of Brown Group, Inc.

Tony Sanna, Vice President Marketing, Saco Foods

Tim J. Warner, Manager Marketing and Business Development, Stanford University Medical Center

We also want to thank Harry M. Briggs, former manager of Crain Books/NTC Business Books for giving us the opportunity to write this book and providing valuable suggestions in subsequent drafts of the manuscript.

We also cannot overlook saying thank you to our students with whom we first tested this book in manuscript form, giving us the opportunity to improve its usefulness in the classroom. Their many suggestions improved its worth as a teaching tool.

Finally, we want to thank all our clients who believed in us over the years and gave us the opportunity to apply again and again (in whole or part) our marketing methodology to their organizations. They provided us with valuable learning experiences and continually challenged us to develop innovative marketing programs that delivered results.

From Scott

There are many people to thank for their assistance in this project. First and foremost I thank my family. My wife, Liz, who encouraged me to undertake this project, pushed me when I didn't feel like writing anymore, and throughout the past ten years has remained my best friend and confidant. To our four sons, Seth, Birk, Reed, and Cale (who was born in the midst of the third draft) for giving me the excuse to grow up all over again, keep my enthusiasm, and see the world in an entirely different light. To my favorite in-laws who bailed me out time and time again by coming to help Liz when I was virtually working and writing around the clock. And finally, to my parents who have always encouraged but never pushed.

A special thanks goes to Margaret Hiebing. On some of those long days with Roman writing, discussing, writing, and rewriting some more, Margaret's upbeat attitude and fantastic cooking was definitely the most positive experience I had.

Finally a huge thanks goes to Roman Hiebing. I have had the opportunity to work closely with Roman for the past seven years. I've known few people who are as smart, work as hard, and care as much. Roman's childlike belief in honesty, and his appreciation of each person's talents has created an environment which allows individuals to live up to their potential. I consider Roman a teacher, my mentor, a pain in the ass, one of my best friends, and business partner. Above all, he's the one other person I know who is crazy enough to take over two years to write a book—and still think it was one of the best experiences of his life.

From Roman

I personally have many many friends, colleagues, and family members to thank for helping me over the years and who directly or indirectly had a hand in making this book possible.

Thank you to my two mentors. Harry Dean Wolfe (now deceased), who was my major professor in graduate school at the University of Wisconsin, from whom I learned that theory and practice are *both* necessary. Harry was instrumental in my taking a first job out of school with the Leo Burnett Advertising Agency in Chicago. And thanks to Rogers W. Zarling, entrepreneur extraordinaire, who from my boyhood to adulthood taught me business by what he called the best school, "the school of hard knocks."

Thank you to the Leo Burnett agency for instilling in me true advertising ideals and the quest for the best.

Thank you to all the McDonald's people that I have worked with over the years for what they taught me and for the confidence they placed in me, specifically Kathy Henry, now in Frankfurt, Germany, handling the marketing for McDonald's Systems of Europe.

Thank you to Brian Cook, friend and President of Famous Footwear, who helped me complete this book by continually badgering me, asking, "When are you going to get that damn book done?"

Thank you to my brothers, Al and Dick, partners with me in a group of restaurants, for giving me the opportunity to try new things. In most cases they had to make the new ideas work and pay for them.

Thank you to my parents. To my father, Roman, for teaching me to "finish what I started" and "if you are going to do something, make sure you do it right the first time." To my mother, Charlotte, for encouraging me "to go for it" and to take the chance to try something new.

Thank you to my wife, Margaret, for her understanding and constant support, who has sacrificed many vacations and weekends because she (thank God) accepts my need for a continual challenge.

Finally, thank you to Scott, my friend, partner, and the best coauthor anyone could ever have, whose wife encouraged him while he pushed me to do this book. And we did it. Because we know there is a better way.

Roman G. Hiebing, Jr.
Scott W. Cooper

Contents

Contents xiii

THE SUCCESSFUL
MARKETING PLAN

INTRODUCTION

The purpose of this book is to provide you with a detailed step-by-step guide for preparing your own marketing plan. This is not a discussion of marketing theory, but a book with real world answers to help you meet head-on specific marketing challenges, whatever your level of marketing expertise or the size and type of your organization. In addition, you will find this book not only a realistic guide to preparing a marketing plan, but a very useful reference resource that will help you find the marketing solutions on an everyday basis.

What the Reader Can Expect

This book provides a comprehensive approach to writing a marketing plan—from describing what background information is necessary and how to analyze it, to writing the marketing plan specifics and evaluating the results of the plan.

Whatever the marketing challenge, this how-to approach will have direct application because it is based on proven marketing principles and hundreds of real business experiences. A wide variety of actual examples, drawn from the authors' experiences, have been included to help the reader understand the marketing principles and the step-by-step marketing plan development process.

This book focuses primarily on the most important part of any marketing program—on the *preparation of a marketing plan*, not the implementation. It includes helpful planning and research tools; it does *not* dwell on specific execution.

The authors have found that if a marketer takes the necessary time and makes the required effort to prepare an effective marketing plan, arriving at the actual executional elements is the easy part—as they flow naturally from the strategic framework of the marketing plan. In our opinion, far too often marketing failures are the result of marketing executions that were *not* rooted in a well thought out marketing plan prepared in a disciplined fashion.

Disciplined Marketing Planning

The key to writing an effective marketing plan is disciplined marketing planning. However, before defining disciplined marketing planning, it is necessary first to describe what is a *marketing plan*. And, we will describe it by defining each word separately. In this book we define *marketing* as the process of determining the target market for your product or service, detailing the target market's needs and wants, and then fulfilling these needs and wants better than the competition. The *plan* is an arranged structure to guide this process.

1

Disciplined marketing planning is a sequential, interlocking, step-by-step decision and action process. In using this disciplined approach you follow a prescribed logical pattern so that you define issues, answer questions correctly, and make decisions. Each major step, as depicted by a box on the disciplined marketing planning chart in Exhibit I.1, should be completed before going on to the next. Further, each major step is broken down into individual, ordered steps providing a clear and efficient road map for preparing an effective marketing plan.

The disciplined approach, although initially more time consuming, dramatically increases the chances of your product's or service's success, because the marketing plan prepared in this manner is just that—totally planned. It is a databased plan that is very encompassing, yet feasible to execute.

How the Planning Process Works

Disciplined marketing planning has two major components. The *first*, marketing background, includes the business review, commonly referred to as a situation analysis, and problems and opportunities segments. The business review is a comprehensive analysis of the marketplace and of your own organization broken down into sequentially ordered sections; the problem and opportunities segment is a summary of challenges emerging from the business review. The *second* major component is the marketing plan itself, which is developed from the information gathered and analyzed in the marketing background section. The marketing plan is totally inclusive, beginning in sequential order with the sales objectives and ending with a budget and calendar of marketing activities necessary to realize the sales objectives.

Once the plan is prepared, it must be executed and then evaluated. And, though evaluation is the last step in the process, with it begins anew the whole disciplined approach, as evaluation becomes a major part of the background section in the preparation of next year's marketing plan. In this book each element within the marketing background and plan sections, along with the evaluation process, is discussed in detail.

How to Use This Book in Your Marketing Planning

We recommend that before you begin writing your marketing plan, you read through the entire book to understand the complete process and all that goes into preparing a comprehensive marketing plan. Next, as you actually prepare your own marketing plan, go through each chapter again and very diligently attempt to follow the step-by-step disciplined marketing planning process as presented in this book.

As you use the disciplined marketing planning process, keep in mind that while you should understand the basic marketing principles provided throughout this book and follow the recommended methodology, you can adapt the review and planning process to best fit your product or marketing situation. The point to remember is that you want to be open minded and innovative, but also methodical and consistent as you prepare the marketing background section and write the marketing plan.

As you go through the whole process, you will come up with all types of ideas for different areas of the actual marketing plan that might not relate to the specific section of the plan you are currently writing. Don't lose these ideas, because they will be very helpful when you prepare the particular section to which they apply. As you prepare the background section and the marketing plan itself, have separate sheets of paper handy with headings of problems, opportunities, and each step of the marketing plan (including a separate sheet of paper for each marketing mix tool) under which you can jot down relevant ideas as they occur to you. Don't evaluate the worth of each idea as you think of it, but jot it down. Evaluate its application as you actually write the section of the marketing plan to which it pertains.

Also keep in mind that many of the principles, procedures, and examples provided in this book will have application to your particular marketing situation even though

Exhibit I.1   Disciplined Marketing Planning

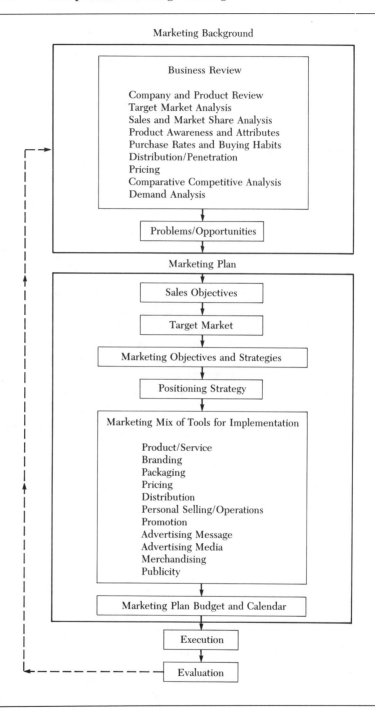

it has not been written just for your specific product or service. In fact, this book is written for broad application by the marketer of a consumer/package goods product, business-to-business product, service, or retail outlet(s) with a private, public, or nonprofit organization. For simplicity and brevity, however, the word *product* is usually used throughout this book in generic planning discussions for whatever is to be marketed. When there is specific reference to consumer or business-to-business products, services, or retail, it will be singled out accordingly.

While this book does not deal directly with execution in terms of writing a newspaper ad or buying a radio schedule, you will find the "Idea Starters by Marketing Situation" grid. This unique marketing idea grid includes hundreds of business building idea starters, categorized by most common marketing situations and presented separately for each marketing mix tool—from product, branding, and packaging to advertising, merchandising, and publicity. This grid section, located in Appendix A at the back of the book, can be of major assistance to the reader who is beginning to develop the actual marketing plan and its executions.

The Marketing Plan Takes Time to Prepare and Continually Changes

Writing a comprehensive marketing plan based on a thorough marketing background document is a time consuming project, particularly if it has not been done before. Therefore, it is wise to begin the disciplined marketing planning process far enough in advance of when the plan is due. It seems to take twice the time originally estimated to prepare a complete marketing plan. To do it right, you can estimate 50 to 100 hours, *or more*, to prepare the marketing background section, and half this number of hours to prepare the first draft of the marketing plan section. Although the background section is usually the most demanding, without this database you have no real objective source from which to make your current and future marketing decisions.

As a side note, you will find that updating this background data and revising a marketing plan year to year is considerably less time consuming and easier than gathering the initial background information and writing the first marketing plan. This is particularly true if the initial marketing background section is prepared in a thorough and comprehensive manner.

Once you have completed the background section, you will be continually revising the marketing plan as you write the first draft, reworking elements in the marketing plan so they effectively interface with each other. Once the plan is written, you must allow adequate time to review the plan, make major changes, and rework the fine points. The time and rewriting is necessary to arrive at a marketing plan that is comprehensive, understandable, supportable, implementable, and in the end, successful.

MARKETING
BACKGROUND

THE BUSINESS
REVIEW.

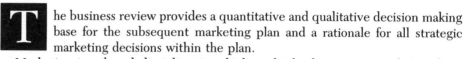

T he business review provides a quantitative and qualitative decision making base for the subsequent marketing plan and a rationale for all strategic marketing decisions within the plan.

Marketing is a broad discipline in which multiple desicions must be made—decisions such as which customers should be targeted, through what specific combination of product features, with what price, through what distribution channels, with what type of service, and via what type of communication. However, these decisions cannot be made without a systematic review of all known facts. The business review provides these facts so that sound decision making can be achieved.

From This Chapter You Will Learn

Suggestions for preparing a business review.

How to develop an outline to use as a roadmap for completing your business review.

The ten major steps necessary to complete a business review.

How to utilize primary data (developed through your own company's research) and secondary data (existing in trade journals, government publications, etc.) in the development of your business review.

Where to find the information necessary to complete the charts and answer the questions in each step of the business review in Chapter 2.

OVERVIEW

This summary is intended to organize your work on the business review you develop in Chapter 2. Following these suggestions will save time and help create a more effective database from which to make decisions.

A well developed business review should be utilized as a daily reference piece. Each year, your business review should be updated to reflect the most recent changes in your industry and company. Therefore, if this is your first business review, don't be overwhelmed. If you don't have time to complete all sections, work on those that most affect your business. Then, next year, update those sections and further complete some of the others which you didn't have time for previously.

Completing the business review can be more than a one-person job. Request assistance from other people in your company to help compile the information. The step-by-step process of completing the business review in Chapter 2 allows for a marketer to easily manage the information gathering process.

Follow the suggestions listed below, paying particular attention to those steps of the business review that have greatest impact on your business.

Suggestion 1
Prepare an Outline

Always start by developing a written outline. The outline should be as specific as possible, covering each major area of the business review. This outline of steps to be covered in a business review helps you stay focused and ensures that critical data needed for actionable marketing plans will be obtained in a disciplined and sequential process. The outline serves as an overview for what is presented in Chapter 2. Each section is a step with topical points discussed and explained so the reader has a full understanding of how to develop this information for use in the marketing plan. An example of what the outline of your own business review should look like follows.

Step 1   Corporate philosophy/description of the company and products
   A.   Corporate goals and objectives
   B.   General company and product history
   C.   Organizational chart
Step 2   Review of the consumer target market
   A.   Demographics
      1.   Sex
      2.   Age
      3.   Income
      4.   Education
      5.   Occupation
      6.   Family/household size
      7.   Region/geography
      8.   Lifestyle factors
      9.   Demographic measures: volume versus concentration
      10.   Demographic measures: national category versus company/product target market
   B.   Product usage
   C.   Heavy users
   D.   Potential primary and secondary target markets
Step 3   Review of the business-to-business target market
   A.   Target market segmentation and Standard Industrial Classifications (SIC) categories
   B.   Other methods of segmenting
      1.   Dollar size
      2.   Employee size
      3.   Heavy usage rates
      4.   Product application/use
      5.   Organization structure
      6.   New versus repeat buyer

       7. Geographic location

       8. Decision makers and influencers

Step 4 Sales analysis

  A. Reference points of data for comparison purposes

     1. Company sales compared to previous years

     2. Company sales compared to the industry or product category nationally

     3. Company sales compared to the top two or three major competitors

  B. Sales data

     1. Total sales

     2. Sales by brand or department

     3. Market share

     4. Store-for-store sales for retailers

     5. Seasonality of sales

     6. Sales by geographic territory/target market segments

Step 5 Product awareness and attributes

  A. Product awareness

  B. Product attributes

  C. Product life cycle

     1. Introduction phase

     2. Growth phase

     3. Maturity phase

Step 6 Purchase rates/buying habits

  A. Purchase rates of the product category and your company's product by geographic markets

     1. Category Development Index (CDI)

     2. Brand Development Index (BDI)

  B. Trading areas

  C. Brand loyalty

  D. Buying habits

  E. Trial and retrial

Step 7 Distribution

  A. Retail

     1. Channel type/trends

     2. Geography

     3. Penetration

  B. Package goods

     1. Channel type/trends

     2. Market coverage/all commodity volume percentage

     3. Shelf space

     4. Geography

     5. Sales method

  C. Business-to-business

     1. Channel type/trends

     2. Geography

     3. Personal selling method

        D.   Service firms
           1.   Type of office
           2.   Geography
           3.   Penetration

Step 8   Pricing
        A.   Price of your product relative to the competition
        B.   Distribution of sales by price point relative to the competition
        C.   Price elasticity of your product

Step 9   Historical marketing review of your company versus the competition
        A.   Developing competitive information
           1.   Market share/sales
           2.   Target market
           3.   Marketing objectives and strategies
           4.   Product positioning
           5.   Product/branding/packaging strengths and weaknesses
           6.   Pricing
           7.   Distribution/store penetration/market coverage
           8.   Personal selling
           9.   Promotion
          10.   Advertising message
          11.   Media strategy and expenditures
          12.   Customer service
          13.   Merchandising
          14.   Publicity
          15.   Testing/marketing R&D
        B.   Summary of strengths and weaknesses of your company and major competitors

Step 10   Demand analysis
        A.   How to estimate demand for your product
           1.   Target market
           2.   Geographical territory
           3.   Consumption constraints
           4.   Average purchase per year per customer
           5.   Total purchase per year in category
           6.   Average price
           7.   Total dollar purchases
           8.   Company's market share of purchases
           9.   Additional factors affecting demand

Suggestion 2
Develop Questions

List questions which need to be answered for each section of the business review outline. The questions will provide direction in determining what specific information you need to accumulate.

Suggestion 3
Develop Data Charts

Develop data charts with headings to help structure your search for relevant information. When completed, the charts should enable you to answer the major questions included in Chapter 2 pertaining to each step of the business review outline.

Organize the headings and columns of the charts first to determine what information needs to be found prior to the data search. This forces you to look for data and numbers that will provide meaningful information. Remember, if you look for data before developing your charts, you may tend to construct the charts around what is easy to find, not what should be found.

Suggestion 4

Develop Reference Points for Comparisons

Always develop charts that have reference points for comparison so that the data are actionable. If you state sales growth for your company, provide sales growth for the industry. In this manner, the company's sales growth can be judged against a reference point. And whenever possible, include five-year trend information so that the current year's performance can be judged relative to past years' performance.

Suggestion 5

Conduct Data Search

Institute a disciplined data search. Stay focused on what needs to be found by constantly reviewing your outline. This will allow you to feel confident that you have compiled all existing data necessary to complete your charts.

Suggestion 6

Write Summary Statements

After the charts have been completed, write brief statements summarizing the major findings and answering the questions you developed in Suggestion 2. Include summary rationale when needed. Keep it objective by strictly reporting the findings; don't provide solutions at this point. The business review is not for developing objectives and strategies. It is for providing facts from which to develop a marketing plan and to provide rationale for that plan.

Organizing the Business Review

The sections of the final written business review should be ordered in the same sequence as the steps developed in your outline. Each section should include summary statements followed by completed, detailed data charts.

Finally, write the marketing background and plan in the third person, being as objective as possible, not interjecting your own personal feelings that cannot be documented by fact. Write in a very clear, concise manner so there can be no misinterpretation of what is presented. Don't assume that everyone who reads the plan will have the same base of information as the writer; include all available information pertinent to the issues being discussed, so everyone reading the plan will have the same frame of reference.

CONDUCTING RESEARCH

In preparing your business review, data can be obtained through both primary and secondary research. If you employ a research firm, an advertising agency that conducts research, or an in-house research department, primary research is the most effective way of obtaining data specific to your market, your product, and your competitors. If you do not have access to a professional researcher, however, we recommend that you do not try to do primary research yourself but rely on secondary research—data compiled by outside sources.

The business review examples presented in Chapter 2 rely heavily on secondary research and your own company sales and marketing data to provide you with a marketing information base. We strongly recommend however, that if possible, both secondary and primary research be utilized in preparing a marketing data base and business review.

Primary Research

Original research compiled to meet your specific data requirements is broken down into two categories, quantitative and qualitative.

Quantitative Research

The data and information are usually obtained through surveys with data gathered from a representative random sample of a given universe. The samples are large enough to make inferences that are statistically significant. We refer to two types of quantitative research methods most often throughout this book. One is customer based research, which provides information about a company's own customers. The other is marketwide research, which is used to provide information about the overall category user/purchaser base.

Qualitative Research

Research methods, such as focus groups, that do not statistically represent the target market universe provide qualitative data. Qualitative research typically involves small groups of consumers who are asked to provide insights into their likes and dislikes of a particular product and why and how they purchase or use one type of product versus another. Qualitative research is also used to gain insights into the strengths and weaknesses of advertising and other forms of communication.

Qualitative research is used to add depth and richness to quantitative findings. For example, quantitative research may determine that a company has a perceived customer service problem relative to the competition. Qualitative research can be used to help further explain what consumers feel customer service entails in the company's particular industry and what specifically is lacking in the company's customer service compared to other companies.

Qualitative research can also be very useful in determining the key issues to include in a quantitative research study. Particularly if there has been no previous research, a company may want to utilize a focus group to provide added insights into consumer thinking prior to formulating a quantitative study. The information and insights gained from initial qualitative research can then be verified through quantitative, statistical research.

Finally, a word of caution. Used by itself, qualitative research can be very misleading. It is not statistically based; a roomful of 10 people is often a poor representation of what the marketplace really thinks. Qualitative research is most valuable when used as an enriching tool to quantitatively defined observations.

Secondary Research

Secondary research, which may also be quantitative or qualitative, is not specifically compiled for your company but rather is existing information, and is available through outside sources. An example of a secondary research source is census information. Combining this type of secondary research information with your company's data will allow you to develop insights into your customers, your market, and the problems and opportunities facing your company, just as is done with primary research. The only difference is that primary research is conducted to answer specific questions a company may have. To answer these questions with secondary research you may have to dig a little more and be willing to analyze multiple studies instead of just one to find your answers. And even then, sometimes you may not be able to answer all your questions and will have to rely on judgment.

Exhibit 1.1   Indexing Example

Age Category	Home Ownership*	Index
18 to 24	20%	33
25 to 34	48	80
35 to 44	60	100
45 to 54	74	123
55 to 64	70	117
65 to 74	50	83
Average—all ages	60	100

*These numbers are used only for example. They do not reflect current home ownership rates.

INDEXING

Indexing is used extensively in the business review and is a process that presents a number or group of numbers in relation to a specific number—an average, or base. It is a method of showing a relationship between two sets of numbers or percentages. Indexing is based upon using 100 as the average. Anything over 100 means the index is greater than the average; anything below 100 is less than the average.

When indexing, a base number is established and all other numbers are compared to it. For example, assume 60 percent of the population owns a home and home ownership is further broken down by age category as shown in Exhibit 1.1. Since 60 percent is the average percentage of home ownership, it becomes the base number from which to measure any subset of the population. For example, among 18 to 24 year olds, only 20 percent own homes, so 20 percent divided by 60 percent equals .33. (For purposes of clarity and easier communications, the decimal is then multiplied by 100 to give a round number, .33 × 100 equals an index of 33. From this point on in the book we will not explicitly show the multiplication by 100.) Thirty-three is substantially below 100; thus 18 to 24 year olds own homes at one third the average across all ages.

In another example, 30 percent of a national company's consumers live in Chicago. So you'd expect them to consume 30 percent of the product (30 divided by 30 = an index of 100, or average). But if Chicago consumers consume 60 percent of the company's product, they are consuming at a rate of 60 percent, divided by the base of 30 percent, for an index of 200. Thus, the Chicago market would compare at twice the national average, or 100 points above the expected consumption pattern.

When using indexing, we usually consider an index meaningful if it is plus or minus 10 from 100. In other words, we look for numbers 110 and above or 90 and below. If all age groups index between 95 and 105 in terms of consumption, we determine that our target market is flat across all age groups. However, if the 25 to 34 and 35 to 44 age groups indexed at 115 and 180, respectively, and all other age groups were at or below average (or below 100), then we would determine that those two age groups consumed at significantly higher levels.

SOURCES OF INFORMATION

The following are commonly used sources of information available to most any marketer. They will help you obtain the necessary data to complete the business review portion of your marketing plan. This is by no means an exhaustive list of information sources, but one that can be utilized by most marketing professionals without incurring large costs. Many of the sources listed can be found in a public or university library, can be obtained free, or can be purchased at a reasonable cost. Addresses and information on where to find the reference are provided for each listing.

Product User Characteristics/Size of Market/ Demographics

Mediamark Research, Inc. (MRI)
341 Madison Avenue
New York, NY 10017
212–599–0444

Simmons Market Research Bureau, Inc. (SMRB)
380 Madison Avenue
New York, NY 10017
212–916–8900

Information on the demographics, size, and media habits of the user and purchaser groups for various products, product categories, and brands.

Demographics and size of demographic groups using product.

Heavy user/light user by demographic break.

Brand loyalty measures.

Media usage by demographic break.

Approximate market share by brand can be derived.

Where to Find Advertising agency

Standard Rate and Data Service (SRDS)
3004 Glenview Rd.
Wilmette, IL 60091
708–256–6067

The *Newspaper Rates and Data* provides population, income, and general household expenditures for individual states, counties, and metro areas.

Population and households

Income per household

Household expenditures across eight categories

Number of passenger cars

Black and Spanish population

Where to Find Library; advertising agency

Dun's Marketing Services (a company of the Dun and Bradstreet Corporation)

A business list company that provides relatively accurate direct mail lists as well as information pertaining to the number and size of businesses within specific Standard Industrial Classification (SIC) categories and geographic territories.

Number of businesses by SIC by territory

Dollar size of businesses by SIC by territory

Employee size of businesses by SIC by territory

Listing of businesses within specific SIC, size, and territory parameters. Also available: trending of sales per employee, address, phone number, and listing of key personnel.

Where to Find Phone book in major U.S. cities

Dun's Million Dollar Directory

The directory provides a listing of businesses $.5 million in net worth and larger.

Where to Find 1–800–526–0651 or phone book under Dun's Marketing Services in major U.S. cities

Nielsen DMA Test Market Profiles

A.C. Nielsen Company
1290 Avenue of the Americas
New York, NY 10104
212–708–7500

Contains demographic, retail sales, and media information for each DMA.

Demographics

Circulation of magazines, newspapers

TV audience data

Retail purchasing rates

County population

Where to Find Advertising agency

Fairchild Fact Files

Fairchild Books
7 East 12th Street
New York, NY 10003
212–741–4280, 1–800–247–6622

Each fact file provides sales, market trend, and buying habit information for product categories. The information is based on the U.S. Bureau of the Census, financial reports, *Sales and Marketing Management Survey of Buying Power*, and other trade publications/government studies specific to the product category.

Market trends

Production/unit volume

Sales

Sales by price range

Sales by geography

Sales by distribution method/outlet type

Margins/financial information

Advertising expenditures

Consumer expenditures/spending data/buying habits

Demographic profiles

Where to Find Advertising agency; library

Survey of Buying Power

Sales and Marketing Management
633 Third Avenue
New York, NY 10017
212–986–4800

Published in July of each year and details buying power by product category on a market by market basis. The data are divided into national and regional summaries and market rankings. Metromarket data by states and county/city data by states are also available.

Income

Buying power index

Sales by merchandise line/product category

Population by people/households

Retail sales

Where to Find Library

Government Publications

No one collects more data on business than the government through its agencies. The Department of Commerce has reference libraries in more than 40 field offices in major cities throughout the United States. The Small Business Administration can also help with information questions and is located in over 80 cities throughout the country. Examples of some of the government sources available are:

County and City Data Book. Provides a variety of statistical information for counties, cities, standard metropolitan statistical areas, incorporated places, and urbanized areas.

*County Business Patterns.*Details summary of number, dollar size, and employment size of businesses by county, state, and country. Breaks information into Standard Industrial Classification (SIC) categories.

Census Data. Includes census data on agriculture, housing, general population characteristics, social, and economic characteristics, retail trade, manufacturing, wholesale trade, etc.

Where to Find Library

Trade and Consumer Publications

Multiple trade publications with research departments are waiting to help. SRDS business, trade, and consumer publication issues have listings of those applicable to your industry.

Where to Find Library; Standard Rate and Data Service, Inc.

Media Spending Data/Competitive Data

Leading National Advertisers (LNA)
136 Madison Avenue
New York, NY 10016
212–725–2700

LNA provides competitive spending data by medium.

Summary of national advertising expenditures by brand and industry category (class).

Includes network TV, spot TV, magazines (consumer only), newspaper supplements, network radio, and outdoor.

Where to Find Advertising agency

Rome Report
136 Madison Avenue
New York, NY 10016
212–725–2700

A resource that provides business-to-business and trade advertising expenditures.

Where to Find Advertising agency

Media Representatives

Media representatives serve as valuable sources of competitive spending information. Contact local print, radio, television, and outdoor representatives.

Where to Find Telephone book

Radio TV Reports, Inc.
41 East 42nd Street
New York, NY 10017
212–599–5500

This service provides copies of competitive radio and television ads. It will monitor specific industry categories or specific competitors.

Where to Find Advertising agency

In addition, many advertising agencies have access to *Media Records* for newspaper information, *Broadcast Advertisers' Report* for network and spot television information, and *Publishers' Information Bureau* for consumer magazine information.

Miscellaneous

Encyclopedia of Associations
Gale Research Company
Book Tower
Detroit, MI 48226
1–313–961–2242

Covers over 2,500 subjects, details over 19,500 national associations. Provides contacts to develop leads on how to find difficult information specific to a certain industry and customer groups.

   19,500 national organizations

   2,000 international organizations

   4,000 consultants, research centers, information services

Where to Find Library

Trade Shows Worldwide
Gale Research Company
Book Tower
Detroit, MI 48226
1–313–961–2242

A guide to conferences, conventions, trade and industrial shows, merchandise marts, and expositions.

Where to Find Library

Management Information Guides
Gale Research Company
Book Tower
Detroit, MI 48226
1–800–233–GALE

Each volume includes books, dictionaries, encyclopedias, film strips, government and institutional reports, periodical articles, and recordings on the featured subject. Guides are available from this series in almost every field.

Where to Find Library

Information USA
Viking and Penguin Books
Viking Penguin Inc.
40 West 23rd Street
New York, NY 10010

This reference is billed as the "ultimate source of information on earth." It is a guide for direct access to government experts. It is a reference book for all the information you can obtain free or almost free from the government, from department of commerce to census information to information from individual committees and agencies.

Where to Find Library

Media and Production Costs/ Availability

Standard Rate and Data Service Publications
Standard Rate and Data Service, Inc.
3004 Glenview Rd.
Wilmette, IL 60091
312–256–6061

These publications provide information required by advertisers for buying media and print production. The following source books are available:

Consumer Magazine and Farm Publication Rates and Data

Direct Mail List Rates and Data

Network Rates and Data (National TV and Radio Rates)

Newspaper Rates and Data

Spot Radio Rates and Data

Spot Television Rates and Data

Transit Advertising Rates and Data

Business Publication Rates and Data

Business Publication Rates and Data: Classified

Community Publication Rates and Data

Print Media Production Rates and Data

Where to Find Library

The Circulation Book
P.O. Box 994
22619 Pacific Coast Highway
Malibu, CA 90265

Shows circulation and penetration by county, metro area, and TV viewing area for every daily newspaper, Sunday paper, all regional sales groups, national newspaper supplements, and leading magazines.

Where to Find Ad agency; library.

Additional Tips on How to Find Industry Specific Data

In addition to the above sources, many additional references of information exist that will help you complete a business review consistent with the outline you establish. We suggest that following methodology to help you find *additional* sources of available information that pertain to *your* specific industry.

Go through the SRDS (Standard Rate and Data Service) and write down all trade and consumer publications pertaining to your industry.

Contact each trade publication, talk to the research department, and ask what information is available. Send them copies of your outline and charts. Ask for the specific information required for completion of your business review as detailed in your outline and charts. Ask about other available sources. Many times trade publications' research departments are aware of other studies that may help you. One publication told us about a consultant who has made it her life's work to learn about the plumbing and sink business. She saved us many days of searching by referring us to timely studies that helped us fulfill required data needs as specified in our outline for a national sink manufacturer.

Call the library and have them do a subject search, pulling all available reference materials. Utilize your local public library, along with the nearest college library. Many public universities have special reference services dedicated to compiling secondary research for private industry.

Dig, dig, and dig some more.

2

HOW TO PREPARE
A BUSINESS
REVIEW

The business review is organized into ten steps. Remember, as we stated previously, completing the business review does not have to be a one person job. Get other people in your company to help compile the information. Take advantage of the fact that the business review is presented as a step-by-step process. Each step includes charts organized so that the data is captured in a format that assures that the information is actionable when later writing the marketing plan.

Within each step are questions to be addressed that ensure the information collection activity is properly focused. These questions and charts are organized so that the marketing manager can effectively delegate some of the data collection function, allowing for a faster compilation of the necessary marketing information. In summary, while it is beneficial to have one person actually write the business review summary statements and the resulting marketing plan, it is most efficient to have several people compile the information and data for the business review.

Some of the sections may not directly apply to your business. We suggest you start by reading the whole chapter to get a good understanding of the focus and material in each section. Then follow the steps of the business review, paying particular attention to those which are most relevant to your type of business.

Finally, a well developed business review should be utilized as a daily reference piece. Each year, your business review should be updated to reflect the most recent changes in your industry and company.

From This Chapter You Will Learn

The data requirements and material that needs to be analyzed in each of the ten business review steps.

The key marketing issues and questions which need to be answered in each step of the business review.

How to write succinct summary statements describing the findings.

OVERVIEW

Now that you have an understanding of what is involved in a business review, you are ready to read through each step of the review. Each of the ten business review steps contains three main components.

- *A general background discussion* that details each area covered in the step.
- *Marketing questions* that must be answered in order to provide an adequate quantitative database for each section.
- *Charts* to help you organize your information in a disciplined manner, so you will be able to answer the marketing questions accurately. The charts are examples of a format you can easily adapt to your own situation. Worksheets for each of these charts are provided in Appendix B, located at the end of the book, to organize the data so the questions can be answered in a most efficient manner. Information is included on each worksheet on where data can be found to complete the charts.

The charts are intended to help you organize your data search. They are not exhaustive and cover only the major topical areas. Therefore, it is not intended that all the questions at the end of each business review section will have a corresponding chart. Many of the charts provide multiple pieces of information when completed. One of the sales charts provides sales trending for the industry and for your company, demonstrates differences in industry growth compared to your company's growth, and provides company market share data.

While the charts are used primarily to assure that your information is organized in a manner that allows you to answer the questions following each business review section, they can also be used as support for business review conclusions during presentations. In addition, you may want to consider transferring the information in the charts onto graphs for presentation purposes. Graphs provide a better visual interpretation than charts, which tend to get very busy with numbers. Finally, please note that two of the ten steps (1, Corporate Philosophy, and 5, Awareness and Product Attributes) do not require further detail and charts.

HOW TO DEVELOP YOUR BUSINESS REVIEW

In developing your own business review, it is important to realize you may not have the resources or time to complete all portions of the business review. At a minimum try to answer the questions to be addressed for each topic. There will also be portions that do not pertain to your business. Remember that this chapter covers information important to business-to-business firms, consumer goods firms (firms that manufacture consumer goods and sell to retailers who in turn sell to the ultimate consumer), retailers, and service businesses. While most marketing questions apply to all business categories, there are some that are clearly applicable to only one or another of these business categories. This should be evident to you as you go through the chapter.

Step 1

Corporate Philosophy/ Description of the Company and Product(s)

Different companies are unique in the ways they do business, their historical backgrounds, and their organizational structures—all of which have some level of impact on the development of a marketing plan. It is important to briefly describe, up front, predetermined corporate objectives, pertinent company and product history, and current product information and organizational parameters. By considering the culture and aspirations of the organization prior to writing the marketing plan, you stand a better chance of developing a plan that will be effectively implemented throughout the organization.

Corporate Goals and Objectives

The marketer should have an understanding of existing sales goals, profit goals, and marketing objectives prior to the development of a marketing plan. The marketer should also review the operating budget to gain an understanding of each product's margins, costs, and potential profit contributions.

If your company does not yet have a mission statement or company philosophy, it is important to provide a written description of your company's overall business philosophy as it relates to marketing, growth, and business goals. All companies are different. If the marketing plan does not reflect the company's basic philosophy, its chances for success are slim.

In stating corporate objectives and philosophies up front, the marketer will have a base to build upon when determining future marketing objectives and strategies. More importantly, through a thorough review of the market and company in the latter steps of the business review, the marketing manager will be able to judge whether the original overall business goals and philosophies are realistic and consistent with consumers' wants and needs. In this manner, the marketer is making himself or herself responsible for determining the feasibility of achieving the corporate goals given the market conditions. Thus, this step provides the first of many bases against which subsequent business review information can be compared to draw conclusions.

Questions to Be Addressed

- What are the long-term and short-term goals, mission, and objectives of the company? Are there existing sales goals, profit goals, marketing objectives?
- What is the operating budget for the company? What are the margins and what are the planned profit contributions of each product?
- Is there a corporate philosophy on how to do business? What are the principles of the business in regard to working with customers, developing and selling product, and internal management?

General Company Product and History

A discussion of the history of both your company and the product is necessary. Since the company and product are what you are selling, provide as much pertinent information as possible. Describe the product to be marketed through this plan. Include a historical and evolutionary perspective, and summarize your company's and product's results to date. Also provide insight as to what the future may hold in terms of marketing and product innovation for your company, product, and the total industry or product category.

Along with a review of the company and its product from a historical perspective, an analysis of future trends also serves to establish guidelines. It helps to understand both where a company has been and what its potential may be before you develop plans for its future.

Questions to Be Addressed

- What is the history of your company? Why was it started, how did it grow, and why is it successful?
- What products does your company sell? What is the makeup of your product(s)? What advantages do your products have over the competition?
- What is the history of your products? Have they always been as successful? Why were they first marketed? Over the years, how have your products changed?
- What is the sales volume, margin, and profitability of each product or product line (five-year trend)? What product categories are most important to the company?

- Do the products your company manufactures or sells have any potential manufacturing problems? Are specialized parts, labor, or manufacturing processes necessary? Are the products vulnerable to shortages or other consumer, environmental, or economic factors? If so, how?

- What plans are there for growth and expansion among *existing product categories?* New products? More markets geographically? New product uses? Market share development within current categories?

- Are there plans for growth and expansion among *new product categories?* Do you plan to go into any new additional categories?

- What single thing does your company want to be known for? What are you best at? Why do consumers purchase from you?

- How has your product category done nationally? What are the trends over the past five years in terms of product innovation, marketing, distribution, pricing, and merchandising? What is expected for the future?

- Where has your company succeeded and failed? Why?

Organizational Chart

Organization structure tells a great deal about a company and its chance for successful marketing. Study your company's organizational chart. Analyze whether the marketing department is set up to develop and implement marketing plans efficiently. Determine where your marketing department fits in relation to the rest of the business. Determine who you have to work with and who makes the final decisions regarding marketing direction or the company's marketing policies.

It is extremely important that you understand how the marketing department interfaces with the rest of the organization. Our feeling is that all areas of the marketing mix should be the direct responsibility of the marketing director, and this person should report directly to the president of the company. This means that the marketing director has decision making impact on the sales, product, pricing, distribution, advertising, media, promotion, publicity, and merchandising functions. If this situation does not exist, there is less of a chance for cohesive implementation of the marketing plan; marketing strategies that should affect sales, product, pricing, and advertising might be interpreted and executed differently. This diminishes the synergistic effect of the marketing tools working together to achieve the companywide sales and marketing objectives established in the marketing plan.

Later you may want to develop a plan to reorganize your department, or to improve communication with other departments in the company so your department has more positive impact. If the individual responsible for marketing does not have access to key decision makers in merchandising or operations, create a structure that forces this.

You won't change the way your department communicates and has input into corporate decision making overnight. The purpose of reviewing the organizational structure is that you are aware up front of the ability of your department to provide marketing direction. You must develop a plan to make sure marketing has the ability not only to formulate marketing plans and get them approved, but also to work with the rest of the company in effectively implementing them, and assuring their success.

Questions to Be Addressed

- Is your marketing department sufficiently organized to develop and execute a disciplined marketing plan? Do you have enough resources to plan, implement, and analyze results?

- To what degree is the company committed to marketing? Where does marketing fit in your overall organizational structure?

- Does your marketing department have the ability to communicate with and have a positive impact on other departments within the company?

- Does your marketing department have influence over all the marketing tools and the decisions made regarding sales, product, pricing, distribution, advertising, media, promotion, publicity, and merchandising?

- Is the company operations driven, finance driven, merchandise driven, product driven, sales driven, or marketing driven? In other words, what area of the company is most responsible for the company's success? Will that be true in the future? How does the marketing department fit in? How will this affect your ability to develop and implement effective marketing plans?

Step 2
Review of the Consumer Target Market

Target market definition is the most important step in preparing a business review. Effective marketing is impossible without a thorough understanding of your *current* and *potential* customer base. The more the customer can be understood, the better the marketer is able to fulfill the customer's needs.

The business review provides a format that sorts current and potential customers into segments. Segmenting allows customers to be grouped according to common demographic, product usage, and purchasing characteristics. This allows for the analysis of which customer group is currently most profitable and which consumer group has the most potential for your company. The end result of segmenting is that a company is able to focus its marketing resources against an ultimate target market that has common demographic and product usage characteristics, purchasing habits, and product or service needs. Instead of trying to be all things to all people, the company can direct its energies toward satisfying essentially one person as characterized by the target market segment or segments.

The business review further provides a format which describes the profile of the current *category consumer* as compared to the *company's current customer*. This allows the marketer to determine if the company's customer is different from the general product category consumer. The similarities and differences will be important when determining future marketing strategies. A company may find that its product is consumed by a far older population than the general product category's consumer. This important information can be used in the marketing plan to further target this older age segment or to develop plans to attract more of the younger, mainstream consumer.

Demographics

The marketer's traditional method of defining purchaser and user groups and segmenting markets is by utilizing demographic factors. Demographics can be determined for either individuals or households (the configuration of individuals making up a living unit). Following is a brief discussion of the demographics that should be analyzed to determine if current or potential consumers can be segmented or grouped according to common similarities and to determine your company's customer profile as compared to the category customer.

Sex

There are often major differences between male and female purchasing and usage habits. Many times sex is used in conjunction with another demographic descriptor to define the target market. For Famous Footwear, a national chain of off-price, brand name shoe stores, The Hiebing Group research determined that women with families are the single largest purchasers. Marketing, communication, product, and in-store merchandising decisions reflect the particular needs and tastes of this segment.

Age

Target markets can be broken out by age. Many times age determines the needs and wants of a specific product brand or service. Most beer companies recognize the importance of young adults (from legal drinking age to age 34) in the consumption of beer. Studies have shown that within this age group are above average and heavy users. More importantly, many beer drinkers form lifelong brand preferences during this time period. Thus, age is a very important demographic variable not only for beer companies, but for many marketers.

Whenever possible, try to gather demographic information by media age breaks (2 plus, 2 to 11, 6 to 11, 12 to 17, 18 plus, 18 to 24, 18 to 34, 18 to 49, 25 to 54, 54 plus). This will allow for more accurate media planning and buying. It will also allow for a better direct link from target market definition to actual purchasing of media designed to reach the target market. Unfortunately, media breaks don't always correspond to secondary sources of target market information such as SMRB and MRI, but whenever possible, for consistency, try to use media demographic categories.

Income

Income can predict in broad terms what a family's lifestyle will be like. There are many product categories, such as cars, appliances, and leisure goods, for which purchases rise with increase in income. Yet purchase rates for other more basic product categories, such as food, remain fairly stable regardless of income size. Often income is combined with geographic information to further determine the location of specific consumers. Marketers often pinpoint geographic census tracks that have households with approximately the same income range. Identification of these clusters can determine location of new outlets for retailers who do well against the income range identified. The clusters can also be used in media selection such as targeted direct mail or for the advertising or promotion of income sensitive product offerings.

Education

In general, the higher the individual's education, the higher the income. Thus, education and income are often analyzed in tandem.

Occupation

Similar to education, income is also a function of occupation. While some of the major differences between white-collar and blue-collar purchasing habits have diminished due to double incomes, there are still major buying patterns affected by type of job. For example, the carpenters/craftsmen/foremen professions spend less for clothing and purchase different clothing than do service/professional/clerical workers.

In working with a regional menswear store, it was determined that there were differences in purchasing rates of suits not only between white-collar and blue-collar professions, but within white-collar professions as well. The salesman, for example, purchased suits at greater rates than some other business professionals. In addition, occupation combined with age further delineated purchasing segments. Young professionals spent at greater rates than average on suits, because they were establishing wardrobes far different from the clothes they wore in college. Conversely, the number of suits purchased drops slightly as the younger person ages and starts a family. Purchases increase again as that individual gets older, reaches the top of his profession, and can afford to purchase suits more often.

Family/Household Size

Family size often determines the quantity sold to the household, with larger households purchasing greater amounts. Family size may dictate that greater quantities of a product are used within a given household, but each person within a family may or may not use more of the product than an individual living alone. Thus, per capita rates of purchasing should also be taken into consideration when developing target markets.

Many times, family size is also combined with the age of the family to determine the family's lifestyle as ascertained by its life cycle. At The Hiebing Group, we tend to break the family life cycle into five categories: single under 35, married under 35 with no children, married with children, married 35 or over with no children, and single 35 or over. Each has different purchasing patterns and often purchases similar products in different quantities. For example, households with small children purchase products like quick, easy-to-prepare meal packages, appliances, diapers, hot dogs, and household cleaners at greater rates than other family groupings.

Region/Geography

Many products are not sold evenly across the country due to distribution capabilities of the manufacturing company or to the unique and differing tastes, lifestyles, and needs of consumers. You should determine the geographic location of your potential consumers as well as the varying levels of usage by geographic area. There may exist a situation where a region has very few actual consumers but they consume higher than normal levels, making that region more important than the small number of customers would indicate. (Actual usage levels by geographic region are determined through Category Development and Brand Development indexes discussed under Purchase Rates and Buying Habits in Step 6.)

Lifestyle Factors

Marketers sometimes use lifestyle factors or psychographics to help develop target markets. Lifestyle descriptors attempt to define a customer segment in terms of the attitudes, interests, and activities of the consumer. This is an attempt to go further than demographic descriptors, to really get inside the consumer's mind. A brief description of your customers, taking into consideration some of the following, is helpful in further describing and defining the target market.

- *Personality Descriptors*. Do your customers tend to be affectionate, likeable, dominating, authoritative, passive, independent, self-assured, sociable, stubborn, followers, leaders, conformists, experimenters, individualistic, etc.?
- *Activities*. Do your customers engage in outdoor/indoor sports, cultural events, environmental activities, political activities, volunteer groups, social clubs, home entertainment, travel, etc.?
- *Purchase Attitudes*. Are your customers economy minded, impulsive, planners, price conscious, style conscious, value conscious, quality driven, self-service oriented, status conscious, purchasing with cash or credit, etc.?

Demographic Measures: Volume versus Concentration

Two measures by which target markets can be determined from demographic data are volume and concentration.

- *Volume:* The total number of purchases or percent of total purchases attributable to any given demographic target market segment. An example would be: Total sales in a category equal $1MM, and 18 to 24 year olds constitute 15 percent of the total purchases, or $150M. (Throughout this book M = thousands; MM = millions.)

■ *Concentration:* The percent within a given demographic target market segment that purchase the product. An example would be: Of all 18 to 24 year olds, 80 percent are purchasers of the product.

The volume measure is the most critical of the two measures from the standpoint that a company must have a large enough target market base and resulting sales base to sustain an ongoing business. At this point in the business review, your job is to analyze the potential target market by determining segments based upon similar demographic and purchasing characteristics. However, keep in mind that the segments must be large enough to assure adequate volume potential. (This is covered in more detail in Step 10, Demand Analysis.)

Volume can be measured in terms of *purchases* (units or dollars). Or volume can be measured in terms of actual *numbers of consumers* (purchasers or users). In the chart shown in Exhibit 2.1, for matters of consistency, we use the term purchases.

This chart demonstrates the demographic profile of the product category nationally from a volume standpoint. If more than one brand exists or if there are segments within your business, a chart for each should be developed. If you sell shoes, a chart should be developed for total shoe purchases along with separate charts for athletic, dress, casual, and children's shoe purchasers.

The easiest way to determine a volume measure is to look at the "percentage of total purchases" column to determine the percent of purchases each demographic category is responsible for.

Exhibit 2.1   National Demographic Description of Product Category Consumers: Volume Measure

Demographic Descriptor	Percent of Total Population (210MM)*	Percent of Total Purchases ($900MM)†
Age		
Under 18	18%‡	36%‡
18 to 24		
25 to 34		
35 to 44		
45 to 54		
55+		

*This number provides a total population number. In this example, the total universe of teens through 55+ is 210MM. (Throughout this book, M = thousands and MM = millions.) With this total figure you can calculate the total population for each demographic category. For example, the total population for 18 to 24 year olds would be 18% × 210MM = 37.8MM.

†This number provides the total dollar volume or unit volume of the category depending upon which measure you use for percent of total purchases. In this example, the total dollar purchases for the product category are $900MM. This information allows you to calculate the dollar volume potential for each demographic category. For example, the total purchases for 18 to 24 year olds would be 36% × $900MM = $324MM.

Note: A similar chart would be developed for all products, product categories, or services your company sells.

These numbers will be useful for future demand analysis and in reviewing the total size of the market to make certain there are enough consumers to meet primary target market volume criteria. Use the blank chart provided in Appendix B, to complete with information specific to your company.

Exhibit 2.2 demonstrates the demographic profile of the product category nationally from a concentration standpoint. A chart for you to fill in with data pertinent to your own business appears in Appendix B.

Volume numbers are often a function of category size, while concentration numbers are a true measure of the propensity to purchase. There may be more 25 to 34 year old purchasers of shoes than 18 to 24 year old purchasers because of the large number of 25 to 34 year olds in the population. Yet, for *particular styles of shoes*, while there are fewer total 18 to 24 year old purchasers, the age category may demonstrate greater concentrations of purchases. For example, 25 to 34 year olds may constitute 22 percent of total purchases for a particular style of shoe and 18 to 24 only 15 percent (volume measure), yet the data may show that only 20 percent of the 25 to 34 year olds purchase the style of shoe, compared to 40 percent of the 18 to 24 year olds (concentration measure).

Thus, the marketer may find it more profitable to concentrate on the younger 18 to 24 year olds when selling specific styles of shoes. A high concentration of purchasers within a specific demographic category allows for a more efficient and effective marketing effort. The marketer can focus on addressing the similar needs and characteristics of the consumers in the category. And there is not much wasted effort, since a vast majority of the people in the category demonstrate a propensity to purchase the product.

In summary, both volume and concentration must be taken into consideration when developing a target market database. Volume is a benchmark type of variable. There have to be enough people interested in purchasing the product in order to justify any business. Once volume levels are deemed sufficient, concentration numbers can further define demographic target market categories by showing strong propensities to purchase within given demographic categories.

Exhibit 2.2   **National Demographic Description of Product Category Consumers: Concentration Measure**

Demographic Descriptor	Percent of Category that Purchases Product (75%*)	Concentration Index: Category/Total
Age		
Under 18	40%	53
18 to 24	50*	66*
25 to 34	75	100
35 to 44	90	120
45 to 54	100	133
55 +	50	66

*Nationally, 50 percent of the 18 to 24 year olds purchase the product; 75 percent of the total population purchase the product. The index of 66 is derived from dividing 50 by 75 and tells the marketer that 18 to 24 year olds have a lower propensity to purchase the product category than does the whole population.

Demographic Measures: National Category versus Company/Product Target Market

It is important to develop target market databases for both the product category nationally and for your company's purchasers. In this manner you will be able to compare the two profiles to see if your company's target market description matches that of the product category. If not, you can spend time determining why and how the differences might help or hurt your situation. One of our retail clients determined that their target market skewed younger (18 to 34) than purchasers nationally, even though the client's market was planned to correlate to the heavy user in the category, women 25 to 44 with children. While our client did well against the heavy user target market, the data showed that they could improve relative to the competition through new marketing and merchandising strategies.

Exhibit 2.3 demonstrates the demographic profile of your company's purchaser as compared to the average purchaser profile nationally. A chart that you can complete with information specific to your own business is included in Appendix B.

Questions to Be Addressed

- What is the consumer demographic profile of the product category nationally? What is the profile of the individuals who consume or purchase the most from a volume standpoint? Do some demographic categories have a higher concentration of purchasers?

- What is your customer's demographic profile? How would you describe your customers in terms of age, sex, income, occupation, education, number of children, marital status, geographic residence, ownership of home?

- What are your customers' attitudes, interests, and activities? How would you describe them from a lifestyle standpoint?

- Are your customers different in terms of demographic and lifestyle characteristics from the overall category consumer profile?

Exhibit 2.3   Demographic Description of Company Purchasers Compared to Category Purchasers

Demographic Descriptor	Percent of Purchasers of Product Nationally ($100MM)*	Percent of Purchasers of Company Product ($20MM)*	Index: Company to National Purchasers
Age			
Under 18	10%	10%	100
18 to 24	20†	10†	50†
25 to 34	40	30	75
35 to 44	10	20	200
45 to 54	10	20	200
55+	10	10	100
Total	100%	100%	

*This provides a total dollar volume figure to help calculate total dollars for each demographic category. For example, the total dollar volume for the category is $100MM. Total dollar volume for the company is $20MM. Company purchases among 18 to 24 year olds is $2MM (10% × $20MM).

†20 percent of the purchasers of the product are 18 to 24 nationally, while 10 percent of your company's purchasers are 18 to 24. This results in an index of 50, meaning that your company sells to 18 to 24 year olds at half the expected average (the average being an index of 100).

- How many consumers purchase your product? How many potential consumers exist? Is the number of consumers growing or shrinking over the past five years?

- Do religious, political, or other socioeconomic factors make a difference in the purchase of your product or service?

Product Usage

For some products, demographics aren't as important as why the product is purchased or how it is used. Many times purchasers with similar demographics purchase the product for different reasons. This offers the opportunity to segment consumers based upon usage of the product. Baking soda is purchased by women who bake from scratch and need the product in the baking process. It is also purchased as a refrigerator deodorizer. Many of the purchasers of baking soda as a deodorizer do not bake on a regular basis and so do not purchase the product for baking. Thus, usage of this product helps define customer segments and knowledge of the customers' usage is critical as to how this product would be marketed to each of the two customer groups.

Questions to Be Addressed

- How is your product used? Are there multiple uses?

- Why is your product purchased? What are the benefits inherent in your product that encourage purchase from consumers?

- If there are multiple uses of your product, are there consumers who use the product for one type of use or benefit but not another? Are there multiple, independent user groups?

- Do the different user groups have differing demographics? What is their size in terms of volume or purchases and number of consumers?

Heavy Users

Most product categories have a group of heavy users—consumers who purchase or use the product at far greater rates than that of the average consumer. According to our definition, a category has a meaningful heavy users segment if approximately one third or less of the consumers account for approximately two thirds or more of the purchases. A retail example of this can be found in the shoe business. One third of the purchasers buy more than 63 percent of the shoes. The demographic description of the heavy user shoe purchaser is women 25 to 44 with children. A heavy user shoe purchaser is further defined as someone who purchases seven or more pairs of shoes per year. (The average person purchases fewer than three pairs per year.)

Heavy users are important because they offer the potential of marketing to a smaller, more defined group of people who account for the majority of purchases. If you do not have primary research that determines the percent of purchasers attributable to the heavy user, you can make direction estimates by using Simmons Market Research Bureau (SMRB) or other secondary sources. Exhibit 2.4 presents an example of how to calculate heavy user definitions from the SMRB resource. Similar methods can be used with other secondary research information. If nothing is available to you, make the best estimate based upon your knowledge of the market.

In summary, it is important to determine if there is a heavy user group in your product category. Then develop a demographic profile of the heavy user group to determine if it is similar to your customer profile.

The chart in Exhibit 2.5 compares the heavy user demographic profile to the total demographic profile (see Appendix B for a worksheet). This is an essential starting place to help you in making such decisions as whether you want to specialize against a smaller, specialized segment of the market or cater to those individuals who are responsible for the majority of the consumption. Companies have done well using

Exhibit 2.4   Example of How to Calculate Heavy Users from SMRB Data

Number of Home Plastic Files Purchased per Year*		Number of People Purchasing (M)		Total Product Purchased ($ or Units) (M)
1	×	5,000	=	5,000
2		4,000		8,000
3		1,000 ⎫		3,000 ⎫
4		1,000 ⎪		4,000 ⎪
5		1,000 ⎬ 4,500		5,000 ⎬ 22,000
6		500 ⎪		3,000 ⎪
7 Plus		1,000 ⎭		7,000 ⎭
Total		13,500		35,000

*Heavy user for home plastic files defined as three plus purchases per year.

Heavy User Percentage: To compute add number of people purchasing three plus divided by total number of people (4,500/13,500 = 33%).

Heavy User Percentage of Purchases: To compute add total product purchased by people purchasing three plus divided by the total product pruchased (22,000/35,000 = 63%).

Heavy users represent 33 percent of the total population of purchasers and account for 63 percent of the total dollar or unit purchases.

Exhibit 2.5   Heavy User Demographic Descriptors Compared to All User Demographics Descriptors

	Heavy User Demographic Profile	Total Demographic Profile
Age	24 to 35	18 to 45
Sex	Female	Female
Household Income	$40M-$50M	$24M-$50M
Education	Graduated College +	Graduated High School-Plus
Employment	White-Collar/Professional	White- and Blue-Collar
Family Size	4 plus	2 plus
Geography	Western United States	Midwest and Western United States
Home Ownership	Yes	Yes

Lifestyle Description of the Heavy User Compared to the Average User

The heavy user is far more social oriented than the average user. The heavy user is more style conscious and quality driven than the average user. Overall the heavy user is more upscale with attitudes and purchasing habits shaped by concern over family, neighborhood, and social expectations.

both approaches, but in either case you need to make sure that there are adequate numbers of potential customers in your defined target market and that you will be able to attract a sufficient number to purchase your product frequently enough to assure profitability. (See Step 10, Demand Analysis, for further detail.)

Questions to Be Addressed

- Is there a group of heavy purchasers of your product? What percent of the purchasers do they constitute and what percent of the purchases are they responsible for?

■ What is the difference in demographic and lifestyle profile of the heavy user and that of the overall user?

Potential Primary and Secondary Target Markets

Primary Target Market

A primary target market is your main consuming group. This group of consumers are the most important purchasers and users of your product and will be the mainstay of your business. In some cases, it is the heavy user. For other companies who are more specialist oriented, it will be a smaller though viable section of the market which requires unique goods and services.

Many times the purchaser of a product is different from the user. If this is true, you need to decide who has most influence over the actual purchase. If the wife does the grocery shopping, does the husband who drinks the beer request his brand preference or does he drink what his wife buys him? In most cases, the individual who does the purchasing becomes the primary target market. However, when the purchaser primarily buys what the user requests, then the user receives primary attention.

The following criteria should be fulfilled before you finalize a primary target market choice:

■ Make sure the customer base is large enough in terms of actual numbers of consumers and dollar volume of purchasers. What percent of the product category's volume does your primary target market consume? Given your projected market share, is it enough to support your business? (See Step 10, Demand Analysis, for further detail.) In general, we require a user/purchaser target market profile to be accountable for approximately 50 percent of the category volume. For example, if 18 to 24 year olds accounted for only 30 percent of the consumption, the marketer would need to expand the age criteria beyond 18 to 24 year olds until the age group was broad enough to account for approximately 50 percent of the volume. Finally, the 50 percent criteria can be less if you are going to specialize against a more narrow purchaser/user base but obtain a larger market share against this segment.
■ Make sure the target market is profitable. Determine that the target market purchases sufficient quantity to assure profitability (this is further discussed in Step 10, Demand Analysis).
■ Try to estimate the growth of your primary target market. Is it a growing or shrinking segment? If it is shrinking, will the market be large enough to support your business at its current market share in five years? If not, this should be a danger signal.
■ Make sure that your primary target market can be as narrowly defined as possible by one unified profile. The primary target market should be a group of individuals with the same basic demographic characteristics and purchasing behavior. This will allow your marketing effort to be focused against essentially one type of individual.

The primary target market becomes the company's reason for being. You are in business to determine the primary target market's wants and needs and to provide for those wants and needs better than your competition. This pertains to providing the product, service, shopping environment, distribution channel, and price structure that is required by the customer for purchase. The better the definition and description of the consumers in your primary target market, the better you will be able to market to them.

Secondary Target Markets

Secondary target markets are important because they provide additional sales to the company beyond that of the primary target market, as well as future sales to the company. This group of people can also help to influence the usage rate and purchases of the primary target market. A secondary target market can be one of the following:

- *Influencers*. Influencers can be both a primary or secondary target market, though in most situations they are a secondary target market. These are individuals who influence the purchase or usage decision of the primary target market. A good example of this is the influence children have on their parents in the purchase of many consumer goods, from toys to fast food restaurants.

- A *demographic category with a high concentration index*. Often there is a distinct demographic category that accounts for a small percentage of the volume, but contains a high concentration of purchasers. For example, 18 to 24 year olds may account for only 10 percent of the total product category purchases, but 50 percent of the 18 to 24 year olds may purchase the product. This could happen for two reasons:

  The small size of the target market relative to other target markets.

  Smaller purchasing rates or purchases of more inexpensive product models.

- *Subsets of purchasers or users who make up the primary target markets*. As stated in the primary target market section, ideally your primary target market should be one unified profile of customers. This allows for a focusing of resources and message in the marketing effort. However, there are situations where the volume of any one target market is not substantial enough to qualify it as a primary target market. In this case, the marketer is forced to develop a broader primary market profile in order to meet the primary target market criteria of accounting for approximately 50 percent of the product category volume. In doing this, the primary target profile encompasses many unique subsets of users who have slightly different demographics, needs, wants, product usage, and purchasing behavior. These subsets should be delineated in greater detail in the secondary target market section. An example of this is in the target market we developed for a regional menswear retailer. The retailer was selling primarily suits and sport coats. There were many purchasing profiles, but no single profile group provided enough volume to allow for targeting against that group. In order to meet the volume criteria, the target market became very broad and encompassed all white-collar males who were 18 to 54 years of age. However, the following secondary target markets were developed with subsequent marketing emphasis and programs against each one:

  Men, 18 to 24, college graduates, entering the working world and looking for affordable suits.

  Men, 45 plus, higher income at the top of their profession, interested in quality menswear and needing to update their wardrobes.

  Women 18 to 34. Women have a great influence over men's purchases of suits and sport coats. Both married and unmarried women also purchase a substantial number of sport coats as gifts and accompany men in more than 50 percent of their shopping trips, serving as advisors.

  Blue-collar male who needs an all occasion suit. Price is a concern.

  Target markets were also broken out by type of profession, as this helped dictate quantity and style of suit purchases.

In another example of secondary target markets, we did work for a national package goods company whose primary target market was the consumer and secondary target market was the trade. Obviously, consumer demand for the product was critical and had to be established. But in order for the consumers to purchase the product, the trade, or in this case grocery stores, had to display the product and provide shelf space. Thus, a whole separate marketing program was developed and implemented against the trade as a secondary target market.

Questions to Be Addressed

- Are there several distinct types of consumer descriptions? What is the size of each target market? Do you have multiple consumer profiles or one main one?

- Are users of the product also the purchasers? If not, who has the most influence over the purchaser's decision?

- Does your primary target market account for approximately 50 percent of the sales volume, or are you going to specialize against a very narrow segment? If so, can this segment support your company; is it large enough, based upon sales volume projections of the segment and market share projections for your company? (See Step 10, Demand Analysis, for further detail.)

- Can you define one narrow and focused profile of your target customer? What is it?

- Is the primary target market growing, stable, or shrinking?

- Are there distinct secondary target markets for your product that have common characteristics apart from the primary target market?

- When the product is purchased, are there individuals who, although they do not make the actual purchase, have a substantial influence on the purchaser? To what extent? How would you describe these?

Step 3

Review of the Business-to-Business Target Market

Business-to-business firms typically have far fewer potential customers than consumer companies. In addition, each business-to-business customer usually generates larger sales than does the typical consumer customer. As with consumer target markets, it is important to segment so you can determine which type of business is most profitable and has the most potential for your company.

Target Market Segmentation and Standard Industrial Classification (SIC) Categories

One of the best ways to segment businesses is by utilizing Standard Industrial Classification (SIC) codes. Businesses are classified into ten different broad two digit SIC categories: Agriculture/Forestry/Fishing, Mining, Manufacturing, Construction, Transportation/Communication/Public Utilities, Wholesale Trade, Retail Trade, Finance/Insurance/Real Estate, Services, and Public Administration. Within each two digit SIC category there are further breakouts into four and eight digit classifications. Within the Retail SIC there is category 56, Apparel and Accessory stores; and within category 56 there is 5611, Men's and Boy's Clothing.

Firms such as Dun's Marketing Services specialize in providing mailing lists and other market information for businesses according to any SIC classification. We have used Dun's to target specific types of business by industry type. We helped generate incremental sales for a statewide CPA firm by creating individual campaigns for small businesses within each SIC code. Different tailored messages were developed for retailers, the service industry, financial institutions, etc. Each industry received multiple marketing pieces explaining why specialized accounting practices were important for their specific business. The campaign was so successful that for every $1 the CPA firm invested, it had a return of $2—a 100 percent return on investment over a two-year period.

The first step in developing business-to-business target market segments is to break down your customer base by SIC. Next, determine how many different business categories you sell to. List the categories in which you have the most customers or clients first, and then continue listing the categories in sequential order from most customers to least. Finally, determine the penetration of each category (percent of the total category that you can classify as a customer). Worksheets for completing these charts are found in Appendix B.

You may be surprised that you are doing business with multiple categories of businesses. You may also find that there are some categories that can provide a large degree of growth potential, categories where you do business with only a small percentage of the total. This information will help you define target markets and develop marketing strategies later in the plan.

Questions to Be Addressed

- To what SIC categories do customers who purchase your product belong?
- What is the demand potential for your product? What is the penetration of your company in each SIC category? How many businesses are there in SIC categories that purchase product in your category but are not purchasing from you? Why aren't they?

Other Methods of Segmenting

Once you have your target market broken into SIC categories, there are additional criteria you should evaluate to further allow for a complete understanding of your target market.

Dollar Size

Determine the total company sales volume for each SIC. Then calculate the average dollar size of each client in the category(ies) by dividing the total company volume in each SIC by the number of clients you have in that SIC. This can tell you a lot regarding current and future potential of the different categories when combined with the penetration information developed earlier. Exhibit 2.6 provides an overview of clients' revenues by SIC category. Compare this chart to previous charts breaking out customers and total businesses by SIC categories (see Appendix B for worksheet to complete with information specific to your company). If an SIC classification averages substantially above other SIC classifications in terms of average dollar per

Exhibit 2.6   Revenue Distribution of Clients by SIC Category

SIC	Number of Customers	Total Company Sales per SIC Category	Average $ per Client ($M)	Index to Average (Average $ per Client/Average All Categories)	Index to Average (Total Sales per SIC Category/Average $ per Client All Categories)
Agriculture/Forestry/Fisheries					
Mining					
Construction					
Manufacturing					
Transportation					
Public Utilities					
Wholesale Trade					
Retail Trade	100*	$100,000*	$1,000*	50*	100
Finance/Insurance/Real Estate Services					
Public Administration					
Total	500	$1,000,000			
Average All Categories	50	$100,000*	$2,000*		

*The company has 100 retail trade customers worth $100,000 in sales with the average dollar sales per retail client being $1,000. Based upon the norm for all categories, the retail trade indexes below the expected, or 50, for average dollars per client ($1,000/$2,000) and the expected, or 100, for total sales generated by SIC category ($100,000/$100,000). Thus total sales potential in this category is a function of the large number of businesses in the SIC, not the average sales per client.

client and your company has not fully penetrated the classification (your company's clients represent a small percentage of the total businesses in the SIC)—then that classification should be targeted for further expansion.

Employee Size

Another way to segment business is by the number of employees or employee size of the firm. Employee size often is an indicator of the company's volume *and* how they do business. For example, large companies tend to be more centralized with formalized organizational structures, while smaller companies tend to be less formalized. Pricing, product, and service requirements often differ between large and small companies. Thus, the marketing approach may differ due to a function of the size of the business customer.

Heavy Usage Rates

Are there heavy or light user categories? Determine the reasons why. Maybe a category of light users would become heavier users if you were to modify your product, service, or pricing. Or perhaps you should consider narrowing your firm's focus to concentrate on just the heavy user categories, especially if the earlier analysis determined that there was potential growth in these categories.

The chart in Exhibit 2.7 provides the business-to-business firm with an alternative way to look at its business. This chart is for the firm with many types of customers not necessarily by SIC code, but across dealers and distributors or within one SIC. Worksheets for these analyses appear in Appendix B.

Product Application/Use

Essentially this is how the organization uses your product. If you find that there are multiple different uses for your product, you can segment target markets by usage type and begin to provide more focused service and expertise to each segment.

Organizational Structure

Different companies have different organizational structures. Find out if your company sells better to one type of company than another. You might find you get more business from centralized organizations with formalized bidding procedures and thus

Exhibit 2.7   Product Category Purchases by Outlet Type

Outlet Type	Where Crafts Are Purchased	Percent of Total Outlets
Craft store	86%*	21%*
Needlecraft store	67	16
Discount store	64	15
Mail order	63	15
Department store	62	15
Craft supply chain store	41	10
Art material store	36	9
Total	419%	101%

*86 percent of craft purchasers utilize craft stores to purchase crafts (most craft purchsasers utilize more than one outlet, which is why the total equals 419 percent). However, craft stores account for only 21 percent of the total craft outlets.

want to target these types of businesses within the SICs you currently service. Or you might analyze why you don't do as well with decentralized entrepreneurial firms and make changes to increase your success with them. Subsequently you may do well targeting headquarters but perform poorly in generating sales from branches. In summary, you may need to develop independent marketing strategies and executions for different target groups as defined by their organization structure, purchasing habits, and purchasing requirements.

New versus Repeat Buyer

Some companies are good at getting new business and poor at developing long-term relationships. For others it's just the opposite. Determine the percentage of your business that comes from new buyers versus repeat buyers. Correct your weaknesses if it becomes evident that you either aren't getting new business or can't develop long-term clients. This area is a good client satisfaction check and should be analyzed yearly. It also allows you to develop alternative marketing strategies depending upon the type of customer (new versus repeat) you are targeting.

Geographic Location

In analyzing sales, you may determine that you are strong in one part of the country but weak in another. It could be because of your distribution system. It might be a competitive situation, or you may find that demand is higher in some geographical areas than others. In addition, you might discover that you do very well against a particular SIC category in one region of the country but haven't marketed to that SIC category elsewhere. By analyzing where your current business exists and where you have potential to expand, you can segment your target market by geographic location. Worksheets for these analyses appear in Appendix B.

Decision Makers and Influencers

Finally, you need to determine who actually decides to purchase your product and who influences the purchase of your product. Analyze the purchase decision making process. Describe who makes the ultimate purchasing decision, how they arrive at the purchasing decision, what the purchasing criteria are, and to what degree people influence the purchaser. The purchaser may in fact be a committee, which means you will need to target many individuals if all have an equal role in the decision process. Typically, the decision maker or purchaser becomes your primary target market, and those individuals influencing the decision become the secondary target market.

Questions to Be Addressed

- What is the total company sales volume by SIC, and what is the average sales volume per customer?
- What is the revenue distribution of your customers by SIC? Does it correlate to the number of clients in each SIC or do some categories have a higher average dollar per client figure?
- What size are the companies that purchase from you? Do large companies respond differently from small ones? If so, why?
- Are there heavy users *within* SIC categories? Are some SIC categories heavier users than others?

- Do different SIC category businesses use your product for different purposes? Why do SIC categories need/use your product? Is your product used more by some industries than by others? Can you expand use to others?

- Are purchasers of your product original equipment manufacturers (OEMs) who utilize your product in the manufacturing of another product? And do they sell to another business or directly to the consumer? How exactly does your product fit into the OEM's manufacturing structure? Why is your product important? How is it used?

- What is the organizational structure of your customers' companies? Do you have more success with centralized companies than with decentralized? Why? Do purchasing procedures differ among customers? Do you get more business from companies with a single purchasing agent versus a purchasing committee that requires more formalized bidding?

- Are the majority of your customers new or repeat buyers? Why?

- Where are your customers located? Are there areas of the country that have businesses from SIC categories that you are successful with but which you currently are not covering? Are there potential customers that match your customer profile, but you are not reaching? Do some parts of the country provide more business for you than others? If so, why? Is it due to servicing, distribution, sales efforts, or competitive factors? Or do some parts of the country use more product than other parts for other reasons?

- Who are the decision makers and influencers in the purchase of your product? What is the decision maker's function and role in the purchase decision? What is the decision sequence and purchase criteria?

Step 4
Sales Analysis

Sales data can be analyzed many different ways. Properly analyzed, the data can provide the marketer with a wealth of information. The key, however, is to break down total sales into actionable segments of information in order to gain a clear understanding of what is taking place within your company as compared to the industry or product category as a whole. We provide you with a methodology to analyze sales data.

Utilize Reference Points of Data for Comparison Purposes

The objective, as with other portions of the business review, is to develop two reference points of data. Company sales by themselves mean nothing; *but* company sales compared to previous year's sales or company sales compared to national category/industry sales provide actionable data. Whenever possible, try to provide the following three reference levels of sales analysis:

- Company sales compared to previous years.
- Company sales compared to the industry or product category nationally.
- Company sales compared to the top two or three major competitors in your field.

In addition, whenever possible, collect five years' worth of data for each reference point category. This allows for an adequate amount of time to determine trends which may be occurring in your business.

Finally, if possible, look at sales figures in conjunction with profit figures. There are situations where sales goals are being met but profits are relatively weak. In other situations, profits might be strong but total sales are below expectations. Both situations need monitoring and call for different marketing actions. Yet, only through analyzing both sales and profits together can a marketer get a total picture as to the health of the product or company.

A marketer may determine that while sales are trending up at levels above expectations, profits have been below plan. This may require a review of the expense structure. Perhaps there is a more efficient channel through which to sell the product or a more efficient selling method. Maybe it would be determined that too much was being spent on advertising or promotion. Or maybe the price could be increased without hurting demand. In any case, this knowledge would direct the marketer toward a more in-depth review of sales and profit trending and the potential solutions.

Sales Data

The following sales categories should be analyzed across the reference points outlined above.

Total Sales

Total sales for *company, industry,* and *competition* should be analyzed (see Exhibit 2.8). The sales analysis allows the marketer to establish a clear picture of the sales trends for competitors and the industry as a whole compared to the total sales of the marketer's company. A comparison may find that the industry is doing very well, yet the company is doing poorly. Or the findings may determine that while the individual company is doing quite well, the industry growth is minimal or declining. Each situation would take the marketer in vastly different directions in regard to the development of marketing objectives and strategies (discussed in Chapter 6).

Sales by Brand or Department

Sales for each product or brand, company division, or department should be analyzed. The sales analysis provides insights to specific company product or department categories through a comparison to national industry data. A worksheet for product/brand sales comparisons to industry trends is provided in Appendix B. A recent business review for Famous Footwear showed that the tremendous growth of athletic running shoes over the past five years was slowing and that the growth areas would be women's aerobic, walking, dress, and casual shoes. This information was then compared to Famous Footwear's department sales trends by individual shoe categories to determine if Famous Footwear's performance was following or deviating from overall market trends.

Exhibit 2.8   Industry Sales Compared to Company Sales

Year	Total Industry Sales (M)	Change	Total Company Sales (M)	Change	Your Company's Market Share
1986	$100,000	—%	$4,500	—%	4.5%
1987	110,000	10	5,500	22	5.0
1988	120,000	9	7,000	27	5.8
1989	130,000	8	8,000	14	6.2
1990	150,000	15	9,000	13	6.0

Estimated Sales by Competitor	Sales 1986 (M)	Market Share	Sales 1987 (M)	Market Share	Sales 1988 (M)	Market Share	Sales 1989 (M)	Market Share	Sales 1990 (M)	Market Share
Competitor A	$6,500	6.5%	$7,500	6.8%	$9,500	7.9%	$11,000	8.5%	$12,000	8.0%
Competitor B	3,000	3.0	4,000	3.6	7,000	5.8	8,000	6.2	9,000	6.0
Competitor C	7,500	7.5	8,000	7.3	9,000	7.5	10,000	7.7	10,000	6.7
Total Market Sales		100 %		100 %		100 %		100 %		100 %

Market Share

Market share is your product's sales as a percent of the total market or category's sales. Market share can relate to total company dollar sales as a percent of total market or category dollar sales; total unit sales as a percent of total market or category unit sales; or total product sales as a percent of total market product or category sales. It is a measure that quickly tells you how well your company or product is performing from a sales standpoint relative to the competition.

The sales analysis should provide market share information. What percent of the market does your company have? Is it growing, shrinking, or stable? Market share information is used to help you develop a point of reference from which you can evaluate and plan your future marketing efforts.

The chart in Exhibit 2.8 demonstrates industry performance and percent change in growth relative to your company's performance. The result is a market share figure for your company. The worksheet in Appendix B also allows you to compare the market share growth of your company with the estimated market share growth of your major competitors. Note that the chart could also be utilized for individual products, departments, or product categories. In addition, company profit could also be included in the same manner as sales.

Store-for-Store Sales for Retailers

Total retail sales for a company often reflect growth that comes from the opening of additional outlets rather than increases from individual stores. Sales need to be monitored on a store-for-store basis in order to determine the relative health of each unit/outlet as well as the total system of stores. The chart in Exhibit 2.9 shows total sales and per store averages (see Appendix B for worksheet). Charts would be developed on an annual basis over a five-year period for comparison. For example, there would be a separate chart for 1985, 1986, 1987, 1988, and 1989.

Seasonality of Sales

It is also important to ascertain the strength of the industry, the company, and each individual brand or department on a monthly basis (and even a weekly and daily

Exhibit 2.9   Store-for-Store Sales

Market	Sales Volume (M)	Change from Previous Year	Number of Stores	Per Store Average (M)	Change from Previous Year	Per Store Average Indexed to System Average ($569.2M)
Tulsa	$2,202.7	+12%	2	$1,001.4	+12%	$176
Minneapolis	6,147.5	+54*	8	768.4	+35*	135†
Milwaukee						
Atlanta						
Tampa						
•						
•						
•						

*The percent change for total sales volume is higher than per store average volume due to a decrease in per store averages and an addition of stores. For example, this would be evident if there were a 1988 chart showing seven stores versus eight in the Minneapolis market during 1989.

†Minneapolis stores do 35 points better on a per store basis than the system average, which is $569.2M.

Break-even per store average for total system: $500,000. (Include this figure as another comparison point to be utilized when analyzing market performance.)

Note: Make sure your year-to-year analysis of per store averages includes comparable stores that have been open for the full year.

basis for retailers). This will allow the marketer a description of what months are typically strong-selling months and which are weaker-selling. The chart in Exhibit 2.10 tracks seasonality of industry sales as compared to company sales. The chart shown in Exhibit 2.11 demonstrates performance of individual brands or departments within your company on a monthly basis. The chart provides seasonality of sales by month for each brand or department. It is helpful to develop five-year trends of these charts to compare and note any significant movement or changes in the seasonality from year to year. See Appendix B for worksheets to complete with information specific to your company.

The sales analysis provides answers to seasonality questions regarding sales performance by time of the year. This type of data is used to determine how you will budget on a monthly basis and when specific products will receive marketing emphasis.

Exhibit 2.10   Sales Seasonality by Month

Month	Company Percent of Sales	Company Index to Average (8.33)	Industry Percent of Sales	Industry Index to Average (8.33)
January	10%*	120*	8%*	96*
February				
March				
April				
May				
June				
July				
August				
September				
October				
November				
December				

*10 percent of the company's sales occur in January. If sales are equal each month, 8.33 percent of the sales would occur in January (10/8.33 = 120); January was above average for sales. The industry index of 96 was slightly below average, demonstrating that company sales for the month of January are substantially above the norm when compared to industry sales. Another way to do this would be to take *total* sales and divide by 12 to get an average. Use this average as the base and divide each month's sales by the base to get an index.

Exhibit 2.11   Brand Seasonality by Month

	Base*	November		December		Etc.
		Percent of Total Dollars	Index to Total Year	Percent of Total Dollars	Index to Total Year	
Company Brand X	38.2%†	41.9%†	110†			
Company Brand Y	18.5	22.8	123			
Company Brand Z	6.2	11.2	181			

Base equals total figures for the year. Brand X accounts for 38.2 percent of the total company business.

†Brand X accounts for 38.2 percent of the sales volume during the year. During November, Brand X accounts for 41.9 percent (41.9 percent/38.2 percent = 110). This means that Brand X does better than it normally does throughout the year during the month of November, while accounting for 41.9 percent of the company's total business.

Sales by Geographic Territory/Target Market Segments

Finally, you can look at sales across a number of additional bases. The following will provide you subsequent information with which to make marketing decisions:

Sales by geographic territory.

Sales by target market segment:

Total households.

Males.

Females.

Different ages.

Income levels.

Heavy users/light users.

Combinations of the above or other demographic variables.

Questions to Be Addressed

Wherever possible use five year trend data.

Total Sales

- Is the overall product category strong? Is it growing or declining? What are industry sales for the past five years? What is the percent increase over that period?

- What are the total company sales and profit levels for the past five years? What is the growth rate? What is the growth rate compared to the industry, compared to your key competitors?

- Are market sales likely to expand or shrink in the next two, five, or ten years? How will this affect your company?

Sales by Brand or Department

- Now that you have charted your company's total sales, what are the sales and profit trends for your individual products, services, or departments over the past five years? What is the growth rate relative to the national average or key competitors' products, services, or departments? Why?

- What products, services, or departments show the most potential in relationship to sales and profit within your *company?* What products, services, or departments show the most potential in terms of sales and profit relative to the *national category and competitive products?*

- Which products are above or below the budgeted margin over the past five years? Which products have the highest margin and the lowest margin?

Market Share

- What is the market share of your total company sales within your industry over the past five years? Are you gaining or losing market share? Why?

- What is the market share for each of your company's products or departments relative to the national product category or relative to key competitors' products or departments market share over the past five years? Are you gaining or losing market share? Why?

- What competitors have gained/lost the most market share? Why?

Store-for-Store for Retailers

- What are store-for-store sales over the past five years? Have they been increasing or decreasing? How do they compare to total sales?
- Is there a certain per store sales average that must be met to break even?
- Which markets are above the break even point and which are below?
- Which stores/markets are above or below budgeted sales and profits?

Seasonality of Sales

- What products sell during what times of the year? Does demand vary by season, business conditions, location, weather?
- How do your company sales differ from the total category's sales? Is there a time of the year in which you don't do as well or in which you outperform the industry as a whole? What is the seasonality of your company's product and the product category as a whole?
- Do specific products have strong seasonal selling periods that differ from the category nationally?
- For retailers, what are the weekly and daily seasonality trends of your product? Which days of the week are strong in sales relative to others? Which weeks are strong in sales relative to others?

Sales by Geographic Territory/Target Market Segments

- Are there areas of the country that provide more total sales and profits and/or sales per capita than others? Why?
- Are there target market segments that account for more total sales and profits, sales per capita than others? Why?

Step 5

Product Awareness and Product Attributes

We have documented in case after case that an increase in awareness of a quality product leads to increases in purchase rates or, in the terminology of our agency, *increased share of mind leads to increased share of purchases*. Therefore, awareness of your product or service is an important barometer of its future success.

Product Awareness

Typically, awareness is measured through primary research on two levels, unaided and aided. *Unaided* is generally considered a more accurate measure. It involves consumers recalling specific product names without any assistance. *Aided* awareness is the awareness generated by asking individuals which product they are familiar with after reading or reviewing with them a list of competing products.

Awareness measures allow the marketing manager to fine tune advertising message and media strategies. Some examples of how awareness is used to help formulate subsequent marketing strategies are:

- Low awareness levels signal the need for a more aggressive or effective advertising and promotional plan. Often, the primary problem is that the product has low awareness among consumers, not that the product necessarily needs a repositioning. This is especially true if the product has positive attribute ratings from current users and it has a high trial/repeat usage ratio.
- Markets with high levels of awareness often don't need as much media weight to

sustain existing sales levels as those markets that have low awareness. And many times it requires less media weight to generate successful promotions in established markets with high awareness than in newer markets where a customer base is not yet established and a minimal number of potential consumers have heard of your product or company. As an example, markets in which a product has low awareness often require larger print ads than markets with higher awareness levels. Our experience has shown that small newspaper ads are more likely to be seen by current users, and it takes larger ads to attract the attention of infrequent users or individuals who are not aware of your product.

- Markets with falling awareness levels often indicate isolated market specific problems such as increased competitive activity. These problems may require an individual market plan tailored to the specific market situation along with investment spending over the short-term to stabilize and increase awareness levels.

If you cannot afford primary research, we would encourage you to informally conduct an awareness study for your product. Randomly call individuals in your geographic selling area. Ask them if they have used products and frequented stores in your category in the past year. If they have, ask them to name all the stores in the area where they can purchase the product category, or to name all the brands they are familiar with in the product category (unaided awareness measure). Try to get between 100 and 200 responses. Also keep track of first mentions (those products/stores mentioned first by each respondent without receiving assistance) as this is a good prediction of your company's market share relative to the competition.

With this information you can infer what percent of the potential customer base is aware of your product and where it ranks relative to the competition. This will provide a rough approximation of unaided awareness levels for your product and that of the competition. You can also determine the first mention level, a strong indication of market share, actual use of the product, or propensity to use, since customers will most often mention first a brand or company name they normally use the most.

Questions to Be Addressed

- What is the unaided and aided awareness of your product compared to the competition? Have awareness levels been increasing or decreasing over the past five years?

- What is the first mention level (first product mentioned) by consumers without receiving assistance?

Product Attributes

Product attributes or benefits are derived from consumers' perceptions of the product. This step of the business review is critical to developing future marketing plans, for it allows the marketing manager to define the strengths and weaknesses of the company's product relative to the competition. It is necessary to find what attributes are important to purchasers and users of your product and then determine how your company or product compares to the competition on these attributes. There may be attributes that you need to improve. Or you may find there are certain needs that no one in the marketplace is fulfilling, providing your company the opportunity to dominate an important niche. The repositioning of a menswear chain we worked with was brought about because the retailer determined that the most important attributes to the target market were quality and value, not low purchase price, which was being emphasized. The repositioning emphasized value (a good price on perceived quality brands). The theme line became "Ross and Ross for Businessmenswear," which denoted a special quality and expertise and labeled a specific group of people identified with quality men's clothing.

Questions to Be Addressed

The information to answer these questions is normally obtained through primary research. If your company cannot afford to undertake primary research to answer these questions, then you should use available secondary research and attempt to answer them yourself in as much detail as possible. Also, have other individuals in your organization answer them to see if your perceptions match those of your co-workers. Perhaps even get other individuals outside of your company to answer the questions to compare with answers from people within your organization.

- How is your product used? What is the product's primary benefit to the consumer?
- What are the important product attributes of your product's category? What are the important attributes of your competitors' products? How do your company's products rank on those attributes versus the competition?
- What do purchasers and users like and dislike about your product?
- Are there differences between heavy users' likes and dislikes compared to the overall user of your product category?
- Are there substitutes that can be used in place of your company's product or the product category?
- Is there anything unusual about how your product is manufactured or designed that would be of interest or benefit to consumers? Is there anything about your product that can help differentiate it from the competition? For example, how is it manufactured? Does it have a unique color, shape, or texture? Does your product last longer than others like it? What about guarantees? Are there unique performance attributes that make it superior to the competition? Is there unique packaging? Is your product more convenient to use than the competitor's? Is your product of better quality? What about the competitors' products?
- Are there any inherent product qualities that have not been communicated but are important to the buyer? (Same for your competition.)
- If you have many competitors, how does your product rank in terms of overall quality? How does your product rank in terms of value (the combination of quality and price)? Where does your product rank in terms of performance, durability, serviceability, and aesthetic appearance compared to the competition?
- What is the history of your product? When was it first marketed? What changes have been made to the product and why? (Same for your competition.)
- Is your product accepted by a broad consumer base or a narrow segment? Why?
- Does your product have any patents that are active? Does your unique advantage depend upon a specific design, formula, or manufacturing capability that could be readily copied? Or is your product unique due to patent protection or some manufacturing process that is difficult or costly to duplicate?

    What are the new developments in your product category? What will be the next big innovation? What product improvements are consumers looking for?

Product Life Cycle

Most products go through a product life cycle. Understanding your product's stage in the product life cycle will help predict anticipated target markets, competition, pricing, distribution, and advertising strategies. The following is a brief outline of how we view the product life cycle and how each stage affects these five areas.

Introduction Phase

Target Market Usually innovators try new products. The goal is to get opinion leader types of people to try and use the product. It is usually more difficult to sell a new product or concept to a mass audience during the introduction period.

Competition Typically there are few competitors in the introduction stage, as the technology and start-up costs for a new product or product category are high.

Pricing Usually the company that first introduces a product has the freedom to set prices as desired. Companies can "cream the price," setting it high for maximum profits on each unit, or set a low price attempting to obtain as many customers as possible. The pricing decision is often a function of the company's ability to produce the product, product availability, and the amount of anticipated competition.

Distribution During the introduction stage, distribution is usually through specialized channels, rather than mass distribution channels. This is because a good deal of attention needs to be paid to educating consumers about the product and how to use it.

Advertising Advertising of a new product is usually educational in nature, convincing people to try the product and explaining how the product will provide benefits not currently found in the marketplace.

Growth Phase

Target Market The market is still growing, with new users purchasing the product for the first time. The product is becoming accepted by a wider profile of consumers.

Competition As product acceptance gains, the number of competitors increases.

Pricing While competition is focused primarily on product attributes, pricing variations are introduced along with diversification and differentiation of the product. Price cutting occurs, and discounters try to steal market share and broaden the customer base by making the product or service more affordable. Higher priced, higher quality products are also introduced and marketed.

Distribution Distribution expands from specialty stores to more mass distribution channels, such as chains.

Advertising The communication focus moves away from selling the product category and educating consumers. Advertising takes on the role of positioning particular products with specific attributes or benefits against the competition as a result of product differentiation and increased competitive levels.

Maturity Phase

Target Market The product is now accepted by all or most consumers. When bank automated teller machines were first introduced, only young innovators used them, with older adults preferring to go into a bank for transactions. Now, after a prolonged introduction period, people of all ages more readily use the machines.

Competition The market is very competitive at this stage.

Pricing In this stage, pricing becomes very important. Products are often standardized, with fewer product innovations and fewer discernable differences that haven't already been seen. Thus, the selling emphasis is not as much on product attributes as on price and customer service.

Distribution All channels now have access to the product.

Advertising The communication strategy shifts toward keeping and improving brand name awareness and differentiating your product from the competition's. By this time, share of mind equals share of market. The company needs to communicate its brand name and have it included in the "evoke set" of brands that comes to mind when a customer is thinking of purchasing.

Questions to Be Addressed

- Where is your product in the product life cycle? How will this affect your marketing decisions?

Step 6
Purchase Rates/ Buying Habits

The marketer should analyze purchase rates and buying habits to further determine where, how, and why consumers are purchasing the company's product. Buying habit information can provide invaluable insight into the target market and provide impact for marketing decisions during the writing of the marketing plan. These decisions revolve around either trying to change current consumption patterns (which is most difficult) or recognizing the patterns and modifying the product, or the way in which the product is sold to better meet the needs of the target market.

Purchase Rates of the Product Category and Your Company's Product by Geographic Markets

Geographic markets should be analyzed for their importance in sales for the category (Category Development Index, or CDI) and sales for your company's product (Brand Development Index, or BDI).

The Category Development Index (CDI) determines the *product category's* strength on a market-by-market basis. It provides a quick index of whether the geographical area or any given market's purchases are at above or below the average, given the size of its population in relation to the total country's population. CDI information allows the marketer to determine markets that have strong per capita sales potential. This information can be used in recommending expansion markets, predicting sales, or as rationale for investment-spending decisions.

The formula for calculating the CDI is

$$\text{CDI} = \frac{\text{Percentage of product category's national}}{\text{dollar volume in a given market}} \Big/ \frac{}{\text{Percentage of U.S. population in a}} \text{given market}$$

Exhibit 2.12 presents a chart that can be used to develop this information and how the calculations are done. A blank worksheet is provided in Appendix B.

The Brand Development Index (BDI) provides an index that determines whether a geographical market purchases your *company's product* at above or below average rates given its population in relation to your company's national market population. For example, if your company only did business in three cities—these three cities and their surrounding trading area population would define your company's national market population. BDI information is used to help formulate geographic spending strategies. Strong company markets can be protected, and weak markets can be targeted for growth.

The formula for calculating the BDI is

$$\text{BDI} = \frac{\text{Percentage company's dollar volume in any given market}}{\text{Percentage of company's national market population that lives in any given market}}$$

Exhibit 2.13 presents a chart that can be used to develop this information. See Appendix B for a blank worksheet.

Often the CDI and BDI numbers are used together. High CDI markets mean the potential exists for good sales as the product category as a whole does well. If these same markets have low company BDI indexes with adequate product distribution and store penetration/market coverage, the markets are often targeted for aggressive marketing plans. Thus, strong category sales (high CDI) and low company sales (low BDI) can mean potential for your company's growth.

Questions to Be Addressed

- Where exactly do your customers reside? Do they live nationwide or are they limited to certain regions? Are they living in large cities, suburbs, rural areas (C and D counties)?

Exhibit 2.12   National Category Development Index (CDI)

DMA*	Percent of U.S. Population	Percent of Product Dollar Volume	Category Development Index: CDI (Volume/Population)	Population Number (000)	Dollar Volume of Product Category Nationally (000)	Per Capita Consumption
Chicago Madison Philadelphia Mineapolis Atlanta	3.5%†	4.5%†	129†	8,493‡	$827,548‡	$97.4‡

*DMA = Designated marketing area defined by television viewing audience.

†3.5 percent of the U.S. population lives in Chicago; 4.5 percent of the category's national sales volume (for example, all shoes sold nationally) is from the Chicago DMA. The Chicago DMA does better in category business than the average DMA as is indicated by the CDI of 129 (4.5/3.5 = 129).

‡Further, 8,493,000 people live in the Chicago DMA. The Chicago population consumes $827,548,000 worth of the product for a per capita consumption of $97.4.

Exhibit 2.13   Company Brand Development Index (BDI)

DMA	Percent of Company's National Market Population	Percent of Dollar Volume	Brand Development Index: BDI (Volume/Population)	Population Number (000)	Dollar Volume Company (000)	Per Capita Consumption
Chicago Madison Philadelphia Mineapolis Atlanta Etc.	11.2%*	10.0%*	89*	8,493†	$200,000†	$23.55†

*11.2 percent of the company's total market population lives in the Chicago DMA: 10 percent of the company's sales are from the Chicago DMA. The BDI for Chicago is 89 (10/11.2 = 89) which means the DMA has a below average BDI as compared to other DMAs in the system.

†Further, 8,493,000 people live in the Chicago DMA. Company sales in Chicago are $200,000 or $23.55 per person.

- Where are sales for your *product category* strongest and weakest nationally (CDI)? Where are your *company's sales* strongest and weakest (BDI)?
- What markets have above or below average consumption per household or per person (CDI)? Does your company have different geographical distribution from that of the category in general?
- What are the markets at above or below average purchase rates on a household or per person basis (BDI)?
- Are national sales increasing at greater or lesser rates than the population growth? Are there specific markets where this is different?

Trading Areas

In addition to CDI and BDI information, the retail/service marketer should determine the trading area for the product. A trading area is the geographical territory where your customers live. This is important not only from a media purchasing standpoint but also for determining future store locations, as discussed in Chapter 10, Distribution.

Through a simple in-store customer survey, as shown in Exhibit 2.14, you can determine where your customers come from. Or, if you keep accurate customer mailing lists, they can allow you to construct trading areas.

Questions to Be Addressed

- What is the trading area for your product? How far do consumers travel to purchase your product?

Brand Loyalty

Brand loyalty is a measure of how loyal your customers are over a period of time. If your customers primarily use only your company's product, they are brand loyal. If they use your product a majority of the time, but occasionally use your competitors' products, they are moderately brand loyal. And, if brand or product switching occurs regularly, there exists low brand loyalty.

Brand loyalty is analyzed to provide insights into the following types of issues:

- How difficult it will be to keep your own customers.
- How difficult it will be to steal market share from competitors.
- The degree of promotional offers that will be needed to induce trial.
- How much media weight will be necessary to increase trial, retrial, and sales.
- Whether a true product difference or innovation is needed to compete.

Exhibit 2.14   Trading Areas by Store

Zip Codes Surrounding Store	Percent of Customers Over 1 Week Period
53704	20%
53705	30
53703	20
53702	10
53711	10
53708	5
53709	1
Other	4

Exhibit 2.15   Brand Loyalty

Brand	All	Sole	Loyalty Index	Sole and Primary	Loyalty Index
Cooper	16.4%	2.7%	16	11.6%	71
Hiebing	12.9	2.6	20	9.5	74
Dorton	11.5	1.2	10	6.9	60
Michaels	9.9	1.9	19	6.0	60

Obviously a product category with extremely high brand loyalty will require more media weight, larger promotional offers or inducements, and perhaps even a product innovation in order to be able to steal market share from existing competitors. With a low brand loyalty type of product category, it is extremely difficult to keep your own customers but it is also easier to steal market share.

The chart in Exhibit 2.15 provides a measure of the brand loyalty that exists within the product category. For example, 9.9 percent of all purchasers use Michaels brand, while 1.9 percent use only Michaels brand. The resulting loyalty measure of 19 (1.9/ 9.9) compares favorably to the other brands in the category. However, the category as a whole does not exhibit strong loyalty.

When adding sole and primary loyalty figures together, it appears that Micheals slips in loyalty relative to the other brands. In other words, there exists a group of loyal Michaels users, but it is not as much of a widely accepted brand/alternative than the other brands in the category. Dorton, on the other hand, has fewer loyal users but is considered a strong second choice or accepted brand in the category. The worksheet in Appendix B can be used to develop information specific to your company.

Questions to Be Addressed

- Is buying by brand name important to consumers in your category? What percent of the consumers in the category are brand loyal—most of the time, all of the time, never?
- How brand loyal are your customers? Is brand switching common?
- Do heavy users have different loyalty than the overall users?

Buying Habits

Buying habits, such as frequency of purchase, also need to be determined. In analyzing the average time between purchases, the marketer can make decisions as to how frequently the business needs to advertise and promote the product. This information also helps when making promotion decisions. If the product is purchased only once a year, a viable strategy would be to provide a strong incentive for purchase prior to the typical purchasing season. Or, if the purchase decision is made frequently at short intervals, a continuity program of lower media weight levels might be required.

In addition to frequency of purchase, the marketer should also determine if the purchase decision is made spontaneously in-store or planned prior to shopping. We did work for a product that was purchased spontaneously in-store 90 percent of the time. Obviously, point-of-purchase advertising and display became critical to the product's success.

Retailers can do *in-store research* to obtain purchase behavior by having customers complete a brief questionnaire. A worksheet for a questionnaire, presented in Appendix B, provides examples of what can be achieved through this type of primary research. A "heavy purchasers" and "all purchasers" category is provided for each question. From this data you can determine purchasing patterns, overall consumer loyalty, and how your store specifically compares to all stores. An example of information you can generate from this data: heavy users visit all stores at a 40 percent greater rate than all purchasers, yet visit your store only 20 percent more than all purchasers. Thus, from this data you may determine that you are not as efficient in attracting the heavy user.

Finally, in looking at buying habits, everything about the purchasing environment, the psychology of the purchaser at the time of the purchase, the average purchase ratio (for retailers this is the number of times a consumer comes into a retail store and purchases versus not purchasing and walking), and the actual purchasing habits should be analyzed. This information will lead to strategic marketing decisions aimed at better meeting the needs of the target market.

Questions to Be Addressed

- What factors are important to the purchase decision making process? What is the purchase decision sequence a consumer makes when purchasing your product? How can you positively affect this?

- How frequently are purchases made? What is the purchase cycle for your product or service? What is the frequency of purchase for all users versus heavy users?

- What is the size and quantity of each purchase? (One, two, three bars of soap per trip/large, medium, or small package sizes?) Do consumers purchase in bulk, stock up, or do consumers purchase your product one at a time?

- What is the purchase ratio? What percent of customers purchase when they visit the store?

- What percent of the product category purchases are on sale or at discount? What percent of your company product purchases are on sale or discounted? What is the average sale or discount percentage? Are there times of the year when sales or discounting occur at greater rates than others?

- How important is customer service, personal selling, salesperson advice/consultation to the purchaser or the purchase decision?

- Is the buying decision spontaneous (made in-store) or planned? What percent of the buying decisions are made at the point of purchase versus at home or over a longer period of time?

- Do the heavy users have different buying habits than the overall users?

Trial and Retrial

Another important area of investigation is trial and retrial. The Hiebing Group did work for a dominant national client that had a specialty line of consumer package good products. The product sold was basically the same but each was packaged for specific uses—packages for the car, the teenager's bedroom, dad's work area, and the woman's purse. The initial thinking was that we would expand usage categories for the products; in other words, find other places besides the car for consumers to use that product. However, after studying the buying habit findings in the situation analysis, we discovered two things:

Overall trial of the family of products was very low.

Of those people who tried the products, retrial was very high.

Exhibit 2.16   Trial/Retrial

Brand	Percent Ever Used	Percent Used Last 6 Months	Loyalty Measure: Percent Used Past 6 Months/Percent Ever Used
Company X			
A	81%	48%	59
Competition			
C	58	22	38
D	43	17	40
E	30	15	50
F	25	17	68

Brand A has a much higher trial (ever used), retrial (used last 6 months) and thus loyalty rate higher than any other competitor with the exception of Brand F. However, while Brand F has strong loyalty measure (68) it has a low initial trial figure, a problem that should receive primary attention in the marketing plan.

In summary, the challenge was not in finding more uses for the family of products, but in promoting trial. Once consumers tried one of the products, the chances were good they would continue to purchase them. However, if we had found that the retrial rate was in fact very poor, we would have had another set of *product-related* problems to focus on, thus taking our marketing emphasis in the direction of finding out why customers weren't satisfied with the product. The chart in Exhibit 2.16 provides a summary of trial and retrial (consumer acceptance) percentages. Use the worksheet in Appendix B to develop information specific to your company.

Questions to Be Addressed

- What percent of the customer base has tried your product?
- How common is retrial? What percent become regular users?
- Do heavy users have different trial and retrial rates than the overall users?

Step 7

Distribution

Distribution is the method of delivering the product to the consumer. In the business review, your job is to determine which method of distribution is used most successfully by the industry, your company, and your competitors. However, the concept of distribution varies depending upon the type of business category.

Retail

Retailers need to be aware of how and where their product is sold in relation to the industry. There are many unique ways to distribute the product to the consumer, and retailers should be aware of which distribution methods are increasing or decreasing in their industry and the advantages and disadvantages of the different methods.

Channel Type/Trends

The retailer has to determine and review the optimum outlet category for the product being sold and the consumer who is purchasing. Common retail distribution outlet categories include mass merchandise, discount, off-price, department stores, spe-

Exhibit 2.17   Purchases by Outlet Type (5 Year Trend)

	Total Sales				Points Change 1986 to 1990	
	1986		1990			
Distribution Outlet*	Units	Dollars	Units	Dollars	Units	Dollars
Specialty store	36.2%†	48.4%†	43.1%†	51.2%†	6.9%†	3.8%†
Department store						
National chain						
Discount store						
Direct mail						
Other						

*The chart for retailers could easily be modified for appropriate use by package good or business-to-business firms by changing distribution outlets to reflect the industry. For example, a package good firm might want to look at sales by chain grocery stores, independent grocery stores, convenience food stores, delis, and specialty grocery stores.

†36.2 percent of the units and 48.4 percent of the dollars were sold through specialty stores in 1986. There was a 6.9 percent increase in units and a 3.8 percent increase in dollars between 1986 and 1990.

cialty shops, chain stores, and direct mail. Each is a unique distribution method a retailer can use to sell the product to the consumer. To do this, it helps to analyze the current channel trends. The business review may determine that for your product category, the two fastest growing methods of distribution are smaller, single-line specialty shops and direct mail. If you were not currently using these channels, you would need to address the industry's shift in emphasis toward these alternative methods of distribution in the marketing plan. This could be done by adapting some of the strengths of specialty store retailing to your channel environment or by experimenting with direct mail. The chart in Exhibit 2.17 details dollar sales and unit sales by outlet type (see Appendix B for worksheet).

Geography

The geographical distribution of outlets should be studied. Try to grade the location of your stores relative to your competitors. Is your firm located in the optimal trading areas of the market? Are they easy to get to and do they have good access? Are they on or near thoroughfares of high traffic counts and other thriving retail locations? Are there markets or specific trading areas within markets that have large numbers of purchases per person and/or household and low levels of competition where you should be doing business?

Penetration

Optimum penetration levels (number of stores per *market*) should be calculated to determine if more distribution outlets are needed. Note that in the broadest sense we define *markets* as DMAs—Designated Market Areas or Television Coverage Areas—but markets can be defined in terms of a DMA, SMSA (Standard Metropolitan Statistical Area), county, or city/metro trading area. Penetration levels are evaluated on three issues:

■ The total number of competing outlets a market can support.

- The number of your stores a market can support before cannibalization (stealing of customers from one of your stores by another) occurs.
- The number of stores that are required in order for mass media such as newspapers, television, and radio to be efficiently leveraged, making the media affordable for your company from a percent of market sales or sales per store standpoint.

We show two methodologies for determining optimum store penetration levels for each market (see Appendix B for worksheets to use in developing information for you company). The chart in Exhibit 2.18 determines the number of stores needed for Group 1 markets. In this example, Group 1 markets are underpenetrated and thus have not received the type of advertising support as the stores in Group 2. Because of this, Group 2 stores have stronger sales performance than Group 1 stores.

In essence, this methodology assumes that if Group 1 markets are more fully penetrated with additional stores, the markets will be able to afford more advertising, and the individual store sales figures will increase. Though it would be unrealistic to expect Group 1 stores to equal Group 2 stores in sales in the near future, ideals are established—the average sales per household and per store of the weaker Group 1 markets and the stronger Group 2 markets.

The number of stores needed calculation is determined by:

- Multiplying the estimated TV market households by the average sales per household figure of the weaker Group 1 markets and the stronger Group 2 markets.
- The end result of this multiplication divided by the average per store sales for the Group 1 and Group 2 markets provides a realistic penetration figure.

The calculations for Market A in Group 1 are

New sales goal based upon expected potential

Estimated TV HHs	×	Average sales per HH in Groups 1 and 2	=	New sales goal for Market A
1,229.6		$4.26		$5,238.09M

Optimum projected stores for Market A

New sales goal for Market A	÷	Per store average of Groups 1 and 2	=	Ideal number of stores required for optimum penetration
$5,238.09		$637.02		8.22 Stores

In addition, Exhibit 2.18 provides an advertising comparison in the form of gross rating points (GRPs, see Chapter 13, Advertising Media, for definition) that could be achieved given a 5 percent advertising budget from the new projected sales and store penetration. Continuing with the examples, Market A will have a new sales goal of $5,238M from eight stores. Five percent of $5,238M equals $261.9M, equating to a media weight level of 2,567 GRPs with a 2/3 TV, 1/3 newspaper mix.

The chart in Exhibit 2.19 shows yet another way to calculate estimated penetration requirements. As with Exhibit 2.18, this chart takes a group of stores seen as optimum and utilizes their performance as the standard. Through this analysis, it was determined that the best performing markets from a sales standpoint have approximately one store per 100,000 households. This was accomplished by reviewing sales of those markets meeting sales and profit expectations. Column 6 shows how many stores would be needed in each market to match this goal.

In addition, this chart looks at how many weeks of television the markets could currently sustain, given the advertising goal of 5 percent of sales. This is then compared to the number of advertising weeks which could be afforded, given the optimum penetration level of 1 store per 100M households, and the subsequent increase (or decrease) in sales this would create in any given market. For example, Market A currently has a per store average of $461.9M ($3,233M/7). With a projection of 12.3 stores (1 store per 100M households), the new market sales figure becomes $5,681.7M (12.3 × $461.9M). A 5 percent advertising budget, given the fully penetrated projected market sales of $5,681.7M, is $284.1M.

Exhibit 2.18   Store Penetration Analysis: I

	Number of Stores	Sales Last Year (M)	Estimated Number TV HH's (M)	Sales per HH
Group 1 Markets (Weaker Markets)				
A	7	$ 3,233.5	1,229.6	$ 2.63
B	9	4,508.9	1,662.1	2.71
C	6	2,292.1	708.9	3.23
D	2	1,597.6	868.2	1.84
E	4	2,079.9	2,518.0	.83
F	4	2,122.1	602.7	3.52
Subtotal	32	$15,834.1	7,589.5	$ 2.09
Group 2 Markets (Stronger Markets)				
G	22	$13,487.1	3,016.8	$ 4.47
H	15	10,746.9	992.9	10.82
I	5	4,350.4	703.7	6.18
J	3	2,407.8	209.5	11.49
K	5	4,323.6	694.9	6.22
L	14	10,004.4	1,156.6	8.65
Subtotal	64	$45,320.2	6,774.4	$ 6.69
Totals/Averages Groups 1 and 2	96	$61,154.3	14,363.9	$ 4.26

Average per store sales groups 1 and 2 $637.02 M ($61,154.3/96)

*⅔ weight in TV, ⅓ weight in newspaper.

Exhibit 2.19   Store Penetration Analysis: II

	Existing Stores		
	Number of Stores	Existing Stores per 100M HHs	Total Sales Last Year (M)	Advertising Budget 5 Percent of Sales (M)
---	---	---	---	---
A	7	.569	$ 3,233.5	$ 161.7
B	9	.541	4,508.9	225.4
C	6	.846	2,292.1	114.6
D	2	.230	1,597.6	79.9
E	4	.159	2,079.9	104.0
F	4	.664	2,122.1	106.1
G	22	.729	13,487.1	674.4
H	15	1.511	10,746.9	537.3
I	5	.711	4,350.4	217.5
J	3	1.432	2,407.8	120.4
K	5	.720	4,323.6	216.2
L	14	1.210	10,004.4	500.2
All Stores	146	.536	$96,445.5	$4,822.3

*200 W18–49 GRPs TV: 30's

Questions to Be Addressed

- Where do consumers shop for products in your category? Where do they shop for your company's product? What channel or outlet type do consumers use most when purchasing?
- What is the importance of department stores, supermarkets, specialty stores,

Current Advertising Plans		Future Advertising Plans			
5 Percent of Sales (M)	W18–49 GRP Media Weight Level*	Average Sales per HH	Number of Stores Needed	5 Percent of Sales (M)	W18–49 GRP Media Weight Level*
$ 161.7	1,587	$4.26	8.22	$ 261.9	2,567
225.4	1,896	4.26	11.12	354.0	2,978
114.6	1,983	4.26	4.74	151.0	2,613
79.9	1,535	4.26	5.80	184.9	3,552
104.0	512	4.26	16.84	536.3	2,641
106.1	1,901	4.26	4.03	128.4	2,301
$ 791.7	1,358	$4.26	50.75	$1,916.5	2,770
$ 674.4	3,148				
537.3	5,055				
217.5	3,191				
120.4	4,391				
216.2	3,947				
500.2	4,023				
$2,266.0	3,704				
$3,057.7	2,461				

Existing Stores		Penetration of 1 Store per 100M HHs		
Estimated 1 Week Cost	Estimated Number of Advertising Weeks*	Minimum Stores 1/100M HHs	Advertising Budget 5 Percent of Sales	New Estimated Number of Advertising Weeks
$24.6	6–7	12.3	$284.1	11–12
27.6	8	16.6	415.8	15
13.8	8	7.1	135.6	10
11.4	7	8.7	347.5	30
48.6	2	25.2	655.2	13
13.8	7–8	6.0	159.2	12
49.6	13–14	30.2	925.7	19
27.0	20	10.0	358.2	13
17.0	12–13	7.0	304.5	18
7.2	16–17	2.1	84.3	12
13.0	16–17	6.9	298.3	23
31.6	15–16	11.6	414.5	13
—	—	272.4	—	—

chain stores, independents, direct mail, discount stores, or other types of outlets that sell your product category or product? What are the sales trends of each outlet type used by your product category? (5 Year Trend)

- What channels or methods of distribution are receiving increased use by the industry? Are new channels emerging? What trends are noticeable in the stores that dominate the sales of your product category?

- What channels or methods of distribution does your competition use? If they use different channels from you, why?

- Do you have adequate penetration of outlets to maximize sales in any given market?

- Does expansion into new territories make sense? Are there additional areas of the country where you should be doing business?

- Does your product require mass, selective, or exclusive distribution? Why? Does it require a combination of distribution methods? Who can best provide this type of distribution? What about your competitors' products; do they require mass, selective, or exclusive distribution?

Package Goods

A package good company views distribution differently from a retailer. Package good companies sell to outlets, which in turn sell to consumers. A cereal company sells to grocery stores who in turn sell to consumers. Unlike retailers, package good companies don't own the channel of distribution; thus, there is more emphasis placed on making sure the package goods product is accepted and sold into the channel, and receives proper shelf space and merchandising support relative to competitors' products.

Channel Type/Trends

The package good marketer has to determine the type of channel(s) best suited for the product. For example, it may be chain grocery stores, independent grocery stores, mass merchandisers, specialty stores, or convenience stores.

Market Coverage

As with retailing, you need to determine the number of outlets required to cover a trading area efficiently. But since the package good firm doesn't own the outlets, there is less concern with over penetration. In some cases, the goal is to reach 100 percent market coverage of grocery store outlets in a given market. At the other extreme, some manufacturers offer exclusive distribution to a chain in return for greater sales and merchandising support. In still other situations, the product is distributed on a more limited basis to outlets that are consistent with the image of the product.

In most cases, package goods marketers do not refer to distribution coverage in terms of total stores. Distribution is referred to as the percent of total grocery store dollar volume that the stores carrying the marketer's product accounts for in all grocery commodities, or all commodity volume (ACV). Thus the term 65 percent ACV means that the marketer's brand is carried by grocery stores doing 65 percent of all commodity grocery store volume.

The chart in Exhibit 2.20 provides information detailing market coverage. This process is used primarily by manufacturers. The example is for a package goods firm but could easily be adapted to business-to-business. (A similar chart would be created for each business-to-business SIC.) From this chart you would determine that your product was represented in eight of the nine major outlets but that those outlets accounted for only 60 percent of the total product category business in the market.

Exhibit 2.20   Market Coverage Chart—Rockford

	Coverage for Your Product	Percent of Total Product Business in Market (% ACV)	Percent of Shelf Space Given Your Product in Store	Percent of Shelf Space for Main Competitors in Product Category	
				Competitor 1	Competitor 2
Outlet A	x*	10%*	10%*	15%*	10%*
Outlet B	x	20	15	15	10
Outlet C		40	N/A	20	10
Outlet D	x	5	10	10	10
Outlet E	x	5	15	15	15
Outlet F	X	5	15	20	10
Outlet G	x	5	20	20	10
Outlet H	x	5	10	15	10
Outlet I	x	5	10	15	5

Note: An identical chart would be created for each key market.

*Outlet A sells this company's product. Outlet A accounts for 10 percent of the product category's business in Rockford. The company receives 10 percent of the shelf space given the product category in Outlet A while the major competitors receive 15 and 10 percent, respectively.

In addition, an average shelf space figure for your company could be calculated. This number can be compared to the shelf space percentages of your major competitors, and can help you establish future shelf space goals (see Appendix B for worksheet).

Shelf Space

The amount of shelf space a product receives is critical to how well the product will do from a sales standpoint. Limited shelf space and poor positioning on the shelf are both reasons for concern and need to be corrected.

Geography

As with retail, the package good marketer should analyze the geographic territories of the firm's distribution to determine if there are markets that should be further penetrated or new markets that should be entered.

Sales Method

An integral part of package goods distribution is the personal selling method. Some companies choose to use an in-house sales force, others use independent sales representatives, and brokers, and still others use distributors or wholesalers. You should analyze your current method as well as what your competitors use and then decide the best method or combination of methods for your company.

Another issue that needs to be explored is the selling programs your company has in place to sell the trade. The questions are designed to establish the importance of trade deals, co-op advertising, and other allowances in your marketplace.

Questions to Be Addressed

■ Where do consumers shop for products in your category? Where do they shop for your company's product? What channel or outlet type do consumers use most when purchasing?

- What is the importance of department stores, supermarkets, specialty stores, chain stores, independents, direct mail, discount stores, or other types of outlets that sell your product category or product? What are the sales trends of each outlet type used by your product category? (5 Year Trend)

- What channels or methods of distribution are receiving increased use by the industry? Are new channels emerging? What trends are noticeable in the stores that dominate the sales of your product category?

- What channels or methods of distribution does your competition use? If they use different channels from you, why?

- Do you have enough market coverage to maximize sales in any given market?

- What is the ACV in each of your company's markets? What is the ACV for each of your major competitors in those same markets?

- Is the percent of shelf space your product receives in major outlets greater, the same, or lower than your competitors?

- Does expansion into new territories make sense? Are there additional areas of the country where you should be doing business?

- Does your product require mass, selective, or exclusive distribution? Why? Does it require a combination of distribution methods? Who can best provide this type of distribution? What about your competitors' products; do they require mass, selective, or exclusive distribution?

- How many potential dealers, wholesalers, distributors, brokers, or retail outlets are there? What are their distribution trading areas geographically?

- How do you sell your product to the trade or other businesses? Do you use in-house sales staff, independent reps, wholesalers, or distributors? What is the most efficient method of selling to distributors, wholesalers, or the retail trade?

- What is the importance of your product to the retail stores or distribution channel that sells it? Do you need the channel's services more than they need your product? Who has the channel power? How important is your product to the channel in terms of profit, volume (units and dollars)? Does it help build or sustain traffic? Is it prestigious? Does it help sell other goods? How do these points differ from your competition?

- How do retailers or other distributors sell or market your product? Does your product receive aggressive sales support or does your product have to sell itself? Does your product receive prominent display relative to the competition? Does your product get promoted in-store or to the ultimate purchaser by the distribution channel? Does your product receive the same merchandising and promotion support (more or less) relative to the competition? Does your product receive other promotion, advertising, or merchandising support?

- How established is your product with the trade? How well is it known and accepted by the trade? Is it important to them? Do you receive cooperation from the channels you sell to? (Same for your competition.)

- What is the minimum order size you require of your customers/channels? Is this standard in your industry? What are the payment terms? How often is restocking needed?

- Do storage, price marking, packaging, or accounting practices help sell the trade or create problems?

- Do quantity discounts, cooperative advertising, promotion allowances, price discounts, trade promotions, or other deals play a large role in the selling of your product category to the trade? How? Does your company have the same programs your competitors do?

- What is the customary markup of your product by the trade? Does this affect your marketing to the trade or the acceptance of your product by the end consumer?
- Are retail sales or sales to the trade subject to taxes or legal restrictions?
- What are the stocking requirements of the trade? How does your company make allocation decisions? Who gets the best fill rates and why? How are out of stocks handled?
- When and how often are the orders placed and by whom?

Business-to-Business

Business-to-business firms either sell directly to other businesses and/or sell through channels such as wholesalers or distributors.

Channel Types/Trends

The business-to-business firm must decide the most efficient and effective channel method for the company. We did a business review for a national manufacturer of sinks and disposals that clearly demonstrated the trend of more and more do-it-yourselfers to install their own sinks and disposals. Further study demonstrated that a shift in purchasing patterns had accompanied the strength of do-it-yourselfers in the marketplace; home centers and lumberyards were now selling more of this type of product than traditional plumbing channels. Thus, because of the channel trend section of the business review, selling emphasis was placed against home centers and lumberyards with a new channel of distribution established for the manufacturer.

Geography

The same issues need to be addressed here as were discussed in the package good section.

Personal Selling Method

As with package good firms, business-to-business companies must decide how to sell the product through the distribution channels. Company sales representatives, independent sales representatives, or wholesalers/distributors all have advantages and disadvantages. These are detailed in Chapter 11, Personal Selling/Operations. Remember, in the business review, your job is to analyze which method is used most successfully within the industry, as well as by your company and your competitors.

As with the package good section, the business-to-business firm must also address the issues of sales programs to the channels. The importance of deals, allowances, co-op advertising, and other sales program issues are detailed in the questions.

Questions to Be Addressed

- What channels or methods of distribution are receiving increased use by the industry? Are new channels emerging? What trends are noticeable?
- What channels or methods of distribution does your competition use? If they use different channels from you, why?
- Do you have enough market coverage to maximize sales in any given market?
- Does expansion into new territories make sense? Are there additional areas of the country where you should be doing business?

- Does your product require mass, selective, or exclusive distribution? Why? Does it require a combination of distribution methods? Who can best provide this type of distribution? What about your competitors' products; do they require mass, selective, or exclusive distribution?

- How many potential dealers, wholesalers, distributors, or retail outlets are there? What are their distribution trading areas geographically?

- How do you sell your product to the trade or other businesses? Do you use in-house sales staff, independent reps, wholesalers, or distributors? What is the most efficient method of selling to distributors, wholesalers, or the retail trade?

- What is the importance of your product to the retail stores or distribution channel that sells it? Do you need the channel's services more than they need your product? Who has the channel power? How important is your product to the channel in terms of profit, volume (units and dollars)? Does it help build or sustain traffic? Is it prestigious? Does it help sell other goods? How do these points differ from your competition?

- How do retailers or other distributors sell or market your product? Does your product receive aggressive sales support or does your product have to sell itself? Does your product get promoted to the ultimate purchaser by the distribution channel? Does your product receive the same merchandising and promotion support (less or more) relative to the competition? Does your product receive other promotion, advertising, or merchandising support?

- How established is your product with the trade? How well is it known and accepted by the trade? Is it important to them? Do you receive cooperation from the channels you sell to? (Same for your competition.)

- What is the minimum order size you require of your customers/channels? Is this standard in your industry? What are the payment terms? How often is restocking needed?

- Do storage, price marking, packaging, or accounting practices help sell the trade or create problems?

- Do quantity discounts, cooperative advertising, promotion allowances, price discounts, trade promotions, or other deals play a large role in the selling of your product category to the trade? How? Does your company have the same programs your competitors do?

- What is the customary markup of your product by the trade? Does this affect your marketing to the trade or the acceptance of your product by the end consumer?

- Are sales subject to taxes or legal restrictions?

- What are the stocking requirements of the trade? How does your company make allocation decisions? Who gets the best fill rates and why? How are out of stocks handled?

- When and how often are the orders placed and by whom?

Service Firms

The service industry's method of distribution is much like the retailer's. It encompasses the business's office and how the service is sold to customers.

Type of Office

Of consideration for the service business is the type of office used to sell the service. For a service company, one of the only tangible things associated with the company is the actual office. Therefore, the office becomes an important representation of the more intangible service being sold. For many services, the service itself is sold or delivered out of the office. In this case, how and where the service is sold and delivered must be closely analyzed.

Geography

An important decision is where to locate an office or offices within a given market. When The Hiebing Group first began operation, we wanted to be close to Madison's Capitol Square because of the positive image associated with being downtown, adjacent to the center of state government, and close to the University of Wisconsin. When we outgrew our first location we decided to stay close to downtown and the university, while maintaining a positive creative image. We found an historic old mansion overlooking Lake Mendota, close to downtown, achieving our goals and creating an office environment and image consistent with that of the agency.

Another issue which must be addressed is the number of markets in which you do business. What markets seem ripe for geographic expansion, and which ones are not currently profitable and may need to be abandoned?

Penetration

As with retailers, proximity is also important to firms providing service. Accordingly, service companies also have to decide how many locations and sales and/or service people are needed to cover any given market effectively and efficiently.

Questions to Be Addressed

- Where do consumers for services in your category shop?
- What are the current methods of delivery used for services in your category? Are new methods of delivery emerging? Are there noticable trends among the firms that dominate your service category?
- How does your competition deliver their services? If they use different delivery methods than you, why?
- Does expansion into new territories make sense? Are there additional areas of the country where you should be doing business?
- Does your product require mass, selective, or exclusive distribution? Why? Does it require a combination of delivery methods? Who can best provide this new method of delivery? What about your competitors'; do they require different methods of delivery?
- Is there a best way to deliver your service through company owned offices, franchisers, or dealerships?
- What type of office is most consistent with your company's image? Describe the office interiors/exteriors of your competitors; are they similar to or different from yours? Where, when, and how is your service best sold to consumers?

Step 8
Pricing

Price is a prominent part of the marketing decision-making process. A price that is too high may discourage purchase of the product and encourage competition in the form of lower price and more entries into the product category. Alternatively, a price that is too low may be a deterrent to reaching profit and sales goals.

The business review section on pricing is designed to provide pricing data relating to competition, changes in the marketplace price structure, and strengths of consumer

- What is the pricing structure for your product relative to the competition? Does the relationship of your product's price to that of the competition change during different selling seasons?

- In addition to pure price, are discounts, credit, promotional allowances, return policies, restocking charges, shipping policies, etc. important to the ultimate sale of your product?

Distribution of Sales by Price Point

- What is the distribution of sales by price point for your industry and your company? (Five-year trend) Do the majority of sales fall in one price category, or can consumers be segmented by price point?

- What has been the trend in pricing (five-year trend)? Are there price segments that are growing or shrinking?

Price Elasticity

- How price elastic is your product category? When you raise and/or lower the price, how does it affect demand? Are consumers price sensitive to your product category?

- Where is your product priced in relation to your major competitors? Why is it priced where it is?

Step 9

Historical Marketing Review of Your Company Versus the Competition

This competitive analysis section is designed to provide you with a summary of how your company is performing as compared to the competition across key marketing variables. This step forces you to consider strategic and tactical differences and similarities between how your company markets its product(s) versus how the competition markets their product(s). An analysis of your company's marketing activities in relation to the competition can provide *benchmark information* necessary to prepare your marketing plan in Part II. This knowledge will provide insights into potential defensive or offensive strategies which you can include in the marketing plan to curtail or exploit a major competitor's strength or weakness. In addition, by thoroughly studying your past marketing efforts and those of the competition, you may look at successes and failures in a new light. There might be ways to modify some of your competitors' more successful programs and make them your own or there might be changes that can be made to successful programs that will make them even better.

Exhibit 2.23   Annual Competitive Spending Analysis

Institution	Total Dollar Expenditures	Share of Spending— Total Expenditures	Change From Last Year	Television			Newspaper		
				Total Dollar Expenditures	Percent	Change from Last Year	Total Dollar Expenditures	Percent	Change from Last Year
City S&L	$200,000	11%	10%	$100,000	20%	+20%	$50,000	10%	−10%
First Bank									
State Bank									
Farmer's Bank									
United S&L									

Note: The above information should also be obtained on a *quarterly basis* to track seasonality of spending. If available, total dollars for each category should also be obtained.

How to Develop Competitive Information

You must analyze your company and your competitors in terms of sales, target market, positioning, marketing objectives and strategies, positioning, product/branding/packaging, pricing, distribution, personal selling techniques, promotion strategies and expenditures, customer service, merchandising, and publicity. Make sure to review the previous two years, as well as projecting into the future. Past years' successes and failures for both your company and your competitor's can be a great learning tool.

You should also consider the results of your marketing testing or marketing R&D (research and development) program. Did you introduce any new products, line extensions, services, new merchandise, or store concepts? Did you test different approaches in your advertising message? Did you test the use of new and/or investment spending? Did you test various promotional offers? What can you learn from past tests that can be translated into future success? If you have been doing the same things year after year, you should explore new uses of your marketing tools to ensure a competitive edge that will help guarantee increased sales and profits year after year.

Competitive analyses are not easy to complete because it is often difficult to obtain specific information about competitors. However, you can use secondary sources, some of which are listed in Chapter 1 and on the worksheets in Appendix B. We also encourage you to shop your competition by purchasing your competitors' products.

In addition, there is a lot to be learned from media representatives regarding media expenditures of your competitors. Exhibit 2.23 provides a review of competitive spending as compared to your company. The example utilizes banks in a given market and traces share of voice or media spending by dollar amount over a two year period (see Appendix B for worksheet).

Finally, one of the best ways to obtain competitive information is through awareness, attitude, and behavior primary research. If your company uses market tracking surveys, you can determine trends of the following:

- Awareness levels of competitors relative to your company.
- Consumers' rating of key product attributes for your company relative to the competition.
- Market share estimates for competitors relative to your company.
- Purchase ratios/trial and repeat purchases for your product relative to the competition.
- Shopping habits for your product versus the competition (normally shop first, etc.).

Magazine			Radio			Outdoor		
Total Dollar Expenditures	Percent	Change from Last Year	Total Dollar Expenditures	Percent	Change from Last Year	Total Dollar Expenditures	Percent	Change from Last Year
$10,000	15%	—%	$30,000	15%	+4%	$10,000	12%	−30%

Distribution/Store Penetration/Market Coverage

- Does your company use the same distribution channels as your competitors? What are the strengths and weaknesses of your distribution methods versus your competitors'?

- If you are a retailer, what are the penetration levels of stores for your company versus that of your competition? If you are a manufacturer, what is the market coverage of your product? Is it sufficient? How does it compare to your competitors?

- Where is your product sold? Where are your competitors' products sold?

Personal Selling

- What was your sales performance last year? Did you meet your goals?

- How does your company's selling philosophy differ from that of your competitors? Are there different methods you may want to consider in the future? If so, why?

Promotion

- What were the results of your company's promotions and those of your competitors last year? What was successful or unsuccessful? Why? How does your company's promotions differ from those of your competitors?

- What promotions does your competition execute that are particularly successful?

Advertising Message

- How does your advertising compare to your competitors'? Is it similar or different? What is the message of your advertising versus your major competitors?

- How successful has your advertising been relative to your competitors' advertising? What are the strengths and weaknesses of your advertising and that of your competitors?

Media Strategy and Expenditures

- Where, when, and how do you and your competitors use the media?

- What is the media spending in total and by medium for your company and your competitors? Do you dominate any one medium? Where are your competitors the strongest?

Customer Service Policies

- What are your company's customer service policies? Do they differ from the competition's? If so, how?

Merchandising

- What is the merchandising philosophy of your competitors? Are you unique or is your merchandising similar to the competition? Does your merchandising help to communicate your positioning?

Publicity

- Do you have an active publicity program? Does your competition? How much publicity did your product receive versus competitive products?

Testing/Marketing R&D

- What tests did your company and the competition execute in the past year? Were they successful? What did you learn from the tests?

Summary of Strengths and Weaknesses

- Based on the information above, what are the strengths and weaknesses of your company compared to each major competitor?

Step 10
Demand Analysis

The last step in the business review is to attempt to calculate demand for your product. The conclusions will be directional and are intended to provide you with a rough estimate on the size of your market and the potential business you might generate. It should give you a check to make sure the sales goals you set later in the plan are realistic and obtainable.

How to Estimate Demand for Your Product

The following outlines the procedures to take in estimating demand for your product.

1. *Target Market*. Define the target market in terms of numbers of customers. For example, if your target market is women 25 to 49, provide the total number of women 25 to 49. This is the top level figure of potential customers. It can be used for calculating future or potential demand.

2. *Geographic Territory*. Define your geographic territory and determine the number of your target market in this area. You can do this by utilizing the SRDS or the Nielsen Test Market Profile Resource. Or you can calculate the percentage of the total population the target market constitutes and multiply this percent against the total number of people in your geographic territory. Whichever method you use, the end result should be an estimate of the number of target market customers in your geographic territory.

3. *Consumption Constraints*. Determine if there are consumption constraints that will reduce the target market for your product. For example, apartment dwellers have no real need for garden tools or lawn mowers. From this review, develop a final estimate of customers in your geographic territory.

4. *Average Purchase per Year per Customer*. Determine the number of purchases per year. From the business review and the purchase rates/buying habits section, you should have access to the average number of purchases per year for your product category.

5. *Total Purchase per Year in Category*. Multiply the number of customers in your territory by the average number of purchases per year to get total purchases.

6. *Average Price*. Determine the average price of your product—utilize the pricing section of the business review to obtain this information.

7. *Total Dollar Purchases*. Multiply the total purchases from Number 5 by the average price in Number 6 to determine total dollar purchase.

8. *Your Company's Share of Purchase*. Review market share data and trends from the sales analysis and competitive market shares and strengths and weaknesses from the competitive analysis section of your business review. Also, consider loyalty measures from the purchase rates/buying habits section of the business review. Multiply your market share by the total in Number 7. Adjust this number up or down depending upon the increases or decreases of your company's market share versus the competition over the past five years (e.g., if your company has

be objective. This is no place for developing strategy. Keep the statements concise and focused on reporting the facts. Include summary rationale when needed. Examples summarizing major findings for a canning company would be as follows.

Buying Habits Examples

Canned vegetables are used by a high percentage (80 percent) of households.

Canned vegetables are a relatively high usage category.

59 percent of female homemakers use four or more cans per month.

29 percent use ten or more cans per month.

13 percent use 16 or more cans per month.

Target Market Example

Canned vegetable consumption is dominated by the medium and heavy users.

37 percent of canned good female purchasers account for over 65 percent of the canned good vegetables used per month.

Sales Example

While the canned tomato category has increased dramatically (140 percent) for the industry over the past five years, Company X has experienced only moderate growth (20 percent). This is far below the industry growth pattern.

DOS AND DON'TS

Do

- Develop an outline and charts before you start digging for information. This will keep you focused on the important issues.
- Always report data with reference points for comparison—use your company compared to the industry or this year compared to last year.
- Keep your summary statements as objective as possible.
- Take as much time as possible to compile a database. It will make writing the remainder of the plan much easier and far more effective.
- Make sure each chart you prepare has a descriptive title that explains the purpose of the chart.
- Round whole numbers and percentages to the nearest decimal point (200.5 thousand or 13.4 percent). Business review data should be used for directional purposes, and long strings of numbers often get in the way of the implications gleaned from the data. In addition, numbers carried out too far connote an exactness that should not be implied in the business review, where interpolation of numbers is sometimes needed to provide findings when using secondary data. *Remember, it's the trends and the comparisons, not the absolute numbers, that are important.* Whether your company sells 15.2 percent or 15 percent of its product in August is going to make little difference when determining seasonality and media spending strategies.
- As you work on your business review, keep a notebook nearby in which to jot down ideas for the marketing plan as detailed in the Introduction. Also keep a list of problems and opportunities that stem from working with the data. Doing this gives you a head start in writing the plan.

Don't

- Don't use the business review to develop objectives and strategies. Keep your findings objective and report facts. Don't develop solutions.

- Don't give up if you can't find some information you need. Call the trade journals, the library, media reps, etc. The answers are out there.
- On the other hand, don't get discouraged if you can't find all the information pertaining to a specific section(s). Gather as much as you can in the time allowed. Try to answer all the questions even if you don't have quantitative support. The important thing is to *as thoroughly as possible* review your business and your company before starting to write a marketing plan. Remember, you can never have enough meaningful information and you can never have too little information, because even a little background information is better than nothing when developing a marketing plan.
- Don't develop a marketing plan without first understanding your target market, your product, and your marketing environment as thoroughly as possible.

Problem or Opportunity?

Many times what appears to be a problem can also be an opportunity. An example is the following sales analysis problem:

- While Heartland Men's Apparel sales are strong during the holiday period of November and December, sales are below that of the men's apparel category nationally. This situation occurs because Heartland Apparel stores are not located in malls that generate heavy traffic during these periods.

While this is a problem for the company, it is also an opportunity. If national sales are at a peak during the November and December periods, then the opportunity exists to capture a larger percentage of these sales. However, because of the stores' locations, it is difficult to do as well as the average store nationally during this period. Thus, this statement is both a problem and an opportunity.

But the statement has to go somewhere. As a rule of thumb, try to determine if it is more of a problem or an opportunity. In this example, it is very difficult to change locations in retail, so this overriding factor would make the above statement a problem. In either case, however, the marketer would probably choose to address the problem or the opportunity by attempting to increase sales in the months of November and December.

HOW TO WRITE ACTIONABLE PROBLEMS AND OPPORTUNITIES

Problems and opportunities should be concise, one sentence statements that draw conclusions. This sentence would be underlined. If necessary, there can be a brief follow-up using supporting data or rationale.

The rationale should utilize key factual data or findings from the business review. This will enable you to quickly support your problem and opportunity statements during a presentation.

The following are examples of problems and opportunities that demonstrate the writing style to use when formulating these statements. We picked three categories of problems and two categories of opportunities for examples. Remember that in your own problem and opportunity section, there will be problems and opportunities for each section of the business review.

Target Market Problems

- *Multiple target markets exist.* Each one has different demographics, needs, and wants. No single dominating customer group can be targeted.
- *The facial tissue's customers skew very old, with small to nonexistent percentage of users coming from teens and young adults.* The brand is developing virtually no new users from which to regenerate the consumer franchise.
- *General Hospital does not have a religious orientation.* The city of Johnsonville has a high concentration of Catholics (40 percent of the population). Of the two hospitals, the Catholic affiliated hospital dominates market share. Thus, religious factors influence the choice of hospital.

Sales Analysis Problems

- *The men's suit and sport coat market constitutes a relatively limited market.* Total purchases of suits and sport coats by males in a given year are low in the absolute, and the category has lower purchase rates when compared to most other nondurable consumer goods. In addition, while small percentages of males purchase any suit or sport coat in a given year, the majority of those purchasers buy only one suit or sport coat per year.

- *The Reed Company has experienced a market share decline over the past five years.* This loss in market share has primarily been to the market leader, Birkenshire, which increased share during the last five years. The remainder of the market has remained fairly stable during this time period.

	Market Share	Percent Change Last 5 Years
The Reed Company	10	− 12%
Birkenshire	25	+ 15

- *Sales data show that a small number of distributors account for a majority of sales dollars.* Forty accounts provide nearly 70 percent of the distributor's sales, yet these 40 accounts make up only 12 percent of the distributors who purchase from Seth Cooper & Sons Office Supplies.

Historical Marketing Review of the Competition versus Your Company Problems

- *The top three competitors outspend Sweetbriar Inc. by 20 percent.* Furthermore, Sweetbriar Inc. does not dominate any one medium, and its media spending has declined since last year in television, the medium in which the majority of its media dollars are spent.
- *The Sweetbriar advertising messages are inconsistent with no unifying selling theme.* In contrast, the top four competitors each communicate one strong, identifiable positioning in all their advertising.

Purchase Rates/Buying Habits Opportunities

- *While the Southwest consumes more of the product on a per capita basis than any other part of the country, The Torger Company has relatively poor sales in this region.* This is because it has yet to fully expand distribution to this portion of the country.
- *The average shopper is extremely brand loyal.* Brand choice is developed at a young age with a majority of consumers continuing purchases for life.
- *Although total trial of the company's brands is very low, retrial is above the category average.* Thus, greater rates of consumers become regular users than is normal for the category, meaning product acceptance is very high.

Product Awareness and Product Attribute Opportunities

- *Of the top ten competitors, the Kuypers Company ranks second in quality of product relative to the competition.* Quality is the single most important purchase attribute for the category.
- *Very little clear differentiation of accounting firms exist except on the basis of size.* Service offerings, expertise, etc., remain relative unknowns among clients, referrals, and prospects.

Keep Your Statements Factual

Finally, it is important that your problem and opportunity section stay factual by summarizing findings from the business review. Problems and opportunities do not show what is to be done, but point out areas that need attention. They describe the current market environment. Leave the solutions to the marketing plan.

The following is not an opportunity but a marketing strategy:

■ Advertise during the strong seasonal times of the year that exist during August, September, December, and April.

It is a strategy because it is not reporting facts but demonstrating what should be done. Leave that for the marketing plan, when you can review all the problems and opportunities together and then determine what should be done. The correct opportunity statement relating to the above would be:

■ The industry is extremely seasonal, with strong purchasing months of August, September, December, and April.

DOS AND DON'TS

Do

■ Draw as many meaningful conclusions as possible from *each section* of the business review. Read and reread each section. Try to look at each set of facts in as many different ways as possible. Ask yourself, "What are the positive and negative aspects of the data?"
■ Write concise, factual statements summarizing the business review.
■ Organize your problems and opportunities so that they reflect each section of the business review.
■ If it helps you to better see the big picture, summarize all the problems and opportunities into five to ten key problems and five to ten key opportunities, including them at the end of your problem and opportunity section.

Don't

■ Don't try to write objectives and strategies in this section. Keep the statement factual.
■ Don't make the statements too long. Keep them short, and focus each on one single problem or opportunity.
■ Don't shortchange the number of problems and opportunities—compile an inclusive list. Once you have your final list, make sure you go back and eliminate any that are redundant. This will allow you to concentrate on a more focused, manageable list of meaningful problems and opportunities.
■ Don't include problems and opportunities that are not based on information included in your business review.

MARKETING
PLAN

4

SALES
OBJECTIVES

W hen you begin writing a marketing plan, the first task is setting sales objectives. This is one of the most complicated and important steps in preparing an effective marketing plan. The more you understand about the process of arriving at a sales objective, the easier to write a marketing plan that will meet sales objectives.

From This Chapter You Will Learn

The definition and importance of sales objectives.

What is involved in setting challenging yet attainable sales objectives.

Upper management's involvement with the marketing department in arriving at realistic sales objectives.

The quantitative and qualitative factors that affect the setting of sales objectives.

How to set your own sales objectives using a three step process.

OVERVIEW

Definition and Importance of Sales Objectives

Sales objectives are self-defining in that they represent projected levels of goods or services to be sold. Setting sales objectives is critical because it sets the tone of the marketing plan. Everything that follows in the plan is designed to meet the sales objectives—from determining the size of the target market and establishing marketing objectives, to determining the amount of advertising and promotion dollars to be budgeted, to the actual hiring of marketing and sales personnel, to the number and kinds of distribution channels/stores utilized, and, very importantly, to the amount of product produced or inventoried.

Sales Objectives Must Be Challenging and Attainable

Because sales objectives have substantial impact on a business, they must be simultaneously challenging and attainable. If not, they could have a disastrous effect on short-term, bottom line profits as well as on the long-term success of the business. If sales objectives are dramatically increased, the cost of doing business will also rise dramatically to accommodate the projected increase in sales. Accordingly, if your sales objectives are set too high and cannot be attained, your resulting expenses to sales ratio will be very high, causing profits to fall below expectations. Or if you dramatically underestimate your sales objectives and have inadequate production capacity or inventory, you will not be able to sufficiently fulfill demand, meaning opportunity is lost to the competition. Over the long term, this may translate to the loss of good distributors, loyal customers, and first time customers.

In summary, sales objectives should be based upon an accurate estimate of the market opportunity and the capacity of the organization to realize those opportunities.

Sales Objectives Must Be Time Specific

You must set time specific sales objectives in order to provide a start and end date for your marketing program. It is also important to set both short- and long-term sales objectives. Short-term sales objectives generally are for one year or less, while long-term ones usually include sales objectives for a minimum of three years. Long-term sales objectives are needed to plan the future direction of the company or product for such areas as equipment, real estate, personnel, and capital. Further, what you include in your year one marketing plan will affect sales objectives set for years two and three. Testing new products and service programs in year one might be a *must* in order to meet sales objectives in year three.

Sales Objectives Must Be Measurable

Setting measurable sales objectives provides the means for determining what must be included in your marketing plan and evaluating its success. Accordingly, sales objectives are quantified in terms of dollars and units for manufacturing firms, dollars and transactions (and occasionally units) for retail firms, and dollars and persons served for service firms.

You must set sales objectives for *both* dollar and units/transactions/persons served. Dollar sales cover your expenses and provide a profit, and they reflect the impact of any increase or decrease in the price of your product. Units/transactions/persons served indicate the fundamental health of your business. If you are continually projecting increased dollar sales but decreased unit sales, eventually you will probably experience a decline in dollar sales, because price increases will no longer compensate for the loss of unit sales.

Sales Objectives Are More Than Dollars and Units/ Transactions/ Persons Served

Projected profits, a direct result of sales, should also be included along with sales objectives in this plan. Accordingly, as the author of this plan, you must have an understanding of profit expectations to effectively prepare and evaluate the marketing plan.

Further, if you are not operating in a pure business environment keep in mind that sales objectives can be defined in terms other than dollars or units. For a nonprofit organization with programs dedicated to the prevention of child abuse, the goal might be a specific number of phone calls asking for help or reporting cases of abuse. In a government agency such as an employment service, it may be number of job placements. Or for a political campaign manager, it may be percent of votes cast for your candidate by county or district. Whatever the organization, there must be sales objectives or a simulation thereof.

Upper Management Involvement in Setting Sales Objectives

If you report to upper management, make sure you have an understanding of the company's sales and profit expectations and have reviewed the company business plan, if available. Many times upper management dictates the sales objectives to the marketing department. When this occurs, it is even more important for you to have systematically arrived at your own sales objectives. Based on your input, management can adjust its sales objectives (if very different from your sales projections) or, at the very least, gain additional perspective as it reviews the marketing plan designed to meet the dictated sales objectives. In any case, it is a good idea to involve upper management regarding the sales and profit objectives before the rest of the marketing plan is written, to ensure developing a plan that reaches the agreed upon sales objectives.

QUANTITATIVE AND QUALITATIVE FACTORS AFFECTING THE ESTABLISHMENT OF SALES OBJECTIVES

Both quantitative and qualitative factors must be taken into consideration in the development of sales objectives. Quantitative factors are those that can help to numerically calculate specific sales objectives. These are calculated first in order to develop hard numbers based upon objective input. Qualitative factors are more subjective because of nonavailability and difficulty in quantifying certain types of information. Therefore, interpretation of these additional subjective factors leads to an adjustment of the quantitatively based sales objectives.

Quantitative Factors

Sales and Share Trends

In preparing to set sales objectives, a good place to start is with the past. The trending of the market and company sales will be major factors to consider when projecting sales.

Market Sales Review the trending of the market over the past five years in terms of dollar and unit sales. What has been the trending of the marketplace—upward, downward, flat, erratic? Within the total market history of sales and units, what has been the trending of market segments that make up the total market? If you were tracking total market shoe sales, you might have found a flat to slowly upward trending market, but athletic sales as a subset were trending upward at a percentage rate more than twice that of the total market. Accordingly, if you had been selling athletic shoes in your store, you would take this trend into consideration when setting objectives.

Also, if your business benefits from fad or erratic sales volume, you must learn to recognize and deal with it realistically in setting your sales and profit objectives. Fad volume could be occasional, such as a convention or sports tournament that brings an incremental number of people to your town and your restaurant. Or fad volume could be much longer lasting, such as that created by a highly publicized health care study indicating that the use of fish oil and/or aspirin prolongs life. If your company markets either one of these products, you would have to estimate the impact of this information in terms of volume and time. How many consumers will it affect and for how long?

Company versus Market Sales Next, compare how your company's sales are trending year to year versus the total market's sales. In most instances, project your sales to equal or surpass the market rate of growth; otherwise you will be losing share of market.

Market Share Trends Another factor to consider is the trending of your market share—for the company/division, for the product line and each product, or for the retail/service category and each major department. At what rate has your share been trending relative to the market? Has it been growing in a growing market? Has your share been going up in a market that is shrinking? Or has your share of market been decreasing in a declining market? If you find your product is losing share in a market that is declining, it would be unrealistic to project sales increases unless your strategy is to reverse this trend through a major marketing commitment. When setting sales objectives, keep in mind that not only is it difficult to reverse a product's sales decline in a one-year period, but it is extremely difficult to reverse a product's decline within a declining market.

Size and Trend of Your Target Market

Determining accurate sales objectives estimates is also dependent on an accurate appraisal of the size and projected growth of the market for your product or service. Many new business ventures fail because of an overly optimistic estimate of the size of the market. It is very important to review census and industry data in your business review, as well as primary research if available, to determine how big the market really is for your product and how it is trending. The management of a retail chain selling low priced men's suits came to our firm asking why their two year old chain of twenty stores was not doing well. After reviewing business census data we discovered a relatively small market for the product category:

> A limited number of purchasers—only 25 percent of men purchase a suit or sport coat each year.
>
> A limited incidence of purchase—approximately 0.40 suits and sports coats purchased per year per male over 18.
>
> The market category for suits was trending down while casual menswear, which the retailer did not carry, experienced growth.

If this company had reviewed the market data before projecting its sales, it might never have committed itself to the retail concept in the first place.

Many times sales objectives are set too high year after year because the company's management does not recognize a continual erosion of the target market that could have been documented through published industry data, company sales data, and/or primary research. Through primary research, our agency was able to document for a fabric chain that the number of women who sew garments declined approximately 5 percent per year over a ten year period.

Budget, Profit, and Pricing Considerations

In determining realistic sales objectives, it is helpful to have an understanding of your company's historical operating budgets and profit expectations. Ideally, sales cover expenses and provide for profits. And the simple fact is, you need a minimum level of dollar sales to stay in business and grow. For this reason, the cost of doing business or expenses incurred to operate your business is an important quantitative factor to consider when setting your sales objectives.

In setting sales objectives, you should also understand the level of profitability within segments of your product line or retail/service offering. Along with the above, product price increases or decreases must be factored into all sales objectives because they dramatically affect sales volume and profitability.

Qualitative Factors

Economic Considerations

One factor affecting sales objectives that is difficult to forecast is the economy. Adjust your sales objectives based on your estimation of the economic factors that will directly affect your business. Are you forecasting sales for a recessionary, inflationary, or relatively stable period? If you are projecting sales for an inflationary period, you most likely will be estimating dollar sales to increase at a greater percentage than unit sales.

Interest rates are also an important factor in establishing sales objectives. Businesses that rely heavily on their customers purchasing on credit, such as auto dealers and real estate firms, usually see their sales slump as interest rates rise.

In addition, if there are major changes in the tax laws, you must plan accordingly. Elimination of an investment tax credit for heavy machinery would dramatically affect the sales of companies manufacturing heavy equipment.

Review not only national economic factors, but also those that might directly affect your product's market on a more local geographic basis. Pockets of unemployment can dramatically affect your sales objectives.

In summary, remember, although you cannot control economic factors, you can thoroughly evaluate what impact they could have on your business, and then adjust your sales objectives for the short and long term.

Competition

What you identified as a large and growing market can be diluted by strong and growing competition. Before finalizing sales objectives, review the competitive section (Step 9) of your business review. Has a major competitor noticeably expanded its sales force, increased the number of trade deals to retailers, added distribution channels/store locations, changed its product mix, or introduced a new product or service? Based on your competitive review of advertising media, is the competition increasing or decreasing its level of spending? Increased competitive advertising spending, particularly in a consumer marketplace dominated by a few major competitors, can negatively affect the chance of your marketing program meeting its sales objectives.

Many times it is difficult to determine the direct impact on sales by an increase in competitive advertising. At this point, telephone survey research of your potential market can quantify its impact on your sales. Through this type of research, we were able to measure a 50 percent increase in awareness for our client's direct competitor. We then translated this awareness into increased sales for the competition, and an erosion of our client's market share. Accordingly, an anti-competitor plan was recommended for our client along with a revision of the short-term sales objectives.

Your Product's Life Cycle

Another consideration in setting sales objectives is to review where your product is relative to its life cycle. Do you have a new product that is just being introduced with a large untapped target market, minimal competition, and substantial growth potential? If successfully introduced, are your product's sales still growing, have they plateaued, or are they in decline? Your short-term sales objectives should reflect the current life cycle stage of your product, while your long-term objectives could concurrently reflect the stage of the life cycle your product is moving into. Many times, to assure a clearer picture of where your product is in its life cycle, it is wise to stand back and review competitive products or draw comparisons to different products with similar characteristics in other industries. After these companies introduced their products, at what rate did they grow, when did they level off, and at what point in their existence did they decline? Manufacturers and service firms, as well as retailers, by determining if specific products they sell are in a growth, plateau, or declining stage, can more accurately forecast expected sales growth for their companies.

The Mission and Personality of Your Organization

An important qualitative factor to consider is the mission and personality of your organization. What are your company's expectations? What is its reason for being? What is its philosophy of doing business?

Is your company conservative and careful, or a moderate risk taker? Is it an old line, "don't rock the boat" company, or a young and charging, "we can do it" company? Consider also the aggressiveness of your organization in terms of growth and innovation—product improvements, new products, and the opening of new distribution channels and new markets. Take all of the above into consideration when estimating future sales.

Marketing Plan Expectation

Somewhat related to organization personality is another very important qualitative factor—your going-in expectation of the overall marketing effort dictated by your marketing plan. The employment of a well integrated, disciplined marketing plan, never before applied, will usually generate incremental sales, everything else being equal. Further, you would adjust your sales objectives upward if you intended to change the way you previously marketed your product, such as improving your product, investing incremental media dollars, adding promotional dollars, or lowering the price of the product.

HOW TO SET SALES OBJECTIVES

The methodology of setting sales objectives is both quantitative and qualitative, which means your sales objectives will be a composite of data based estimates and educated guesses. If you use a disciplined process in setting sales objectives, these goals will be based more on realistic estimates and less on guessing.

The Process of Setting Sales Objectives

The recommended process to set your sales objective(s) is based on three steps:

- Set individual sales objectives using three different quantitative methods.
- Reconcile these different quantitative goals into composite sales objectives.
- Adjust the quantitatively arrived at composite sales objectives through the interpolation of the relevant subjective qualitative factors, such as the economy, competition, and the personality of your organization.

Worksheets for each step and a marketing plan format for writing the sales objectives are provided in Appendix C.

Step 1

Set Quantitative Sales Objectives

We suggest if the data are available you use the following three different quantitative methods: outside macro, inside macro, and expense plus. Each method will develop a sales objective estimate, and each estimate will provide one of three parameters from which to make realistic judgments in arriving at a final sales objective(s). Each method can be used exclusively in arriving at a sales objective; however, the final outcome will not be as reliable as when you apply all three approaches. By using the three different approaches, you develop sales objectives derived from three different sets of data—a safeguard against using only one set of data that might not be totally reliable or encompassing.

Outside Macro Approach

In this approach, first look outside of your immediate company environment and estimate *total market or category sales* for each of the *next three years*. Follow this with an estimate of your company's current and future share of the market for the next three years. Then multiply the total market or category projections by the market share estimate for each of the next years to arrive at your sales objectives. You should end up with a three-year projection for both unit and dollar sales.

In order to arrive at these estimates, begin with a review of the past five-year trend of each marketplace in which your product, service, or retail store competes. (If you don't have five years of sales data available, use what data you have, and supplement with available data from similar businesses to arrive at a trending of the marketplace.) If the market is trending up at a 5 percent rate, you could project the market to continue to grow at this rate for each of the next three years.

Market Trend Line Sales Projection Other than applying a straight percentage increase to arrive at market volume for future years, you can statistically develop a market trend line. If you were projecting sales in dollars for 1993 and you had a market change from $800,000 in 1985 to $900,000 in 1990, you would do the following:

Market change 1985 to 1990 = $100,000 ($800,000 to $900,000)
Market change period = 5 years (1985 to 1990)
Average $ change per year = $20,000 ($100,000/5)
$ change for 8 year period (1985 to 1993) = $160,000 ($20,000 × 8)
Projected $ sales for 1993 = $960,000 ($800,000 from base year 1985 + $160,000 for change over 8 year period)

This method of projecting sales is referred to as *freehand*, and is the simplest method of determining trend lines. You can use this trend line approach for both dollars and unit sales. If there is a substantial fluctuation in past sales year by year, you can arrive at a mathematically generated trend line by the least squares method. If this is necessary, we suggest you refer to a text on business statistics.

Company/Product Trend Line Share Projection To arrive at a share of market estimate, review the change of your company's share over the past five years and project a similar share change for the future. You can estimate a percentage point change or use the same freehand approach per the above. If you were estimating a share number for 1991 and your share changed from 10 percent in 1985 to 16.5 in 1990, you would do the following:

Share change 1985 to 1990 = 6.5 points (from 10 percent to 16.5 percent)
Share change period = 5 years (1985 to 1990)
Average change per year = 1.3 points (6.5 points/5 years)
Share change for 6 year period (1985 to 1991) = 7.8 points (1.3 × 6)
Projected share for 1991 = 17.8 percent (10 percent share from base year 1985 + 7.8 percentage point change over 6 year period)

Again, once you have arrived at a projected number for market sales and units, and a projected share of the market for each, multiply the total market estimates by the estimated market shares to arrive at a sales objective for dollars and units. You would apply this Macro method in each of the years you are developing sales objectives. Exhibit 4.1 provides an example of how this method can be used. A worksheet is provided in Appendix C that you can use to apply this method. Modify this worksheet to include transactions if you are in the retail business, or from units to persons/companies served if you are in the service business.

Exhibit 4.1   Sales Objectives: Macro Method

Market and Share Data

		Market Sales Volume			Company Share Percent of the Market			
	$ (MM)	Percent Change Previous Year	Units (MM)	Percent Change Previous Year	$	Percent Point Change from Previous Year	Units	Percent Point Change from Previous Year
Previous 5 Years								
1986	$ 952.2	13.3%	449.1	5.1%	5.0%	0.1	4.0%	0.2
1987	1,067.0	12.1	484.0	7.8	5.1	0.1	4.7	0.7
1988	1,135.1	6.4	508.2	5.0	6.1	1.0	5.2	0.5
1989	1,202.9	6.0	527.9	3.9	6.5	0.4	5.7	0.5
1990	1,275.0	6.0	544.0	3.0	6.6	0.1	6.1	0.4
Projections Next 3 Years								
1991	1,355.7	6.3	567.7	4.4	7.0	0.4	6.6	0.5
1992	1,436.4	5.9	591.4	4.1	7.4	0.4	7.1	0.5
1993	1,517.1	5.6	615.1	4.0	7.8	0.4	7.6	0.5

Three Year Sales Projection for Company

	Dollars			Units		
Year	Market Sales Volume (MM)	× Company Share Percent of Market	= Company Sales (MM)	Market Sales Unit Volume (MM)	× Company Unit Share Percent of Market	= Company Unit Sales (MM)
1991	$1,355.7	7.0%	$ 94.9	567.7	6.6%	37.5
1992	1,436.4	7.4	106.3	591.4	7.1	42.0
1993	1,517.1	7.8	118.3	615.1	7.6	47.0

Inside Micro Approach

Having reviewed the broad macro outside market sales, next review your own organization's sales history. Start at the *top* or with a review of your organization's total sales. Using the straight percentage increase or the trend line approach, arrive at projected three-year sales for your company. From the top go further, and using the straight percentage or trend line approach, estimate sales for each product or department, adding the projected sales of each (product/department) together for a three-year company total. Then reconcile this pieced together total with your initial sales estimate for the entire organization for an ultimate top projection.

Next, review your sales by dollars and units from the *bottom up* to arrive at an estimated sales figure. Bottom up means estimating sales from where they are generated, such as sales by each channel, store unit, or service office/center. Based on history and changes in the marketplace, estimate sales for each bottom up sales generator, and add them together for each year's projection. You can use the straight percent change or trend line approach for each year's projection. However, because of the vast amount or lack of data to process, you might have to estimate rather than calculate each sales projection.

Exhibit 4.2 provides an example of how to prepare a top to bottom sales forecast. Worksheets for top and bottom sales forecasting to apply the Micro method are provided in Appendix C.

If you are in a manufacturing business, your bottom up generator becomes the

Exhibit 4.2   Sales Objectives: Micro Method

Projection from Top: Sales Forecast for Manufacturing, Service, or Retail
Category*

		Company Sales Volume		
	$ (MM)	Percent Change Previous Year	Units (MM)	Percent Change Previous Year
Previous 5 Years				
1986	$ 47.7	10.3%	20.2	6.0%
1987	54.1	13.4	22.8	12.8
1988	68.8	27.1	28.8	26.3
1989	78.0	13.3	32.7	13.5
1990	84.2	7.9	34.0	4.0
Next 3 Years Projections				
1991	93.3	10.8	37.5	10.3
1992	102.4	9.8	41.0	9.3
1993	111.5	8.9	44.4	8.3

Projections from Bottom: Sales Forecast by Distribution Channel for Manufacturers*†

	Existing			New		
	Number	Dollars (MM)	Units (MM)	Number	Dollars (MM)	Units (MM)
Direct Accounts	25	$29.2	9.2	6	$5.6	2.4
Wholesalers/ Brokers	74	62.4	26.5	6	2.1	0.9
Other	—	—	—	—	—	—
Total	99	$91.6	35.7	12	$7.7	3.3

Projections from Bottom: Sales Forecast by Store for Retailers*†

	Existing Stores	
Market	Dollars (000)	Transactions (000)
Green Bay/Store Number		
3	$ 773.7	73.6
4	276.8	25.2
5	449.8	41.8
7	285.6	23.2
8	343.5	30.5
Market Total	$2,129.4	194.3
Madison/Store Number		
1	644.1	59.5
2	396.6	35.0
6	534.7	46.0
9 (new, open 9 months)	400.0	36.0
Market Total	$1,975.4	176.5
Grand Total	$4,104.8	370.8

*Based on your type of business, include in your sales projections dollars and units/transactions/persons served, and take into consideration *new* products, distribution channels, stores or services, and price changes. Service organizations use service office/center in place of stores. Manufacturers use net dollar sales to trade/ intermediate markets and retail/service firms use dollar sales to ultimate purchasers.

†For bottom-up projections, develop projections for each year for a three year period.

distribution channel (e.g., direct accounts, wholesaler/distributors, etc.). If you are in the retail business, estimate by store, by market, by district/region, building up to a total sales estimate. Use this same building approach if you are in the service business. Many times it is a good idea to have participation by the sales force or the retail/service people in the field who estimate sales by their area of responsibility.

To arrive at a final micro sales objective, you must then reconcile the organization's sales estimates derived from the top with those derived from the bottom.

Expense Plus Approach

Once you have the outside macro based estimates and the inside micro based sales estimates, it makes good sense to estimate the sales level needed to cover planned expenses and make a profit. This budget based sales objective approach is more short term in nature and is most useful in helping to arrive at your one-year sales objective. A sales objective arrived at from expense and profit expectations can differ dramatically from a sales objective generated from a market or company sales trend projection. This difference in projections may signal the need for a more conservative or aggressive marketing plan. Although very simplistic, it is also very real because it details the sales that have to be generated to stay in business and make a profit.

To arrive at a sales objective using this method, you will need budget data. If your company has been doing business for a number of years, it is relatively easy to estimate expenses and expected profits for the next year by reviewing your historical business data. It is a good learning experience, particularly if you are new in the business, to review the cost of goods, operating margins, expenses, and profits within the industry and for other comparable businesses. Industry guidelines such as this are available from libraries, trade associations, and the Business Census.

A number of methods can be used to develop a budget based sales objective. Using a common approach we apply in our business and labeled expense plus, you first estimate your operating expenses (marketing, administrative, etc.) in total dollars for the upcoming year. Next, from your expected gross margin percentage[1] subtract your expected profit (pre tax) percentage to provide an estimated expense percentage. The gross margin percentage is available from historical company records and/or from industry guideline data. The estimated expense percent is divided into the estimated expense dollars to determine the required sales necessary to meet expense and profit goals. Exhibit 4.3 presents an example of a review of data and calculations for the expense plus approach. A worksheet for your computations is provided in Appendix C.

Exhibit 4.3   **Sales Objectives: Expense-plus Method**
                  (Budget Based for One Year)

Previous 5 Years	Gross Margin Percent of Sales	Profit Percent of Sales	Expenses	
			Percent of Sales	Dollars (MM)
1986	33.4%	4.5%	29.1%	$13.9
1987	35.1	3.1	32.1	17.1
1988	37.2	3.1	34.1	23.5
1989	35.2	1.0	35.5	27.7
1990	31.3	1.0	30.1	28.0

Expected Margin 33.5% − Expected Profit 3.5% = Operating Expense 30.0%

Budgeted Expense Dollars $28.5 (MM)/Operating Expense 30.0% = Sales Objective $95.0 (MM)

---

[1]Gross Sales − Cost of Goods Sold = Net Sales. Net Sales / Gross Sales = Gross Margin.

Exhibit 4.4   Method for Reconciling Sales Objectives

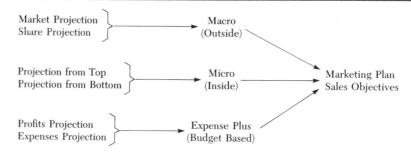

Exhibit 4.5   Reconciliation of Sales Objectives

	Macro		Micro		Expense Plus	Composite Sales Objectives	
	Dollars (MM)	Units (MM)	Dollars (MM)	Units (MM)	Dollars (MM)	Dollars (MM)	Units (MM)
Short Term							
1991	$ 94.9	37.5	$ 96.3	38.2	$95.0	$ 95.4	37.9
Long Term							
1992	106.3	42.0	103.4	40.1		104.9	41.1
1993	118.3	47.0	112.2	45.1		115.3	46.1

Step 2

Reconciling Sales Objectives

Now that you have arrived at outside macro sales objectives, inside micro sales objectives, and an expense plus sales objective, you must reconcile the differences to establish the sales objectives for your marketing plan. This methodology is graphically shown in Exhibit 4.4. After reviewing your sales objective alternatives based on the this methodology, you may decide to go with a pure average of the three or a weighted average, placing more emphasis on one alternative than the other. Or, you may use the (weighted) average of two, or just one. The important aspect of Step 2 is that you have reviewed the data from various quantitative perspectives. This will help you arrive at a sales objective with your eyes wide open and with an understanding of the dynamics that go into setting a sales objective. For the most meaningful sales projections, attempt to apply all three methods, or at the very minimum, two methods that you can use for comparison. Exhibit 4.5 shows how reconciliation of the three methods' goals into a composite sales objective(s) can be accomplished. A worksheet is provided in Appendix C.

Step 3

Qualitative Adjustment of Quantitative Sales Objectives

Now that you have arrived at quantitative sales objectives, you should review again the qualitative factors that will have an impact on the future sales. You need to temper the numerically derived sales objectives with the more qualitative forecasting factors. Using the appropriate qualitative factors, you can increase or decrease the composite dollars and unit/transactions/persons served sales objectives through an assignment of positive or negative percentage points depending on the estimated degree of impact by each qualitative factor. If the economy is growing and the economic outlook is bright, you might increase the composite sales objective by two percentage points. Or, you may decrease the composite sales objective by four percentage points because an aggressive competitor moved into your trading area. If there is more than one

Exhibit 4.6   Qualitative Adjustment of Quantitative Factors

Qualitative Impacting Factors	Point Change	Percentage Adjustment	×	Composite Sales Objective (MM)	=	Adjusted Sales Objective (MM)
1. Economy	+2	1.02		$95.4		$ 97.3
2. Competition	−4	.96		95.4		91.6
Total						$188.9
Final Adjusted Average (Total of adjusted sales objectives divided by number of calculated factors)						$ 94.5

Note: 1. List qualitative factors and to what extent they will impact on the previous numerically arrived at sales objectives. Adjust composite sales objective(s) accordingly to arrive at final sales objective(s).

2. Use qualitative adjustments for units, transactions, or persons served, as well as for sales dollars objectives. However, percentage point adjustment may differ from dollars.

major impacting factor, you can balance their effect through averaging. Exhibit 4.6 illustrates how you would calculate these factors. A worksheet for you to use in adjusting the composite sales objectives by the qualitative impacting factors is provided in Appendix C.

Final Reminders

Include Rationale with Sales Objectives

Once the sales objectives are determined and agreed upon, include a brief rationale along with the sales objectives. This rationale should summarize the processes used, assumptions made, and factors considered in finalizing the sales objectives. Although they are not included in the worksheets for sales objectives, you can also include specific profit objectives for each year as well. Any additional pertinent supporting data related to sales and profit objectives should be included in the marketing plan appendix.

Plan to Revise the Sales Objectives

The sales objectives will most likely be revised more than once as you write the marketing plan. You may uncover greater than expected sales potential among a target market. Or, you may determine that your company does not have the necessary capital, there is greater competition than expected, or there is not enough consumer demand, which could all negatively affect the estimated sales objectives.

Once your marketing plan is written (ideally, two or three months before the start of your fiscal year), it is wise to keep your sales objectives current. Review your sales objectives at two months, five months, and eight months into the marketing plan year in order to adjust the sales objectives for the second, third, and fourth quarters of your fiscal year. This will help you maximize your sales and control your expenses in a timely and profitable manner.

DOS AND DON'TS

Do

- Set sales objectives in a disciplined manner.
- Set short- and long-term sales objectives.

- Make them time specific and measurable.
- Make them challenging and attainable.
- Review your past sales experience.
- Consider the size and growth of your specific target market.
- Determine where your product/service/store concept is in its life cycle.
- Get upper management's agreement to sales objectives before finalizing the marketing plan.
- Review industry averages for cost of product/inventory, expenses, and profits.
- Use more than one method in developing your quantitative sales objectives.
- Realistically plan for pricing changes.
- Qualitatively adjust your numerically derived sales objectives.
- With today's unlimited personal computer potential, investigate the possibility of using computer generated sales objectives based on the methodology provided in this chapter.
- Once you have arrived at your sales objectives, consider developing a range forecast of high and low to give perspective on up-side potential and down-side risk. This will provide for contingency options as the year progresses in order to realize unforeseen potential or cut your losses should the business not perform as expected.
- Depending on your type of business, break down your annual sales objectives into smaller segments such as quarters, months, and/or weeks—possibly even days for retail and service firms. This breakdown will be of major assistance when you formulate your annual marketing calendar.
- Revise your sales objectives, as needed, during plan preparation and after the plan has been prepared as your business year evolves.

Don't

- Don't guess.
- Do not just set dollar sales objectives.
- Do not accept upper management's sales objectives out of hand without independently arriving at your own.
- Do not always believe your company alone can buck a marketwide decline; don't set sales objectives based on achieving unattainable sales increases.
- Do not overestimate the size of the market.
- Do not consider just the qualitative factors presented in this chapter, but consider other qualitative factors that pertain to your specific industry.
- Do not underestimate the impact of competition in setting sales objectives.
- Do not set sales objectives based on what you or the company wants and needs, but rather on what the market will bear.

5

TARGET MARKET

W hile a company's profits are derived from sales, sales are totally dependent on the purchasers and users of your product. In effect, your company exists because of the customers you choose to serve. It is essential to have a complete understanding of who your target market is and how best to fulfill their needs because it is the *key* to all that follows in the marketing plan. Because it is the reason for your product's existence and the key to finding the marketing answers, let your target market drive your marketing plan.

From This Chapter You Will Learn

The definition of target market and segmentation.

How to define your primary consumer target markets.

How to define your primary business-to-business target markets.

How to define your secondary consumer and/or business-to-business target markets.

The form to follow in listing your target market descriptors.

OVERVIEW

Definition

Once you have developed sales objectives, you must determine to whom you will be selling your product. Making this determination is really defining a target market—a group of people with a set of common characteristics. Target marketing allows for a concentration of effort against a portion of the population with similar purchasing needs and buying habits.

Defining your target market will help you develop plans to achieve your sales objectives for an existing product and help you set realistic sales objectives for a new product.

Segmentation

Segmentation is a selection process that divides the broad consuming market into manageable segments with common characteristics enabling you to realize the greatest potential sales at the lowest cost. Develop your target market by first selecting the current and potential purchaser and/or user of your product, and second, by breaking down this broad group into the most relevant segment(s) for the most effective and efficient communication and selling of your product.

In segmenting your target market(s) you define the ultimate purchaser(s) or user(s) of your product, who will become your *primary target*. Further, you also may find it necessary to define and consider *secondary targets*, such as a smaller but high consuming and/or very profitable segment. Other potential secondary targets might be influencers or intermediate markets. If you are marketing a consumer service of a hospital, you would market not only to potential patients, but also to the physicians who, as influencers, refer patients to the hospital. Or, in the business-to-business category, if you are selling craft supplies to retailers as a primary target, you would define the intermediate distributor market as a secondary target.

Target Market Defining Methodology

Before applying the prescribed defining process to your own business, make sure you review the target market section in Steps 2 or 3 of your business review.

As you have previously defined many of the potential consuming market segments in the business review, you now begin the process of determining the segments that hold the greatest potential for your firm and that are most likely to respond to your marketing efforts. There are various methods to determine the target market for your product. Following is a step-by-step process to define your primary and secondary consumer and business-to-business target markets.

CONSUMER PRIMARY TARGET MARKET FOR MANUFACTURERS, RETAIL, AND SERVICE FIRMS

Step 1
Purchaser and/or User Determination

You must determine whether the primary target group will include purchasers, users, or both. However, keep in mind that it is very difficult to effectively market against two primary markets.

Because this is the first and most encompassing step in the defining process, step back and attempt to determine which of these two targets is the driving force, and what makes up their purchase and usage behavior. Consider these five factors in your determination:

The amount purchased and/or used.

The degree of influence on the usage and purchase decision.

The size of the market.

Who the competition chooses as its target market.

The inherent benefits of your product to one target or the other.

If the user and the purchaser are different, whom do you make the primary target for your marketing efforts: The user or the purchaser? Or do you target both? Some examples show how to make this determination. In marketing powdered soft drinks that are consumed primarily by kids age 2 to 11 but are purchased by their mothers, to whom do you market? Ideally both if you dominate the category and have adequate marketing dollars. If you are a low share competitor and have limited marketing dollars, as was the case for one particular client, concentrate on a single target market. In this case, the primary target market was redefined as kids 2 to 11 with marketing focus concentrated against the user rather than the purchaser. The result was a revival in sales and a share increase. Therefore, if you do not dominate the market in terms of sales and marketing dollars (which is most often the case), concentrate your marketing efforts against one target market rather than fragmenting your efforts over many and making minimal impact.

McDonald's, however, being a dominant player in its category and having substantial marketing dollar leverage, puts major emphasis against two primary targets: kids, who as users and influencers are considered the cornerstone of their business; and adults, because they are also users but more importantly, they are purchasers who bring their kids to McDonald's.

In the case of shoe purchasers and users, a mother who buys shoes for her children, herself, and sometimes her husband and is responsible for 80 percent of purchases, she, as the heavy purchaser, becomes the primary target market and receives the major marketing emphasis.

Once you have made your user/purchaser target market decision, make sure your primary target can be defined by a unified profile of similarities from demographics and geography to consumer benefits and purchasing behavior. With a retailer marketing fabric to sewers (the purchaser is usually the user as well), product attributes or benefits became the primary means of defining the target market. Because not all sewers consider both large selection and low prices of fabrics equally important in choosing one fabric store over the other, the retailer made "selection shoppers" its primary target, because it could not profitably deliver the price benefit as well as selection.

Step 2

Compare Your Current Target to the Demographic and Geographic Market Profile

Now that you have determined the primary user or purchaser, compare the demographic profile of the category to the demographic profile of your current customers, which you can quantify through market and/or customer research. Through comparing your customer market to the demographics of the total category, you can determine if you must adjust your current target focus to realize greater market potential for your product. Through an analysis for a retail client experiencing low sales per store, we found that its customer target market was primarily blue-collar with an annual income of under $30,000, while the majority of purchases in the total category were white-collar with annual incomes over $30,000, skewing to $40,000.

Based upon your findings, you may want to alter your initial target market profile description to more closely mirror the product category's target market in order to expand your current customer base. Or, this exercise may simply point out the major differences between consumers of your company's product and those of the category and provide insight as to why your company is successfully capturing a specific segment of the product category and how to attract even more of the same consumers.

Further, based on your business review, you should have determined regions, markets, and/or areas of markets that have the greatest consumption potential for your product by comparing the overall category usage of your product by area relative to the sales of your product. (See discussion of BDI and CDI in Step 6, Purchase Rates/Buying Habits, in the business review.) Based on this analysis, you may want to expand, reduce, or merely refine the geographic focus of your target market.

This geographic comparison can be used for an individual store or retail trading area, as well as for a region of the country. A real estate firm discovered that total population and total home sales outside the city, but still within the metro area, had experienced twice the growth than that in the city. The realtor also found that the firm's share of home sales was high in the city but low outside the city in the metro area, which was the major growth area. Based on this comparative data, the marketing program was developed to target home buyers and sellers not just in the city but in suburban areas throughout the metro area as well. The marketing plan called for a targeted advertising strategy that resulted in the advertising theme, "East side, west side, all around the county, your home is our profession." In addition, the marketing plan recommended broad metro media coverage and the opening of branch offices on the periphery of the city. The results of this geographic targeting were dramatic increases in the realtor's sales and profits, with its market share of home sales going from fourth to first in two years.

A word of caution: Before you go on to develop a new market or modify an existing target, make sure you have profitably exploited the full potential of your current customer base. This is particularly true in retail, service, and business-to-business marketing where you have personal contact with your customers. Your own customers in most cases are your most important and potentially profitable target market, because they are responsible for your firm's current existence and are a prime target for future sales. Target your current customers not only to retain their purchase loyalty, but also to motivate them to make more and bigger purchases and to refer new customers.

Step 3

Is There a Heavy User or Purchaser Target?

Having decided on the broad user versus purchaser market as it relates to current and potential target, analyze the target market data in Steps 2 or 3 of your business review to determine if there is a heavy user for your product. As a guideline, you have a heavy user in your product category if approximately two-thirds or more of total product is consumed by approximately one-third or less of the total users. A few percentage points below 67 percent of total usage and few points above 33 percent of users is acceptable. For example, 35 percent of canned vegetable users consume 65 percent of canned vegetables.

With a *one-third user to two-thirds consumption* determination, this heavy user usually always becomes your primary target, and you define it based on descriptive data available to you. For the consumer market, the heavy user descriptor could include demography, geography, and/or possibly lifestyle and product benefit/usage information, if available.

Step 4

Define a Target Market by Volume and Concentration

Not every product category possesses a heavy user target, in which the majority of product is consumed by a minority of users. If this is your situation, next review the target market data for those demographic and geographic segments that have above average concentration of usage (index at approximately 110 or greater) and cumulatively account for over 50 percent of all volume.[1] Based on the following example, the 18 to 34 age group would become part of your primary market, because the 18 to 24 age segment indexes at 125, and the age 25 to 34 age segment indexes at 120. Together, the two age groups account for 56 percent of consumption.

Adults by Age	Volume/Percentage of Consumption	Concentration Index
18 to 24	23	125
25 to 34	33	120
35 to 54	25	105
55+	19	85

---

[1]As a reminder from the business review section on target markets: Volume measures the amount of total consumption any given demographic segment is responsible for (e.g., 18 to 24 year olds account for 23 percent of all consumption). Concentration is defined as the percent of a given demographic segment that purchases the product (e.g., 70 percent of 18 to 24 year olds purchase the product). A concentration index is derived by dividing the concentration percent of 18 to 24 year olds by the concentration percent of all ages.

Use this selective collapsing process for each of the available demographic and geographic breakouts. On occasion, you will add a category that indexes under 110 in order to arrive at a target market that accounts for a minimum of 50 percent consumption.

It is important to understand that this target market selection process is only one approach and should not be considered inclusive when defining your target audience. In most cases, when there does not exist a heavy purchaser that you can target, it makes sense to assure yourself that your target market accounts for enough sales to justify the continued existence of your company—thus the 50 percent parameter discussed above.

However, while volume and concentration are critical to defining a primary target market, each situation is different. In a specialty retail situation, a small but heavily consuming segment might become a primary market because it provides a profitable niche for the right product or product mix. And though the segment accounts for only a small percentage of total category volume, its needs might be specific enough to be fulfilled by only one or two competitors, assuring them of a continuing source of profitable business because of a limited competitive situation.

BUSINESS-TO-BUSINESS PRIMARY TARGET MARKET

Step 1
Define Your Existing Core Customers

Through your target market analysis in Step 3 of the business review, you should have a clear understanding of your current customer companies in terms of Standard Industrial Classification (SIC), size, geography, application of your product, organizational structure, and new versus repeat usage. You must decide whether to focus your marketing efforts on selling more to your key primary customers or selling more products to lesser purchasing customers who have high purchasing potential. What is most efficient? What holds more short- and long-term potential?

Make sure you segment your current customer base into heavy and light users of your product to determine where you should concentrate or focus your marketing energies and dollars. In working with one of our clients who manufactures craft supplies, we discovered that, although they were spending nearly half their time and marketing dollars selling directly to craft retailers, over 80 percent of their sales were being made directly to distributors. Further analysis showed that 10 out of 400 distributors to whom they were marketing accounted for nearly 40 percent of distributor sales and 33 percent of total sales. The result of refocusing the primary emphasis against these core customers meant more efficient use of available marketing resources and greater sales, along with insight into the need to uncover and sell similar companies.

Step 2
Target High Potential New Customers

After redefining your current customer target market to fully exploit its buying potential, next compare your target customer to the marketplace (national and state SIC charts in the business review), selecting those customer SIC categories with the greatest potential.

New Potential Customers within SIC Categories Your Company Does Business

Within each SIC category that your company does business, target companies that best match your high volume customers in terms of size (sales dollars, employees, number of outlets if retail) and geography, not neglecting application of product and organization structure (one location versus branches). You can select these market potential companies from the individual state industrial directories (available from state government) that provide a complete listing of in-state commercial and industrial firms.

Famous Fixtures, a company that manufactures and installs new store fixtures for retailers, segmented their current high potential retail SIC category by size and geography using their current customer profile as a guide. They targeted retail companies with five or more outlets in a contiguous three state area, so they could market to larger, regionally concentrated store chains that would be most profitable and easy to service.

Potential Customers in SIC Categories Your Company Does Not Do Business

Also, do not neglect the SIC categories in which your company has no or minimal market share if it sells a product or service that would fulfill the needs of companies in those categories. In working with a statewide CPA firm that was strong in serving the accounting needs of companies in the financial field, we found it was also very effective to market their services to retailers, even though this CPA firm originally had only a small share of this category.

After reviewing new company market potential, you might come to a realization that only a few, many, or none of the new companies considered will become part of the primary target market. However, make sure that you again review these market potential, new companies originally discarded as candidates for a secondary target.

Step 3
Define the Decision Maker(s) and the Decision Making Process

Once you have segmented the customer and noncustomer companies, you must target the specific decision makers, as well as determine their function and influence in the decision process. Further, you must determine the decision sequence and the purchase criteria. Which decision maker does the initial screening of your product? Who makes the final decision? Is the decision maker looking for the very best quality product and then the best price, or vice versa? Is service most important?

Many times you cannot answer these questions unless you first define who the real decision maker is, and if there is more than one. In working with a firm that manufactured computer paper, we found through quantitative research that it really was not the manager of the computer department alone who made the purchasing decision; the purchasing agent manager was also part of this decision process, providing an important final approval role. The purchasing agent's decision was based primarily on price, while the computer department manager's decision was based primarily on the quality of paper and the service. Based on this determination, each decision maker was then targeted with a tailored direct mail and personal selling program.

SECONDARY TARGET MARKET FOR CONSUMER AND BUSINESS-TO-BUSINESS PRODUCTS

Now that you have made a primary target market determination, it is wise to consider secondary targets that you originally discarded because they did not account for the majority of sales volume or sales potential.

Consumer Secondary Targets

In the process of determining your primary consumer market you will most likely have discovered target markets that have *heavy concentration* of usage, but do not account for a high percentage of total volume. In this case, you could make these concentration segments secondary targets and place additional emphasis against them. As a result you might develop special promotion programs and add selective media weight for the secondary target. Examples of these secondary targets would be the Hispanic market's heavy usage of flour for meal preparation; college students' heavy beer usage; and salesmen as frequent suit purchasers.

Also affecting purchase or usage is the *influencer* who most often becomes a secondary target. Through primary research for a retail men's apparel chain, we found that spouses influence the suit and sport coat purchases of their husbands in over 50 percent of all purchase decisions. So in this situation, the male who is the purchaser and user should be the primary target, but his spouse cannot be totally ignored, and thus becomes a secondary target.

Influencers are of particular importance in public sector marketing, where outside forces can affect the success of an organization's marketing program. In a statewide bus transit marketing effort, we concentrated marketing efforts against current and potential riders as our primary target, but also targeted as our secondary market such opinion leaders as aldermen, major employers, and education leaders who affect communities' public support of the bus system.

Business-to-Business Secondary Targets

In business-to-business situations, a secondary target many times can be a customer who does not heavily purchase from your company currently but has high purchasing potential. You can delineate the potential of this customer by estimating your competitors' sales to this customer and determining what additional needs your company can fulfill for this customer.

Further, manufacturers must often include an intermediate channel as a secondary target segment. This target might be a fabricator, distributor/ wholesaler, or retailer that should receive special attention in order to make sure the product is available for the end user to purchase. This is particularly true in marketing consumer goods, with minimal retail shelf space available and multiple competitors selling the same type of product. It happens that so much time and money is devoted to selling to the end user that the intermediate channel is taken for granted.

Conversely, many business-to-business manufacturers, because they are selling directly to an intermediate target market (which is their primary target), *push* these products through the primary distribution channel (often using low prices and promotions) and put less marketing emphasis on the end user to *pull* the product through the channels. It might be more efficient in the short term to push the product through intermediate markets. However, ignoring the end user as a secondary target may mean loss of demand and loyalty for your product over the long term.

HOW TO WRITE TARGET MARKET DESCRIPTORS

Once you have arrived at your final target market selection(s), you can use the worksheets provided in Appendix C to list your target market(s). Include a brief rationale under the final target market selection with reference to additional supporting data in the business review. Exhibits 5.1, 5.2 and 5.3 illustrate the format for writing target market descriptors for a package good, retail, and business-to-business firm.

Exhibit 5.1   Target Market for a Packer of Canned
               Vegetables

Primary Market

Heavy users (35 percent of the users and 65 percent of the total consumption) who need on hand large quantities of inexpensive food for their families.
  Female homemakers
  Age 25 to 49
  Blue-collar occupation
  Household income $15 to $30M
  Reside in size B and C counties
  High school education
  Family size 3+ skewing to 5+
  Eastern and Midwest regions

Secondary Target Market

Trade

Buyers for chain supermarkets and independent grocers that cumulatively represent a minimum of 65 percent of total canned vegetable sales.
Current brokers/wholesalers

Exhibit 5.2   Target Market for a Retail Casual
               Apparel Chain

Primary Target Market

Value conscious purchasers of casual apparel for the family.
  Married women
  Age 18 to 49
  Household size 3+
  Household income $25M+
  Employed
  Reside in size B and C counties
  High school education

Secondary Target Market

Purchaser of durable, value oriented casual/work apparel for self:
User/Purchaser
  Men 18 to 49
  Income $25M+
  Reside in B and C counties
  Better education than women's apparel purchasers

DOS AND DON'TS

Do

- Use a step-by-step disciplined process in reviewing target market alternatives so that you consider all viable targets.
- Make sure the target market you select is big enough to meet your sales objectives.
- Make sure you consider both the volume and concentration of the market segments in order to weigh the importance of the quantity of consumption as well as selectivity in your target market determination.
- Compare your customer profile to that of the competition and the market to isolate additional target markets with potential.
- To really understand your target market in terms of demographics, usage, purchasing characteristics, and needs/wants, look to the extreme; look to and thoroughly understand the heavy purchaser/user segment.
- With multiple potential target markets and limited marketing funds, focus your

**Exhibit 5.3   Target Market for a Manufacturer of
                 Computer Form Paper**

Primary Target Market
Firms that purchase customized stock form computer paper.

Current Customers
Companies
   SIC: 20 to 39 (Manufacturing), 60 to 70 (Finance, Insurance, and Real Estate)
   Size: 25,000 cases or more purchased per year per company
   Geography: East Central and West Central regions
Decision Makers
   Data processing managers
   Purchasing agents

Secondary Target Market
Firms that purchase customized stock form computer paper.

Prospects
Companies
   SIC: 20 to 39 (Manufacturing), 60 to 67 (Finance, Insurance, and Real Estate), 70-99 (Business
      Services)
   Size: Minimum 1,000 cases or more purchased per year
   Geography: East Central, West Central, and Atlantic Seaboard Regions
Decision Makers
   Data processing managers
   Purchasing agents

---

marketing efforts against one target market whenever possible, giving secondary
emphasis to other markets with minimal support and only when needed.
- In business-to-business marketing, remember that companies don't buy your prod-
  ucts/services, people do. Market to the specific needs of the individual decision
  maker(s).
- Make sure you can deliver the product sought by the designated target markets.
- Consumer goods manufacturers that have both consumer and trade target markets
  should consider preparing a separate business-to-business trade marketing plan
  along with a consumer marketing plan. In this way the necessary focus will be
  placed against each critical target and each plan will more clearly communicate
  the specific marketing approach.

Don't

- Don't try to sell your product to everybody—segment!
- Don't guess who your target market is; quantify by the numbers whenever possible.
- Don't expand into markets that have low target market product usage and a high
  level of competition.
- Don't assume that the purchaser of your product is also the user and the only
  target market affecting the purchase.
- Don't expect all individuals within the same target market to buy a product for
  the same reasons.
- Don't overlook the potential of your current customers when considering new
  target markets.
- Don't expect the most obvious target to be the target with the most potential for
  your product; the competition and limited marketing resources might dictate otherwise.
- Don't overlook the importance of the intermediate market or the end user, whether
  you sell directly to them or not.

MARKETING OBJECTIVES AND STRATEGIES

Marketing objectives and strategies form the foundation of the marketing plan. Marketing objectives describe *what* needs to be achieved in order to meet the sales goals, and marketing strategies describe *how* the objectives will be accomplished.

Marketing objectives and strategies are developed by reviewing your sales goals, target markets, and problems and opportunities. From this review, you will learn how to determine marketing objectives and strategically how best to meet these objectives. Keep in mind that while this section does not take as much work in terms of writing and number crunching, it does require a great deal of think time. Make sure that the direction you map out for your company is rooted in well thought out logic. Innovative thinking becomes very important in this area of the marketing plan, but keep this thinking channeled by staying within the parameters established by the problems and opportunities, sales objectives, and target market.

From This Chapter You Will Learn

The definition of a marketing objective.

How to develop and write marketing objectives.

The definition of a marketing strategy.

How to develop and write marketing strategies.

MARKETING OBJECTIVES: OVERVIEW

Definition

A marketing *objective* is a statement of what needs to be accomplished. Marketing objectives are ends that need to be achieved. Differentiating between marketing objectives and marketing strategies is not always easy and is a source of confusion even for marketing professionals who have been in the business many years. To show the difference between the two, we have detailed those properties we believe make up a marketing objective. A marketing objective must:

- Be *specific*. The objective should focus on one singular goal.
- Be *measurable*. The results must be able to be quantified.
- *Relate to a specific time period*. This can be one or more years, the next six months, or even specific months of the year.
- *Focus on affecting target market behavior* (encouraging shopping, trial of a product, repeat purchase of a product, larger purchases, more frequent purchases, etc.). Often, objectives are set for individual segments of the target market.

Current and Potential New Users

Marketing objectives relate to target markets and focus on influencing their behavior. Marketing objectives will therefore fall into one of two target market categories: current users or new users. Within each category there are several possible objectives to be achieved.

Current Users

Retention of Current Users A common marketing objective is to retain the customer base at its current size from both a number and a dollar standpoint. This objective is defensive in nature. If your company has been losing customers over the past year or two, it becomes necessary to reverse this trend and maintain your customer base. You need to direct total focus first toward determining why business has been lost, and then toward stabilizing the customer base.

Increased Purchases from Current Users If your customer base is already stable, the objective can take a more offensive direction with strategies designed to obtain additional business from existing customers. This can be accomplished three different ways—by getting your customers to purchase:

- More often or more times in a given month or year.
- A more expensive product or service.
- Greater volume or amounts of product during each purchase.

New Users

Increase Trial of Your Product or Service For retailers, this equates to first getting increased traffic into the store. Most retailers have a fairly consistent purchase ratio (percentage of times a consumer purchases versus leaves without purchasing), which means that the retailer can visually rely on a certain percentage of the increased traffic actually making a purchase.

Increased trial for package goods, service, and business-to-business firms equates to *actual use of the product*. However, in both the retail situation and in package goods, service, and business-to-business, trial relates to obtaining new customers.

Obtain Repeat Usage after Initial Trial If your company has obtained high degrees of initial trial, it is important to make sure you establish continuity of purchase and loyalty. Often large amounts of trial exist, but the repeat purchase ratio is very low. If this is the case, establish an objective of increased repeat purchase and product loyalty, along with a fact finding program to determine why repeat purchase rates are low and what can be done to increase them. Even if repeat purchase rates are fairly strong, there is usually some need to make sure they are maintained. Remember, it is far less expensive and more profitable to keep existing customers than it is to prospect for new ones.

HOW TO DEVELOP YOUR MARKETING OBJECTIVES

In order to develop marketing objectives, first review the sales objectives, target markets sections of your marketing plan as well as the problems and opportunities summaries of your Business Review. Each provides guidance in developing realistic marketing objectives.

Step 1
Review of Sales Objectives

Sales objectives determine the qualifiers or parameters for your marketing objectives. Sales goals were established by taking into consideration the marketing data summarized in the business review. They are a direct reflection of a quantifiable estimate of your company's abilities over the next year. Review your sales objectives and the reasons why your sales goals were established at low, moderate, or high levels. If your sales goals are low to moderate, perhaps you have been losing customers and market share over the past years, or there is increased competitive activity or advertising spending in your territory. These reasons will directly influence the setting of your marketing objectives. They will also help you determine what your marketing objectives should be and whether you need to target new users, existing customers, or both.

Sales objectives provide a guideline for determining marketing objectives, as marketing objectives are established specifically to achieve the sales goals. All marketing objectives are quantifiable and measurable. The numerical quantifier used in the marketing objectives must be large enough to assure success of the sales goals. Assume the sales objective is to increase sales 7 percent, or $7MM. The subsequent marketing objective, to increase current customer purchases from two to three times a year over the next 12 months, would have to assure that this action will guarantee a sales increase of $7MM. In order to calculate this, we need to know the customer base size. This leads us to the next step: target market.

Step 2
Review of Target Market

The target market is the source or generator needed to achieve the sales goals. Sales come from the target market and will be from either existing or new customers. By reviewing the target market sections of the business review and the marketing plan, you will be able to define:

- *The size of your target markets.* This will allow you to determine the number of people in your primary and secondary target markets, or the actual potential universe of customers.
- *The size of your current customer base.* This will allow you to determine the number of customers you have versus the number of potential customers across each target market profile.

The target market information is necessary because each marketing objective is meant to affect the target market's behavior. The marketer must know the number of customers being affected, or it will be impossible to estimate the marketing objective's end results on sales. Again, assume the sales goal is to achieve a $7MM sales increase, and one marketing objective is to increase current customer purchases from two to three times per year over the next 12 months. Without knowing the total number of existing customers, it is impossible to calculate the effect of increasing purchases from two to three times per year. However, if the size of your customer base is known, simply multiply the customer base by the average purchase price to obtain the sales effect of getting your customers to purchase one more time per year.

In another example, assume that a marketing objective is to increase the number of new purchasers by 15 percent over the next 12 months and subsequently to obtain repeat purchase rates at equal to current customer purchase rates of three times per year among 50 percent of the new customers over the next 12 months. Again, without knowing the total number of potential customers versus the number of your own customers, there is no way of knowing if a 15 percent increase is realistic, or if it is enough to obtain a given sales objective.

By reviewing your sales goals and your target market size, you have the potential to calculate the total effect of your marketing objectives and determine whether they are realistic in terms of helping your company reach its sales goals. The next to last step is to review your problems and opportunities.

Step 3
Review of Problems and Opportunities

The problems and opportunities summaries of the Business Review provide insight into the content of the marketing objectives. Review each problem and opportunity that relates to the target market's behavior. Solving these problems or exploiting these opportunities will be the basis for your marketing objectives.

One of the opportunities we discovered while working for a national package goods firm was stated in the following manner:

> Though trial of the product is very low, repeat purchase is above average when compared to the industry standard.

The implication from this opportunity is that while trial was low, consumers liked the product's benefits, and there was a high degree of product acceptance and loyalty. Thus, the marketing objectives from this opportunity became:

1. Increase new trial of the product by 10 percent among the target audience over the next 12 months.
2. Achieve repeat purchase of 60 percent from new users over the next 12 months.

Step 4
Formulate a Rationale

The last step is to formulate a rationale. Assume the product is in the early stage of its product life cycle, the sales objective is to increase sales 50 percent or $25MM, and the marketing objectives are those developed above in Step 3. Here, the work you did in reviewing your sales objectives and target market becomes important.

We can assume that when we started to form the two marketing objectives from Step 3, we weren't sure what percent of new trial was needed to achieve our sales objectives. However, in reviewing the required sales increase of 50 percent or $25MM, we were able to calculate that we would need a 10 percent increase in new trial to achieve the required sales objectives. From reviewing our target market size, we knew that currently only 10 percent of the current target market was using the product. So an additional 10 percent new trial rate was realistic given the product's early stage in the product life cycle and other positive purchasing behavior, competitive, and product information available to us in the business review. Finally, we knew that our normal customer's repurchase rate was 60 percent, and that the average number of purchases per year was four. Thus, the rationale for the marketing objectives became:

> A major problem has been low trial of the product (less than 10 percent of the target market). However, while trial is very low, repeat purchase among users is high (over 60 percent). Thus, consumer acceptance of the product is very positive, and the major problem to overcome is low overall trial of the product by consumers. An incremental 10 percent increase in new customers and the

Exhibit 6.1   Developing Your Marketing Objective Rationale

Sales Goal	Increase dollar sales 10 percent over the previous year, from $250MM to $275MM
Target Market	Women 18+
Total potential target market size	85MM (Does not include existing customers)
Marketing goal	10% New trial; 60% Repeat users from new users
Total new users	85MM × 10% = 8.5MM New users
Repeat users	60% × 8.5MM = 5.1MM Repeat users
Repeat usage by customers	4 Times per year (2 times per year in this calculation because not all new customers will be users for the full year)
Average price of product	$1.33
Total sales	8.5MM × 1 Time use @ $1.33 = $11.3MM 5.1MM × 2 Repurchases @ $1.33 = $13.6MM Total Sales = $24.9MM

Note: This calculation is to determine if additional sales of approximately $25MM will be achieved. It is assumed that the previous sales level will be maintained through existing customers.

maintenance of current customers will achieve the sales objective. This assumes that 60 percent of the new customers repurchase at the average of twice per year. The figure of twice per year is half of the normal purchase rate of four times per year, for the reason that not all the new trial will be generated at the beginning of the year. Thus, new customers won't necessarily have a full year of purchasing.

Exhibit 6.1 illustrates the calculations for developing a marketing objective rationale.

Long- and Short-Term Marketing Objectives

Typically, businesses develop one- to three-year plans while actually operating from the current one-year plan. It is a good practice to develop both long-term (two to three years) and short-term (one year) marketing objectives. Even if you don't have a long-term plan, the exercise of writing long-term marketing objectives forces you to focus on the future and consider the long-term implications of short-term marketing objectives, strategies, and executions. You might realize that while your short-term marketing objectives can be realized through increased sales from the *existing* product line, long-term marketing objectives will be realized only through the development of a *new* product line. With this knowledge you can plan for this inevitability sooner rather than later, and perhaps develop a strategy of testing new products.

In another example, you may realize that in order to meet long-term marketing objectives, you will eventually need to develop new markets in different parts of the country where you do not currently market your product. Thus, a strategy or program can be initiated with this in mind, to study and recommend new geographic markets where you are most likely to succeed. Then, when the time comes, you will be ready to proceed in an orderly, disciplined fashion.

In summary, most plans have long-term objectives that provide overall direction for the next one to three years. Short-term objectives are specific to the current year, as are strategies. However, both the short-term objectives and strategies should be focused toward helping the company achieve both short-term and, in two to three years, long-term objectives.

Differences Between Retail, Package Goods, and Business-to-Business Marketing Objectives

Marketing objectives reflect the major differences between types of businesses. *Marketing objectives for retailers* affect consumer behavior in a retail environment. This means there is a concentration on building store traffic, transactions, items per transaction, dollar sales per transaction, multiple purchases, and greater repeat purchases among both current and new users. The following marketing objectives might help a retailer achieve its sales goals:

Increase purchases per transaction of women 18 to 49, from 1.23 pairs of shoes to 1.35 pairs of shoes during the heavy seasonal sales months of back-to-school in August and the holiday months of November and December.

Increase dollar sales per transaction among the current users by 10 percent, from $22.00 to $24.22 over the next 12 months.

Increase traffic of women 18 to 49 by 15 percent, from existing levels of 180 people per day over the next 12 months. Maintain the current purchase ratio of 45 percent.

Generate a two-to-one purchase to walk ratio among all customers over the next 12 months.

Package goods marketers also focus on affecting consumer behavior of existing and new customers, but the emphasis is really on two different target markets: the consumer and the trade. Marketing objectives must be established to achieve sales goals by affecting purchase rates of the trade and the consumer in the store. The following marketing objectives might help a package goods marketer achieve sales goals:

Trade marketing objectives

Increase trial of the target market by 10 percent over the previous year in the Western region of the country.

Maintain current purchase rates of existing trade customers over the next year.

Consumer marketing objectives

Increase repeat usage of the product from 20 percent to 25 percent among current users over the next 12 months.

Increase new trial of the primary market, females 25 to 49, 5 percent over existing levels during the next year.

Increase trial of the product among the secondary target market of males 18 to 35 by 10 percent over the next year.

Business-to-business marketing objectives are focused on affecting the behavior of other businesses. Remember that in business-to-business marketing, there are often multiple target markets as defined by SIC categories. Each one should have specific marketing objectives which, when added together, will meet the sales objectives. The following marketing objectives might help a business-to-business marketer achieve the sales goals for two specific target markets, construction companies and manufacturing businesses:

Construction companies (Construction SIC): Maintain current purchases and reorder rates of existing customers over the next 12 months.

Manufacturing businesses (Manufacturing SIC): Develop ten new accounts over the next 12 months with average sales of $100M.

Worksheets for writing your marketing objectives and strategies appear in Appendix C.

MARKETING STRATEGIES: OVERVIEW

Definition

A marketing *strategy* is a statement detailing how an individual marketing objective will be achieved. It describes the method for accomplishing the objective. While marketing objectives are specific, quantifiable, and measurable, *marketing strategies are descriptive*. They explain how the measurable objectives will be met.

HOW TO DEVELOP YOUR MARKETING STRATEGIES

Marketing objectives are very narrow in scope, relating to customer behavior. Yet marketing strategies are broader and provide direction for all areas of the marketing plan. Marketing strategies serve as a guide to the positioning of your product. They also serve as reference points for the development of specific marketing mix tool programs in the marketing plan (product, price, distribution, personal selling/operations, promotion, advertising message, advertising media, merchandising, and publicity). What marketing strategies do not do is provide such specifics as use television, which belongs in the actual media segment of the marketing plan. You should review each of the following categories and determine if you need to address the topic by developing one or more marketing strategies. (Note: All of the following categories may not apply to your particular firm.)

Build the Market or Steal Market Share?

A critical strategic decision facing all marketers writing a plan will be whether you plan to *build the market*, or *steal share* from competitors in order to achieve your sales goals. The information in Step 5, product awareness and attributes, of your business review regarding product life cycle will help provide answers to this fundamental question.

A situation with a relatively new product where the current user base is small, the potential user base is quite large, and there is little competition often requires a build the market strategy. Many times the company that creates the market maintains the largest market share into the future. An example of this would be Miller Lite beer. Miller established the light beer category and has been the market share leader ever since. However, remember that it is usually easier to steal market share than to build the market. Building market share takes additional time and money because it is a two-step process. You have to develop a consumer's need for the product and then convince them to purchase your product.

Conversely, a situation where the product is a mature one with little growth (i.e., few new customers entering the marketplace) often calls for stealing market share from competitors. In this situation you have to convince product category users that your product is superior to that of your competition.

This is a very fundamental strategic decision that must be made up front in your marketing strategy section. The decision whether to build the market or steal share will affect all other areas of the marketing plan. A stealing share strategy such as, "steal market share from the leading competitor" requires that your company's target market definitions will closely approximate those of the current market leader's customer profile. Also, the advertising will most likely communicate benefits or an image of your product the market leader doesn't possess. To the contrary, a build the market strategy often requires educating new customers about the benefits of product usage and convincing them first to use the product category, and only then to use your company's products.

National, Regional, and Local Market Strategies

This marketing strategy category is often overlooked by the national, regional, and local marketer. This strategy helps the marketer determine whether there will be a core national marketing plan or a combination of national, regional, and local marketing plans. Having a combination of plans requires a lot of work but is usually worth the effort. This strategy recognizes regional DMA (designated market area or television viewing area) and even local trading area differences by allowing for the application of specific territorial marketing programs. If you are a retailer, you may have a national marketing program as an overlay with special DMA plans and specific local marketing programs for each store. Or, if you are a national package goods company, it may be that to accomplish your marketing objective of increasing new trial by 10 percent, you need to develop a national marketing program. However, to help guarantee your success, you will place special marketing and spending emphasis on specific markets which have demonstrated the potential to grow at far greater rates when given local, tailored types of marketing programs. These local marketing programs often have their own plans with specific marketing objectives and strategies. For instance, the Madison, Wisconsin market may receive special promotions that are proven sales generators in Midwest college towns, while Chicago may receive extra media spending because of its size, sales potential, and the amount of advertising clutter in the marketplace.

Seasonality Strategies

Strategic decisions must be made about when to advertise or promote your product or store. Here, the seasonality portion of the sales section in your business review becomes useful. Several issues are important. The first is whether there are times of the year when your product category as a whole does significantly better than your company does. If so, why? Can you do something to increase sales during that period when customers of your product category are naturally purchasing at increased rates?

The second issue is whether you are going to advertise and promote all year, during stronger selling periods, or during weaker selling periods. If you have a limited budget, it is recommended that you concentrate only on those times of the year when sales are highest, and attempt to capture as many purchases during that period as possible. Often, retail companies utilize in-store promotion strategies such as bounce back coupons during stronger selling periods to entice customers back during down periods; thus using high volume months to help promote lower volume months.

Finally, you need to decide if you are going to advertise and promote prior to, during, or between peak selling periods. In retail, for example, the holiday seasons are heavy purchasing periods. A strategic decision must be made on whether you are going to advertise earlier than your competitors, throughout the whole selling season, or just during the peak selling weeks. It is often recommended to lead the selling season. There will be less competitive advertising clutter, and you can build awareness just prior to the heavy shopping period. An alternative strategy that is also successful is to concentrate advertising during the heaviest weeks of the holiday shopping period. Thus, the advertiser can dominate a critical selling period and be visible when it counts most.

Competitive Strategies

Often there is need for a competitive strategy. The business review may reveal that a single competitor is almost totally responsible for your company's decline in market share; or a single company or group of competitors may have preempted your unique positioning in the marketplace. If this is the case, you will need to develop a competitive marketing strategy in your marketing plan.

Competitive strategies vary depending upon the situation. Sometimes competitive strategies try to be anticategory, establishing your company as better than all competitors in the category. To achieve this, a company often takes a common consumer perceived problem in the industry (such as lack of customer service attention in retail, or delayed flights in the airline business), establishes the problem as inherent to the industry, and then tries to set itself apart as better than the competition in this area of concern.

Sometimes competitive strategies focus on one competitor or a group of specific competitors. You may need to reestablish your product attribute dominance relative to a specific competitor. Or a competitor may have done a better job of creating a lifestyle image in tune with the heavy user consumer in your category. In both these situations, you might consider developing competitive strategies which require comparison advertising or advertising which counters specific competitive claims. You might also consider a competitive media tactic of advertising within the same time frames and media as your competition. Or you might try to dominate a medium which is heavily used, or perhaps not used at all, by the heavy *user* of your industry category.

Another common competitive situation occurs when a strong competitor starts doing business in your trading area or in a market you previously dominated. We developed a competitive strategy for a retail client when an aggressive, nationally known competitor announced it was moving into one of our client's important markets. The competitive strategy centered around taking advantage of the fact that our client was already in business and the new competitor wasn't. To implement the strategy, our client ran a half-price sale for two months prior to the opening of the competitor's stores. This was intended to get customers to purchase prior to the anticipated grand opening of the competing stores. The week of the competitor's grand opening, we mailed a promotional piece to consumers in the five-mile trading area surrounding the competitor's store. We continued heavy promotion during the competitor's grand opening with a grand opening of our own, celebrating the opening of the 240th store in our client's chain of stores. This competitive plan resulted in our client's stores being up 40 percent during the promotional period and maintaining market share over the long run.

Finally, competitive strategies also include the development of a new or improved product, packaging, selling, or merchandising techniques to counter competitive strengths.

Target Market Strategies

Your target market section detailed primary and secondary target markets. You must now discuss the emphasis you will place against the various target markets and how you will market to them. For example, you may decide to target the *heavy user* through the use of a specific product in your product line that has proven appeal to heavy users. Or you may initiate in-store changes that appeal to heavy users. You may target a *secondary target market* only through in-store incentives or point-of-purchase promotional techniques, saving all mass media expenditures for the *primary target market*. Or your company may have recently revised your primary target market to include the heavy user who may have shopped your product only as a second choice in the past. A target market strategy must reflect this change in target market description. This strategy to primarily target the heavy user in all marketing mix decisions affects all subsequent marketing strategies and individual marketing mix tool plans.

Product Strategies

You must make strategic decisions regarding the product. If repeat purchase rates are low, and your company's product ranks poorly across product attributes, you must decide how to improve the product in order to meet your marketing objectives. Another area to consider is expanding alternate uses of the product. This is a viable strategy when you have a mature product with a static or limited customer base. An example is the expansion of the use of baking soda as an odor deterrent in refrigerators. This was a successful marketing strategy to meet the marketing objective of increasing the purchase and usage rates by current customers and providing a reason for new customers to try the product.

The development of new products or new extensions of your existing product line should be addressed if they are necessary to meet marketing objectives. If you are developing new products, you need to establish a new product strategy. Describe in general terms the type of product you will be developing, including the new product's features and attributes. You will also have to address a program to develop a brand or name for the product. This, however, comes after the positioning of the product, and is detailed in Chapter 8, Product/Branding/Packaging. Again, remember that these should be general strategies which provide overall marketing direction.

You should develop a strategy addressing whether you are going to emphasize stronger or weaker product categories/brands in your marketing plan. Selling and emphasizing the products/brands with the greatest potential is particularly viable when growth potential still exists. This strategy can also be used to attract users with product or store strengths and then cross-sell to weaker selling categories via promotions or discounts. Many times a specific target market can also be attracted through utilizing loss leaders or a specific strong selling brand in the product mix. You may have a marketing objective of building new trial among heavy shoe purchasers, women 35 to 44 with children. The problems and opportunities section may point out that women 35 to 44 shop your shoe store not for themselves but for their children. Therefore, your strategy may be to promote children's shoes to heavy user women to initiate trial, and then cross-sell to the women's shoe department in-store. Other incentives and merchandising techniques could also be created to encourage purchasing women's shoes once trial is established.

Alternatively, building weaker product categories/brands is often attempted when it is felt that the company's strengths have been fully exploited. This strategic decision requires more initial money, as it is always more difficult to improve a weakness than to build upon a strength. However, it is very worthwhile if it provides a company with more products that contribute more equally to profits. This also protects a company from major fluctuations resulting from having only one or two strong selling products.

Finally, finding more efficient ways to produce the product might also be a viable strategy to help insure success of a previously stated marketing objective, if the improved efficiency can permit you to achieve a price advantage. In addition, the improved efficiency might also provide greater gross margins, which can help achieve greater profitability or can be invested in implementing stronger marketing programs.

Packaging Strategies

If you are going to develop a packaging plan later in the marketing plan, establish a general packaging direction. A problem identified in the problem and opportunities summaries may point out that the company's packaging makes usage difficult. Therefore, a change in packaging might help achieve the marketing objective of increasing repeat usage and consumption among current customers.

Pricing Strategies

Pricing strategies should also be discussed. One area to address is whether you will use high or low prices relative to your competition, or whether you'll simply match the competition's price and depend upon service or superior product attributes for a competitive edge. Will you maintain margins with high price strategies, or will you allow for lower margins and lower prices to develop trial? Also include whether your pricing will be uniform nationally or whether it will vary market by market, store by store, or customer by customer. Finally, if you are going to use price to help communicate a positioning, state this intent in this section. Some companies follow a strategy of a premium price to help establish a premium positioning relative to the competition.

Distribution of Product/Penetration or Coverage Strategies

The strategic decisions that must be made in this area are different for package goods and business-to-business firms than for those of retailers and service firms. *Package goods and business-to-business firms* must decide in what areas of the country to target their distribution efforts. They also must decide the type of outlet that will carry their product and the desired market coverage among the targeted outlet category.

Retailers and service firms must strategically decide if marketing objectives can be achieved through existing outlets, whether new stores need to be added in existing markets without cannibalizing existing stores, or whether new stores need to be added through opening new markets. If sales per store have not been maximized in low penetrated markets, one way to build sales is to add new stores in existing markets. This allows for greater leverage of advertising dollars. However, if sales have been maximized in current markets, and the markets have been fully penetrated to the point where additional stores/products could cannibalize existing sales, then a realistic strategy is to expand to new markets. In summary, the penetration potential of existing and new markets must be analyzed and strategically addressed.

It is helpful to estimate market strengths (BDIs and CDIs) by reviewing Step 7, Distribution, of the business review prior to completing this section.

Personal Selling/ Operation Strategies

You need to determine whether your organization will incorporate a structured personal selling program in its marketing plan. If you are a retailer, note whether your subsequent selling plan should include specific sales ratios (e.g., develop sales ratio of purchasers versus walkers based upon past history and future expectations).

Like retailers, manufacturers also need to decide whether they are going to establish specific sales ratios. If so, such a statement as "establish specific sales ratios (number of prospects that become customers) to monitor the results of the sales force," should be included as a strategy in this section.

Finally, if necessary, this section should include a strategy for implementing your marketing department's performance. An example would be to create a marketing liaison between purchasing and marketing to assure that the product is purchased and available for marketing promotions.

Promotion Strategies

Promotions should be channeled to meet specific needs and incorporated into the overall marketing plan in a disciplined fashion. The promotion strategies in this marketing section will set the areas of emphasis for the specific promotion plan later in the marketing plan. A retailer may have the marketing objective of increasing number of units per transaction from the target market by 10 percent over the next 12 months. A marketing strategy to achieve this could be to encourage multiple purchases through promotional incentives. This would then be expanded upon in the promotion section of the marketing plan, but it would have been established up front that pairs per transaction increases are going to come from multiple purchase promotional incentives.

Spending Strategies

Spending strategies detail how the marketing dollars will be spent. To achieve your market objectives, you need to decide whether to increase sales of weaker selling brands, stores, or regions of the country, or to attract more customers to your stronger brands or stores. In order to make these decisions, you need to determine spending levels by brand, store, or regions of the country. In most situations you can't increase sales of a weaker selling brand without making an incremental budget commitment to the brand. We know that one way to increase short term sales is to place emphasis on a company's strengths. However, there comes a point when strong brands, stores, or markets can't be expected to provide additional growth. Long-term success requires building weaker brands, stores, and sales territories, and this requires some investment spending. (Note that this strategy category will affect later media spending decisions.)

Overall spending should also be addressed. Does your company plan to spend at a percent of sales for marketing and advertising consistent with past years? Or, because of new aggressive sales projections and marketing objectives, do you need to increase marketing and advertising spending from, for example, 4.2 percent of gross sales to 6 percent?

Advertising Message Strategies

The marketer needs to provide an overall focus for the advertising and communication. It is important to state up front in your marketing strategy section how you are going to use advertising to fulfill your marketing objectives. Are you going to develop image advertising and build long-term sales, or will your advertising promote short-term sales through a harder sell, promotional emphasis? Do you plan to vary your advertiser's message by region? Perhaps you will have both a national advertising program and a localized market-by-market program.

Advertising Media Strategies

The strategies developed in this section should be consistent with the direction established in the product, competitive and spending marketing strategies. The primary goal in establishing an overall media strategy is to provide direction for the upcoming media plan while also establishing geographic and product spending emphasis. You may decide upon a strategy varying media spending by market or spending more in markets with greater potential. You may investment spend in new markets to establish awareness and generate trial. You may also consider exclusively developing a national media plan, or you may develop national and local media plans to support a dual marketing strategy of both national and local orientation.

Merchandising Strategies

A strategy is needed to set the tone for what will be done from a merchandising standpoint. This applies, for example, to in-store signage and point-of-purchase displays for retailers, point-of-purchase displays and packaging for package goods firms, such personal sales presentation devices as brochures and sell sheets for business-to-business firms, and special events for all three business categories. An opportunity identified under problems and opportunities might tell you that 80 percent of purchase decisions are made in-store. Thus the marketing strategy in this situation might be to utilize extensive point-of-purchase merchandising to affect decision making in-store.

Publicity Strategies

You should determine if you are going to make publicity part of your marketing plan. If you are, your publicity effort should be channeled early in the marketing plan. Then there will be an overall direction established when it comes time to develop a specific publicity plan in the marketing mix tools chapter. For example, you might consider supplementing your overall advertising and promotion communication program with publicity. Or you might use media cosponsors of planned promotional events to generate publicity. Or you may decide to develop an extensive publicity plan to take advantage of ongoing publicity opportunities for your company in a specific medium.

Marketing R&D (Research and Development) Strategies

Change is often important in generating trial and retrial of a company's product. A disciplined program to initiate this change is critical. In most businesses there is a need to continually expand and/or refine the company's product offering and marketing in order to continually build incremental sales. This can be accomplished through a planned and disciplined testing or research and development program.

Marketing R&D is the lifeblood in perpetuating the success of your business. It takes work, planning, and perseverance to test and produce readable results, but it is always worth it. It keeps you ahead of the competition and helps you avoid costly mistakes. Testing can help you develop a new product or marketing activity, make it better, provide evidence of your program's effectiveness, and can help eliminate those ideas that aren't going to work before a costly investment has been made.

Once you have committed to some form of marketing R&D, this section should be used to define what you will be testing—new products, services, merchandising programs, store layouts, packaging, media strategies, advertising messages, pricing, promotions, etc. Then fully develop each test program in the respective marketing mix tool objective and strategy sections later in the marketing plan.

Primary Research Strategies

If you plan to conduct primary research, now is the time to establish a research strategy. You may develop a research strategy to solve a specific problem that will help you to build sales and accomplish a marketing objective. Or you may decide to conduct an ongoing awareness, attitude, and behavior tracking study to assist with next year's plan and to provide a benchmark to evaluate the results of current and future marketing plans.

HOW TO DEVELOP YOUR MARKETING STRATEGIES

Step 1
Review Your Problems and Opportunities

Again, go back and review your problems and opportunities. First, read through the list and make notes regarding ideas you have on how to solve the problems and take advantage of the opportunities. Be as creative as possible in this exercise, coming up with multiple solutions for each problem or opportunity.

Step 2
Review Your Marketing Objectives

Review your marketing objectives. Now reread the problems and opportunities, along with your original notes on how to solve the problems and take advantage of the opportunities. Determine which of the ideas will form strategies capable of achieving the marketing objectives.

Step 3
Develop Your Strategies

Make certain that you have developed strategies to cover each of the strategic categories that are necessary to fulfill your marketing objectives. The strategies should provide the direction for use of the marketing mix tools throughout the marketing plan. You will develop specific plans for these strategies later in your advertising, media, promotion, and marketing mix tool sections. You may have a seasonality strategy to emphasize the stronger selling periods with mass communications, and the weaker selling periods with in-store promotions. A spending strategy may be to grow and develop specific markets at the expense of established markets. Both these strategies will be reflected in the detailed media plan later in your plan.

In summary, after reading the marketing strategies, upper management should have a good idea as to how you are going to achieve your marketing objectives from a strategic standpoint. However, the details of these strategies will be fully developed in the subsequent marketing mix tool sections of the marketing plan.

Writing Your Marketing Strategies

In writing your strategies, make sure to focus on one single idea at a time. The strategies should be very descriptive and focus on how you are going to utilize promotion or packaging to achieve the marketing objectives. Following each strategy should be a brief rationale. Some examples for you to follow are presented here. Worksheets are provided in Appendix C.

Store Penetration Strategy

Place emphasis on building sales of existing markets by increasing the number of stores in markets that are efficient and most easily penetrated.

Rationale Research has shown that maximum sales can be achieved in a DMA if it is penetrated at the rate of one store per 150,000 households. There are a number of markets that are not penetrated to this level.

Promotion Strategy

Use promotions to build the slow sales periods of January through June and to build product categories in which the company is not realizing its full potential.

Rationale The strategy recognizes that heavy promotional emphasis is needed to move the market during slow periods of the year and for specific slower moving product categories. However, the decision has been made to obtain full margin sales through pure advertising during times of the year when consumers are purchasing at peak rates.

Advertising Strategy

Use image advertising during times of the year when consumers are purchasing at peak rates and price promotion during down periods.

Rationale While promotion will be used to provide incentive to purchase during slow periods of the year and weaker selling months, the company should use product benefit advertising during key buying periods to capture full margin sales.

DOS AND DON'TS

Do

- Remember that *all* objectives must:
  Be specific in focus.
  Be measurable.
  Relate to a specific time period.
  Relate to a target market.
  Focus on affecting target market behavior.

- Consider sales objectives, target market size, and problems and opportunities when developing marketing objectives.
- Remember that marketing objectives must be responsible for achieving the sales objectives. Hold them accountable and provide quantifiable rationale that they will provide the required results to achieve the sales objectives.
- Keep your marketing objectives to one sentence and the rationale to one brief paragraph.
- Make your strategies descriptive statements of how you will achieve your marketing objectives.
- Include all the meaningful strategies from your problems and opportunities. Then go back and make sure they meet your marketing objective requirements, and that you address each of the strategic categories outlined in the strategy definition and overview section.
- Take considerable time in developing your marketing objectives and strategies. They form the basis of your whole marketing plan. You should give them a considerable amount of thought and review prior to finalizing this portion of the marketing plan.
- Whenever possible, steal market share; it's easier and less expensive than building the market. Also, it's easier to build upon marketing strengths than to improve weaknesses.

Don't

- Don't necessarily limit the number of marketing objectives to one. It's fine to have only one marketing objective, but make sure it will meet your sales objective. If not, you may need multiple marketing objectives, each focusing on a more narrow target market or a specific area of consumer behavior.
- Don't write slogans and think they are objectives. "To be the best," or "to provide the best customer service" are slogans. They are not measurable or time specific. They don't allow for results that can be measured.
- Do not include communication goals with marketing objectives. Increasing awareness or changing attitudes are communication based and should be included in the advertising section of this plan. Concentrate on marketing objectives that change consumer behavior. The key is that *marketing objectives alter actual behavior while advertising objectives alter a thought process*.
- Don't let the strategies become too executional. Keep the strategies broad and directional.
- Don't limit the focus to one or two specific marketing areas. Remember that marketing strategies should include direction across all areas of importance to your marketing plan.
- Don't be stagnant in your strategic thinking and become left behind in the increasingly changing and competitive business environment. Initiate a marketing R&D program so that you are continually developing new and proven marketing programs to replace those programs that aren't working or to help make an existing program even better.
- Don't expect the majority of your marketing R&D testing program to be successful. Remember most new ideas fail. However, only a few successes (and sometimes only one) are needed to keep you ahead of the competition year after year. And, many times one success can pay for multiple failures in a very short time.

7

POSITIONING

T he next step in your planning process is to develop a market positioning for your product, service, or store. The positioning process is both fun and frustrating, because it calls for creative thinking on one hand and a sorting out of multiple sets of data on the other. Be open minded and visionary; think as a buyer rather than a seller.

From This Chapter You Will Learn

What positioning is and why it is important.

What makes a positioning succeed or fail.

The various ways to position a product.

How to develop your own positioning.

How to write a positioning strategy.

OVERVIEW

Definition

Once you have defined your target market(s) and have established marketing objectives and strategies, you must develop a market positioning for your product. By positioning, we mean creating an image for your product in the minds of the target market. Within your target market you must establish *the desired perception of your product relative to the competition*.

If there is no real or direct competition (such as for some nonprofit organizations), the organization still needs a point of reference in order for the target market to understand and remember what is being communicated. In the case of the competitive marketplace, a positioning positively differentiates the product from that of the competition. And remember, it is to a specific target market, not the whole world, that positioning is used to differentiate your product.

Importance of Positioning

No matter what you are marketing, a salient positioning is necessary. It is the basis for all your communications—branding, advertising, promotions, packaging, sales force, merchandising, and publicity. By having one meaningful, targeted positioning as a guide for all your communications, you will convey a consistent image. Each vehicle of communication conveying a common positioning will reinforce the others for a cumulative effect, maximizing the return of your marketing investment. Accordingly, everything you do from a marketing perspective must *reinforce one positioning*. Otherwise, you will not only undermine your marketing efforts, but confuse the target group as well.

Further, because everything you do should reflect one positioning, the positioning must be correct, or your marketing activities will be ineffective. Worse yet, a wrong positioning could even destroy a successful product. Because of the inclusivity of positioning, you must look for a positioning that is not only right for your product now, but will also be adaptable years into the future for both the marketplace and the product. The *macho* positioning of "Marlboro Country" and *a friend as you travel* positioning of "Fly the Friendly Skies of United" are examples of positioning for the long term.

As a side note, if you must develop a new brand name for a product, it must reflect the product positioning. For those of you who need to create a new product name, there is a discussion in Chapter 8, Product/Branding/Packaging, on how to develop a branding program that will be a guide for new name generation.

Positioning Considerations

In order to arrive at a successful long-term positioning, you must take into consideration these factors:

- The inherent drama of the product you are selling.
- The needs and wants of the target markets.
- The competition.

The business review and the problems and opportunities you have completed, along with the target market determination and marketing strategies you developed are key to arriving at the right positioning. You must understand the strengths and weaknesses of your product versus that of the competition. Where is your product comparable to the competition and where is it different? Where is it really unique? And most important, what do these competitive differences, if any, mean to the target market? If the positioning reflects a difference that your product cannot deliver or that is not important to the target group, your positioning will not be successful. And even if your product possesses a meaningful difference, your positioning will not be effective if the target group does not perceive it as meaningfully different. The key point is that as you develop your product positioning, you must deal with the target group's *perception* of the competing products even though it is not altogether accurate, because they are the buyers, and consequently *their perception is truth*.

Further, the odds of arriving at a successful positioning increase dramatically when you have done market research among the potential target market. Primary research will help identify key users/purchasers along with meaningful product attributes. Also, quantitative research will show how the primary market perceives these important attributes relative to the competition. Even without primary market research, if you have diligently employed the disciplined marketing plan process, you should have a good start in developing a positioning that communicates well to the target market.

To repeat, everything in a marketing plan evolves from the target market, and how you strategically meet the needs of the target market with your product. Therefore, no matter how you position your product, the target market must be the reason for the positioning. As you consider various positioning alternatives, let the target market be the focal point and the marketing strategies your guide.

TYPES OF POSITIONING

You can position your product many different ways. Here are some types of positionings to consider.[1]

Position by Product Difference

Ask yourself: What is meaningfully different about what my company is selling? Pillsbury took a commodity product, flour, and put a recipe inside the sack to make it different from the competition, calling it "the Idea Flour." Another example of using a product difference as a feature is Famous Fixtures, a manufacturer and installer of store fixtures selling to retail store chains. It positioned itself as having actual retail experience because its own parent company is a retailer—"Famous Fixtures: retailer owned, retailer built, retailer tested." Thus, their product difference is not just their product but their service as well.

Many times a product difference can be easily duplicated, as in the first example— Gold Medal Flour matched Pillsbury and put a recipe in its packages. However, if the product feature is truly part of the inherent drama of your product, it is not as easy to duplicate, as the second example illustrates. Most fixture companies were not created by a retailer, as was Famous Fixtures, to build its own fixtures, and really don't have a retailer's perspective in building and installing retail store fixtures.

Further, in both of these positioning examples, the product positioning began with a difference, and these differences were meaningful to the target market. To homemakers, the product difference was the inclusion of a recipe which meant new or better baked goods for a family. To retailers, Famous Fixtures, being retail oriented, knew best how to fixture their stores for increased sales and understood the importance of quick installation for the store to open.

Position by Key Attribute/Benefit

Ask yourself: What benefit does my product offer that the target market will consider meaningful? Primary research among consumers for a hospital found that personal care was a benefit patients could evaluate and considered extremely important. Further, no competitor had claimed this attribute. We helped our client position itself as the caring hospital with the basic selling idea, "We care for you . . . A lot." The result: This hospital moved from third place to second in the public's personal care rankings. Here is a case where all four competing hospitals in the market gave various levels of personal care, but only one claimed this important attribute as its own. It might be added that as the new personal care positioning was communicated to the public, the level of personal care given by the hospital staff also improved. Many times the image you position outside your organization can have a major positive effect on those employed within the organization.

In the retail area, the key consumer attributes usually are quality, selection, and price, followed by service and location. Depending on the concept you are retailing, the order of the attributes will change according to their importance to your target market. Quality and price are important not just for retailers, but to the positioning for products and services as well. A key point to remember is that the two attributes of quality and price translate into a third very important attribute: *value*. Value is a good competitive image to own if you can first establish it and then hold it.

We helped successfully reposition our retail shoe client from a chain of stores with an image of low prices to a chain with an image of value. This value positioning

---

[1]The following materials were reviewed by the authors in putting together this discussion: Michael L. Rothschild, *Advertising: From Fundmentals to Strategies* (Lexington, Mass.: D.C. Heath and Co., 1987); Al Ries and Jack Trout, *Positioning: The Battle for Your Mind*, rev. ed. (New York: McGraw-Hill, 1986); and David Aaker and J. Gary Shansby, "Positioning Your Product" in *Business Horizons* 25 (May/June 1982).

translated into an advertising theme of "good prices on *great* shoes," which took a singular emphasis off price and put greater emphasis on quality.

Position by the Users of Your Product

By going right at the users/purchasers of your product, your positioning will become more salient to the target market, creating an image among this group that the place, products, or service is especially for them. We helped a fabric store chain position itself as the store for sewers who take pride in their creativity: "The More Ideas Store" for women who love to sew. A similar example was the positioning of the cigarette, Virginia Slims, just for women, through "You've come a long way, baby."

We employed a user positioning for a business-to-business client that marketed a hot water machine to offices for making instant coffee, replacing the need to brew coffee. In this case, we directly positioned the product to the target: "Office coffee maker, say 'Goodbye' to the office coffee mess." Not having a mailing list of individuals (or title) responsible for making the coffee in the office, a direct mail piece carried the title Office Coffee Maker on the mailing label. Thus the user was directly targeted in both the positioning and the actual delivery of the piece within the office.

Position by Usage

Many times you can position by how and when the product is used. For the Coors young adult summer urban program, we positioned Coors as the summertime, fun time beer for parties. We translated this positioning to "Coors Celebrates Summer in the City," purchasing the music rights to the song "Summer in the City" from singer John Sebastian. Another beer positioning itself on the basis of usage occasion and then expanding the usage occasion is Michelob. Michelob moved from a weekend to every night positioning—"Weekends were made for Michelob" to "The night belongs to Michelob."

Positioning Against a Category

This is a very common positioning whereby you establish your product not at the expense of a specific competitor, but at the expense of a specific category within which you are attempting to steal business. This approach is particularly effective when your product is new to the market—when you are building a new market or subset of an existing category. A classic example was the positioning of light beer against regular, higher calorie beer. This positioning was so successful that it built a whole new light beer category. With its tremendous growth, Miller Lite has redefined its positioning to a more preemptive leadership stance to protect its position against other light beers—"There's only one light beer . . . Miller Lite."

In the public sector area, an example of positioning against a category is an antiauto positioning by a local bus company exploiting the high cost of driving and parking your own car: "The best deal on wheels."

In the business-to-business environment, we as an advertising and marketing agency have positioned our firm directly against other agencies, particularly those that are not truly full-service advertising agencies:

"If your agency thinks all you need is ads, you need a new agency."

"If your agency believes advertising and marketing are the same, you need a new agency."

"If your agency thinks promotion is a dirty word, maybe you should clean house."

Positioning Against a Specific Competitor(s)

In this type of positioning, you go directly at a specific competitor(s) rather than a product category: Avis against Hertz—"Because we're number 2, we have to try harder." In the retail fast food category, we have seen Burger King position its hamburger as tasting better than McDonald's, and Wendy's position against

McDonald's with "Where's the beef?" Hardee's followed with a positioning against the potential weaknesses of all three competitors.

We feel that although positioning against a specific competitor can be successful, particularly over the short term, in the long run it has its limitations. This is particularly true when positioning against a strong leader in the category. The leader didn't get there by blowing smoke and using mirrors. Usually, the leader is very entrenched in its position. Hertz is still number one while Avis is being pushed for number two, and McDonald's is just getting stronger. When going against the leader, ask yourself these questions: Does your company have the necessary resources and management's real commitment to challenge the leader? Will your company spend the necessary dollars to change the target market's perception of your product versus that of the leader? Will your organization be capable of delivering a better product that will make a meaningful difference in the mind of the user? Remember, it's difficult to go head to head with the king when you are only a serf.

Positioning by Association

This type of positioning can be very effective when you don't have a distinct product difference, or if the competition owns the inherent positioning relative to your product. The use of image and emotional type of advertising can successfully implement this kind of product positioning.

Positioning by association is often seen in political campaigns, when a popular elected offical endorses a relatively unknown candidate. This type of positioning can be implemented with limited resources and a limited amount of time to directly challenge the key competition.

As an example in the retail field, this association positioning was used by a small bank in Madison, Wisconsin. This bank was not very progressive and had very limited resources, yet was attempting to compete with major financial institutions with multiple locations and many more services. In this case, the small bank created an association with the people's pride in their city's history. The bank was positioned in the early 1970s as the "caretakers of the community's heritage," a theme that would eventually lead and tie into the country's bicentennial of 1976. The bank's logo was changed to reinforce this positioning, and the bank's barren walls were transformed into a gallery of over sized local historic photos. Along with these changes, a series of inexpensive television commercials was produced, which extolled the city's history, built around the advertising theme, "Take a high interest in Madison with Randall State Bank." The results were almost magical. Within one year of this new positioning being implemented, deposits which had been declining yearly showed an increase. This increase in dollar deposits and share was realized with no major investment in increased services or marketing dollars.

Positioning by Problem

With this type of positioning, the product's difference is not as important because there is minimal if any real competition. In this situation there is a need to position against a specific problem in order to involve the target market, or in some instances, build a market for the product.

To illustrate, in the mid 1970s, utilities, which are quasimonopolies and have no direct competition, experienced major credibility problems with their customers. The credibility problems were exacerbated by the rising cost of energy, stemming from the effects of the oil embargo and escalating inflation. Our statewide utility client was experiencing similar difficulties with its customers. As a result, we helped position this energy company as the utility that understands and acts upon energy related problems with its customers in mind. This positioning translated to a home grown campaign: "We can do it, Wisconsin, if we do it together." This campaign led to a very positive shift in customer attitudes toward the energy company in a short 15 week period of time, documented via pre- and postcampaign research.

Another example of positioning by problem deals with a nonprofit alcohol and drug abuse treatment program that was originally positioned as the program that can help in the treatment of the disease. This positioning was not attracting in incremental numbers those who were addicted, nor those indirectly affected—the affected others such as the spouse, children, or employers of the alcohol/drug user. The positioning needed to be changed, because approximately 40 percent of the adult population is affected directly or indirectly by alcohol and drug addiction, with most not always aware of, nor acknowledging, their own problem. There was a need first to position against the problem, and second against the solution. The positioning was thus changed from "the program's professionals are prepared to help" to "understanding and empathizing with the affected others' problems." The results were quickly evident. Within three months of the implementation of this new positioning program admissions and revenues nearly doubled over the previous year.

METHODS TO POSITION YOUR PRODUCT

Now that you have an understanding of the various types of positioning, you must closely evaluate how your product ties to the target market relative to the competition in order to arrive at a specific positioning. To help you position your own product, you can use the matching and/or mapping step-by-step methods.

Position by Matching

Simply stated, this positioning method matches your product's inherent and unique benefits or competitive advantage to the characteristics and needs/wants of the target market.

Step 1

Analyze Your Product versus the Competition

A good place to start with this method is with the product you are selling and the competition you are selling against. Based on your business review, list your competition on the top left side of the worksheet provided in Appendix C (see Exhibit 7.1 shown after Step 5). The competition could be one major competitor, a number of key competitors, a specific category, or a number of key categories. In the positioning of an off-price menswear retailer, it was determined that specific competition varied by market, but the competitive categories remained the same in all markets—department stores, specialty men's clothing stores, and off-price/discount stores.

Step 2

Identify Product Differences versus Competition

Next, write down the key positive and negative differences of your product versus that of the competition relative to your primary target market. These differences should be listed as they relate to key elements of the marketing mix that are appropriate to what you are selling.

Sometimes a difference, although seemingly negative, can become a positive. A small retailer with limited square footage and thereby limited in variety of product offering can lead to a positioning of specialty selection and personal attention.

For Coors, a meaningful difference was the quality of beer, because it is unpasteurized and fresh, with the beer shipped from the brewery refrigerated. For Cheer, it was the one laundry detergent ("All Tempercheer") that washes all types of clothes in hot, warm, or cold water. For Funny Face powdered soft drink, the children oriented name was the key, which led back to a pure kids positioning. For a retail ski client, being new to a market and offering many innovative customer services led to its positioning as the "new age of ski shops." This was a very appropriate positioning, because the skiing target market was young adult, contemporary, and into "change." For a business-to-business firm selling to office supply stores, its established reputation and many office product innovations led to a leadership positioning, "Organizing the American office since 1949."

For each area, ask yourself, "How is my product different and how is it better?" Is your product different through product superiority, innovation, or size—number of customers, volume of goods sold, number of outlets? Whenever possible, use quantitative research for objectivity.

Step 3

List Your Key Target Market

Insert your key target market on the top right side of the same worksheet (see Exhibit 7.1).

Step 4

List Key Target Market Characteristics

On the right side of the worksheet, now list the characteristics of your target market in terms of wants and needs. With or without research, ask yourself the following questions, listing brief answers below each question:

What is the target market really purchasing—is the product to be used by itself or in conjunction with a number of products (i.e., are women purchasing dress shoes separately or as part of a fashion ensemble)? For what purpose is the target using the product (i.e., is the baking soda for baking a cake, deodorizing the refrigerator, or brushing teeth)?

Where is the target market purchasing/using it—by geography (i.e., in sunny, very warm climates) and by place (i.e., in the home, car, etc.)?

When is the target market using it—time of the year, month, week, day, during or after work?

Why is the target market purchasing and/or using the product or why are they purchasing from one store over the other? Is it because of a particular feature? Is it convenient location or greater selection? Why are they really using the product? Does it save time or money?

How is it purchased/used? Is it purchased/used alone or with other people? Is it a frequent or infrequent purchase? How is it used (i.e., is the tissue used to wipe one's nose or clean the windows? Is the beer used to relax after work or celebrate and party)?

How is the target changing? Is the market changing by demographics and lifestyle? How are purchasing/usage habits of the product changing (i.e., is fashion becoming more important than durability, value more than price, service more than just product quality)?

Step 5

Match Your Product's Characteristics to the Target Market's Needs/Wants

Having listed the differences of your product below the key competition and listed the key needs/wants of the target market, try to match what is unique about your product to the meaningful needs and wants of the target market.

Using a retail fabric chain as an example, in Exhibit 7.1 we have listed the specific competition and retailer's competitive differences on the left, and the target market and its characteristics on the right. A worksheet is provided in Appendix C.

Based on the listing of the competitive differences, it would appear that this fabric retailer has a competitive advantage through offering an abundance of fabric related merchandise in larger, better designed stores. The merchandise selection appears superior not only in amount but in the variety of merchandise necessary to complete a sewing project, as well as related crafting and home decorating projects. Also this retailer could be viewed as a leader with an established reputation offering a variety of quality merchandise, but *not* at the lowest prices or greatest values.

The target market, on the other hand, is a mix of both practically and recreationally motivated sewers who want a large selection of all types of fabric related merchandise that is very competitively priced and is a real value. It would seem that this retailer definitely has the desired selection and quality, but not necessarily the lower prices and value. The target also wants all the required merchandise under one roof to enjoy a fun and rewarding shopping experience, as well as fulfill the needs for both practically and recreationally motivated projects.

Further, the listing indicates changes occurring within the target market. It appears sewers have less time or need to sew regularly, creating fewer garments and becoming more recreationally oriented with a growing interest in craft and home decorating projects.

After reviewing both sides of your worksheet again and again, you hope to find a competitive advantage or advantages coming together to match a clustering of the target's current and changing needs. In this retail fabric chain example, there appears to be a number of competitive advantages coming together under a "superior selection

Exhibit 7.1   Positioning: Matching Product Differences to the Target Market's Needs/Wants

Competition
1. Specialty chains
2. Mass merchants

Differences from Competitor
Product/Store/Service attributes
  Larger selection of fabrics and notions
  Slightly better quality
  Favorite store of sewers
  Always new merchandise
  Carries variety of goods for sewing, home decorating, and crafting

New products/Improvements
  Greater expansion into craft and home decorating merchandise

Packaging/Store appearance
  Best store layout
  Larger stores
  Does not have promotional appearance

Branding/Name/Reputation
  Established reputation

Distribution/Penetration
  Greater number of outlets in most markets

Price
  Perception of higher prices and less value

Advertising
  Have more advertising

Key Target Market
Practical and recreation sewers
Women 25-54
Average household income
3+ household size

Characteristics—Needs/Wants
What
  Wide selection of merchandise from which to choose
  Be able to purchase everything at one store
  Lowest prices/good values
  Quality fabrics

Where
  Sews at home
When
  After work and weekends (seen as recreation)
  Throughout the day (considered part of family responsibilities by practical sewers)

Why (Benefit)
  For fun and as a hobby
  To express creativity
  For herself and children
  To save money
  For better fit of garments
  For feeling of accomplishment

How purchased/Used
  Usually shop alone
  Visit a fabric store on average every two weeks
  Like to shop for deals
  Shop for enjoyment

How the target and its needs/wants are changing
  Less sewing to save money
  More sewing for fun and recreation
  Not enough time to sew
  More sewers working out of the home
  Using fabrics not just for sewing garments but for more crafting and decorating the home
  Buying more fabric related merchandise for special occasions/holidays

offering" (wide variety, quality, fashionable, growing selection, and larger stores). These advantages would appear to match the target's growing desire for a fabric store with a large and complete offering of not just sewing but craft and home decorating merchandise.

By matching the key differences to the key target market needs/wants of the positioning listings, you could arrive at the following positioning statement for this fabric retail chain: "Each store provides *everything* a woman needs to fulfill fabric related sewing, crafting, and home decorating expectations."

After you have prepared your positioning worksheet, if it helps, draw lines from the major competitive positive differences to the paralleling want/need characteristics of the target market. Then ask yourself again what really is important to the target market in terms of how your product is different and better. Based on this, eliminate lines until you have the two or three most meaningful product to target market potential positioning connections.

In some cases you might combine two product differences or advantages to fill an important want. If you were a retailer, you may combine the attributes of brand name products and very competitive prices to arrive at a *value* positioning which ties to an important consumer desire.

In some cases you will draw lines between product and target market characteristics and find that a most important consumer need/want is not being fulfilled by your product or the competition. Virginia Slims was created to fill a consumer void or gap with a cigarette for women. Or, to the other extreme, all the competing products available fulfilled the target's need/want, but no one competitor, including your product, has claimed it as their reason for being.

Position by Mapping

This approach is a practical application of mapping methodology based on multidimensional models. Although theoretical in origin, we actively use the mapping approach in the positioning of our clients' products and services. Using this approach, you map out visually what is important to your target market in terms of key product attributes. The competition's products, including your own, are then ranked on these attributes. This type of mapping is extremely useful in positioning a product and, again, is *most effective when based on quantitative research that is representative of the marketplace*. Your preconceived notions about what the target market thinks can differ dramatically from what quantifiable research reports.

However, if you do not have market research, it is still helpful to use this method when positioning to help sort out what you believe is important to the target market. Further, this positioning approach will help you to more clearly evaluate how well your product and that of your key competition is perceived on each attribute. Because this mapping method is somewhat involved and you will most likely not have research to assist you, read through the three steps before beginning the actual mapping process.

Step 1

List Product Attributes by Importance

Acknowledging your built in bias while being as objective as possible, the first step is to list in order of importance the product category attributes on the right side of the mapping worksheet provided in Appendix C (see Exhibit 7.2 shown after Step 3), top to bottom, from most important (10 value) to least important (1 value).

In the retail category, the most important attribute to the consumer might be quality, followed by selection, price, service, and fashion, with loction listed at the bottom. In business-to-business it might be reliable delivery ranked most important, followed by product consistency, quality, price, and favorable reputation, with knowledgeable sales force being least important at the bottom of the chart.

Step 2

Rate Your Product and Competitors' Products for Each Attribute

Once you have listed the key target market attributes, for each attribute rate each competitor from best to worst. For each rating, place the initial of each key competitor, including your product, on the line of each attribute ranking. Make a master listing of these keys under company/product/store code.

If you do not have available quantitative research before you begin mapping, it's a good idea to gather a number of people knowledgeable about your product category and have each one of them list the most important attributes. Next, have them as objectively as possible, independently assign a number from 1 to 10 (10 being most important, 1 least important) for each attribute. Take an average of these estimates for each ranking. Based on each composite estimate, rank order the attributes.

After ranking attribute importance, ask the participants to agree on the top three to five market competitors, including your product. Then have each of them independently assign a rating of 1 to 10 for each competitor on each attribute, with 10 being best. Average the ratings for each competitor, and insert a rating for each competitor by initial in line with each attribute ranking.

In your plotting of the competitive market, you might have great disparity between competitors on one attribute and no differences on another. Ideally, you want your product ranked the best versus the competition on all attributes, but particularly on those that are most important to the consumer. The more you see your product's initial on the right, particularly on those attributes at the top of the chart, the stronger the position of your product in the marketplace.

A note of caution: Using a knowledgeable group of people to assist in arriving at key attributes and competitive ratings is not very accurate compared to using survey research that will quantify the perceptions of the users and/or purchasers. However, with no research available, this approach will at least give you more perspective than if you just positioned by matching.

Step 3

Visualize Desired Position on Map for Your Product

Once your positioning map is complete, review how your product ranks on the more important attributes relative to the competition. Next, visualize where you want your product positioned on the map based on what the consumer wants and what your product can provide relative to strengths and weaknesses of the competition. Finally, from the various types of positionings previously discussed, select the positioning approach that will positively affect the target market's perceptions and attain your visualized positioning.

To illustrate, we will use one of our clients as a case example. In Exhibit 7.2 our new client, a very price oriented retailer with the code letter H rated second to last competitively on the two most important attributes for the retail category: quality and value. Declining sales had prompted the store chain to do market research among consumers. This research indicated, among other things, that although price was important, quality and value were most important. Based on this data, the company changed its position from a "store with low prices" to "the value shoe store"—a store with quality merchandise at competitive prices. Translating this goal to the map visually would mean it would be the first store from the right for the value attribute. Accordingly, this retailer upgraded its merchandise mix and the appearance of its stores. The advertising was also changed to convey a value image.

The results of this value positioning versus the former low price/discount price positioning were dramatic. Comparable store sales for the year increased more than 30 percent. Market research conducted 18 months after the benchmark research study revealed dramatic positive shifts in how the consumer perceived this retailer versus the competition on the key attributes. As you can see in Exhibit 7.3, the retailer's competitive rating (H) on *quality* moved from second to last to second. Further, its competitive *value* rating moved from second to last to first, while the *price* rating remained virtually the same. Even the retailer's competitive rating on *selection* showed considerable positive movement from third to second place.

Mapping Customer versus Noncustomer Perceptions

When putting together your maps, you must consider the makeup of your target market. Accordingly, you can put together one map for customers and another for target market noncustomers. Many times, what is important to your current customers might not be as important to noncustomers. Noncustomers will usually rate your product more negatively than will your customers.

To illustrate through a business-to-business case, you can see in Exhibit 7.4 how highly *customers* rated Company A (uppercase) versus its key competitor, and how poorly its *noncustomers* rated the same Company a (lowercase). This firm, which originally emphasized price to attract new customers, changed its positioning to one of "best performance" in terms of reliable delivery, product, consistency, and quality—all of which the company said it could or did provide. This new positioning was supported with an aggressive advertising and personal selling program built around the new performance positioning, resulting in a substantial increase in new customers.

Exhibit 7.2   Original Price Positioning

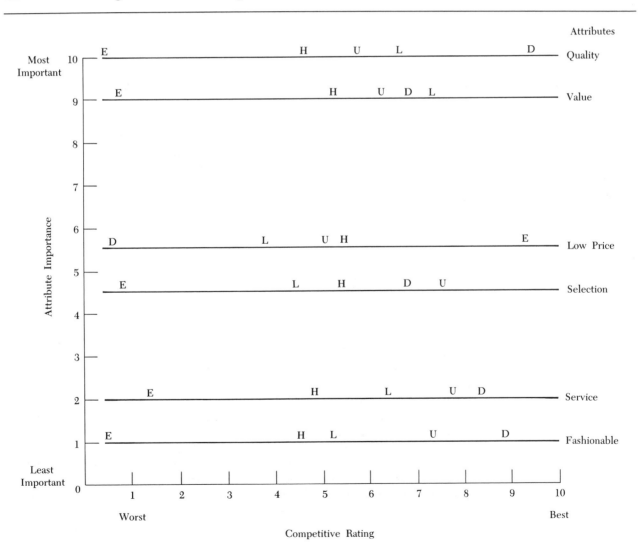

Exhibit 7.3   Original Price versus New Value Positioning*

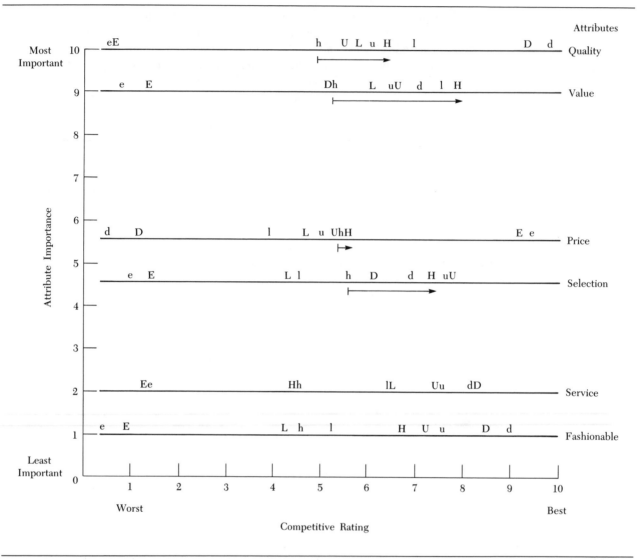

*Lowercase letters represent original positioning; uppercase letters represent new positioning.

Look for Positioning Gaps

Using the mapping approach, you can isolate differences for your product versus the competition that will lead to effective positioning. Often, however, there are no meaningful differences, but only attribute opportunity areas that no one has taken advantage of. To find this type of opportunity gap, review your map for an important attribute vacuum that your product can fill. In Exhibit 7.5 for a business-to-business company B selling its professional services to small firms, we see no one fully satisfying the target market on the third most important attribute, "knowledge of client's industry." Because competitors appeared strong in the two most important attributes, "expertise of personnel" and "competence of staff members," we positioned our client as the consulting firm that understands and tailors its services to the clients' specific business. Accordingly, the target market was segmented by SIC and size. Each industry target segmented by size received its own tailored frequency direct mail advertising. The result was a substantial increase in new clients and a 90 percent return on the marketing investment.

Exhibit 7.4   Positioning by Customers versus Noncustomers*

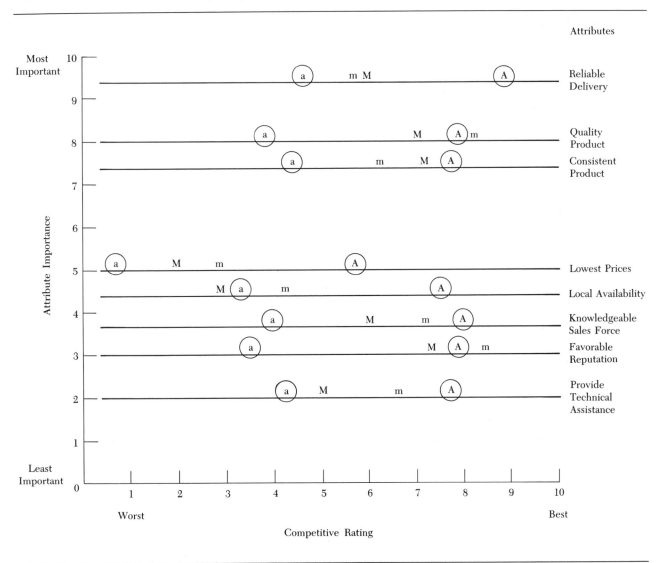

*Uppercase letters represent customers; lowercase letters represent noncustomers.

HOW TO WRITE THE POSITIONING STRATEGY

Once you have determined how you want your product perceived as meaningfully different from the competition by the target market, you are ready to write alternative positioning strategies. It is wise to write more than one positioning strategy in order to make a comparison of strategies and evaluate which positioning best reflects your product relative to the competition and fulfills the needs/wants of the target market. Your alternative positioning statements should vary by the degree of emphasis placed on the product advantage, the competition's weakness, and the target market benefit. All the positioning alternatives relate to product, competitor, and target market, but each alternative will focus on one of the above rather than all.

The key word is *focus* when writing a positioning statement. The tendency is to write a positioning statement that reads like a litany rather than keeping it simple and straightforward. The shorter and more to the point, the better the posi-

Exhibit 7.5   Positioning to Fill a Gap

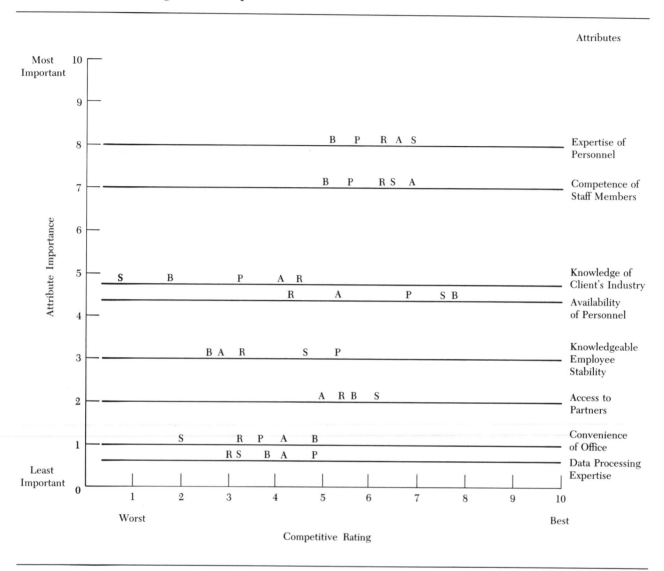

tioning strategy. A succinct positioning will provide clear and specific direction for the advertising and the employment of all the other tools in the marketing mix. For this reason, choose thoughtfully each word that you use in your positioning statement.

Once you have prepared the alternative positionings, select the one that will best suit the target market and fulfill the marketing strategies using the format provided in Appendix C. We show some examples of positioning statements.

Retail Shoe Chain

Position Brady's Footwear as the *value alternative* to purchasing shoes at department stores.

   Same quality

   Better selection

   Lower prices

Note that in this positioning strategy, brief qualifiers or descriptors have been included below the positioning statement. This is not always necessary; however, you should include, along with the positioning statement, a brief rationale based on your product's benefits relative to the competition and needs/wants of the target market.

Consumer Package Goods

Position Funny Face as the *kids'* powdered soft drink for summertime fun.

Position Miller Lite as the only beer with superior taste and low caloric content.

Business-to-Business

Position W.T. Jones as the *established office supply leader*, improving the look and efficiency of the office environment.

Consumer Real Estate

Preemptively position the Lake Condominiums as the *most rewarding alternative* to conventional home rental or ownership.

> More amenities with less hassle for homeowners
> Low price ownership for renters

Position Star Realtors as the *most professional realtor* for home buyers and sellers *throughout Dane County*.

Political Campaign

Position the Democratic candidate for governor as the *only wise choice* for the unprecedented challenges facing the state.

Repositioning of Retail Concept

Reposition Big Jake's as *the* store with *quality, casual apparel* at *everyday reduced prices* for active families.

This example of repositioning from a men's work clothes store to a family casual apparel store was included because it represents major restructuring in terms of target market and product offering. It presents a major and immediate shift of the image to be projected representing a repositioning of the retail concept, not just a refinement of positioning emphasis.

It might be mentioned at this point that this type of total repositioning of your product should be considered carefully. Once the repositioning decision has been made, however, execute this repositioning in a manner that retains a maximum number of current customers while still expanding your target market.

Further, when it is necessary to change your positioning dramatically in terms of changing the target market and the product being marketed, it is wise to at least consider changing the name as well. A name change would seem in order with the repositioning for Big Jake's—although Big Jake's might be an appropriate name for a men's work clothing store, it might not be an appropriate name for a family clothing store. However, a name change is a high risk stragetic option to be pursued only when continuing to use the current name means certain failure.

DOS AND DON'TS

Do

- Position with a meaningful difference.
- Position to take advantage of normal usage, not to try to change it.
- Position from your product's strengths and competitors' weaknesses to fill a target's need keeping in mind that you could possibly change a product weakness to a strength if it leads to a stronger positioning for your product.
- Consider combining your product differences for a stronger positioning.
- Use quantifiable market research whenever possible.
- When confused on how to position your product, let your target market and their needs/wants be your guide.
- If you have a parity product, look hard and long for a meaningful need or want that has not been taken by a competitor.
- Use the product's name whenever appropriate for successfully positioning.
- Make sure all elements of the marketing mix reinforce your positioning.
- Give your positioning a chance to reap success by supporting it with a substantial investment in time and marketing resources.
- Make your positioning statement as simple and succinct as possible.

Don't

- Don't try to position everything about your product/service to everybody. To position means to sacrifice.
- Don't position against a follower if you are a leader.
- Unless you can deliver a lower price on a consistent basis, don't position only on price because that position can easily be preempted.
- Don't change your positioning if it has proven successful and there have been no major changes (or you anticipate no major changes) to your product, that of the competition's product, or the target market. However, attempt to sharpen the focus of your established positioning to present a clearer perception of your product in the minds of the target market.
- Don't position directly against another competitor if at all possible.
- Don't position directly against a leader unless you plan to settle for less than first or you have product superiority and sufficient marketing resources to outlast the leader.
- Don't use two different positionings for the same product to the same target market.
- Don't position your product in such a manner that it cannot deliver on the positioning.
- Don't, if at all possible, change your positioning in one large leap, if you anticipate losing a substantial portion of the current customer base. Position one step at a time, but still think long term.
- Don't take the first positioning that comes to mind, but review a number of alternative positionings.
- Don't expect to arrive at your product positioning immediately. Positioning might seem to be a simple concept to understand but it is extremely difficult to apply. To arrive at the right positioning takes time and concentration. Don't settle for an "almost on" positioning. Perserve for the best positioning and almost magically the right positioning for your product will come to you, seemingly from nowhere.

PRODUCT/
BRANDING/
PACKAGING

Y ou have just finished developing the positioning for your product. Now you must make sure the product lives up to your planned positioning. Effective communication of a positioning may induce trial of a product, but beware—nothing will ruin a company faster than selling a poor product or a product which is not consistent with its positioning. Customers may be convinced to purchase once, but they won't be fooled again.

The product, the product's brand name, and the product's packaging are the most fundamental elements of the entire marketing mix. They make up the reality of the positioning. Since the product is so closely identified with its name and packaging, we have included all three (product, brand or name, and packaging) in one chapter.

Before you write the product/branding/packaging segment of the marketing plan, you must review the direction provided by the problems and opportunities and the marketing strategies affecting each of the three areas. If you are *not* modifying or developing a new product, brand name, or package, there is *no* need to address these marketing mix tools in your plan. However, for background and perspective in writing the remainder of the marketing plan, it is recommended that you read through this chapter.

From This Chapter You Will Learn	**Product**
	The definition of product.
	Issues affecting your product plan.
	How to establish product objectives and strategies.
	Branding
	The definition of branding.
	How to develop a branding program.

Packaging

The definition of packaging.

Issues affecting the packaging of your product.

How to establish packaging objectives and strategies.

PRODUCT OVERVIEW

Definition

In the case of consumer package goods, retail, and business-to-business companies, the *product* is a *tangible object* that is marketed to customers. However, for service businesses, the product takes the form of some *intangible offering*. Often for a service business the product is a future benefit or future promise. Thus, while all products are offerings to the customer, there is an inherent difference between what is sold by a service firm and what is sold by a retailer or manufacturer.

Issues Affecting the Product

Product Attributes

A major focus should be to determine if there is a need or an opportunity for product modifications, new products, or extended product lines. In order to accomplish this it is important to first determine what attributes consumers find most important in the purchase decision for your product category, and how your product ranks along these attributes compared to your competitors' products. (Review your Business Review, your Problems and Opportunities summaries, your Marketing Strategies, and your Positioning statement.) If there are critical areas where your product is less competitive and/or there is a product void in the market, then you must develop product objectives and strategies to address the situation.

Product Segmentation

The desirability of segmenting your product to meet specific demographic and life-style needs should be addressed. Especially for the manufacturer, one method is to develop different product sizes based on product usage. Smaller sizes are often requirements of singles or light users and larger sizes are often needed by families or heavy users of the product category.

Another way of segmenting products is by utilizing different product features to attract different target markets. Many times new products are developed with a basic appeal to a broad, homogeneous market. As competition increases and the product reaches the growth stage in the product life cycle, differentiation occurs and marketing must more closely target the needs and tastes of specific target markets. Cross-country skis are a good example. Back in 1970, the sport of cross-country skiing was relatively new. There was basically one style: all-purpose wooden cross-country skis. However, by the next decade, there were touring skis, racing skis (skating and traditional), deep-snow skis, telemarking skis; not to mention multiple options on bindings, poles, boots, and ski construction. As the sport of cross-country skiing grew, manufacturers targeted specific needs. Product segmentation is often achieved through product innovation, the topic of the next section.

Product Innovation

Another important portion of the business review is the analysis of change and innovation in the product category. Change is critical for all marketers. Product innovations allow you to map out changes in your company's product. They compel you to determine how your product should evolve to meet consumers' needs and the competitive pressures of the future. We view product innovations as falling into four categories:

New Uses of Old Products Many times marketers can expand the user base for a product by developing new uses for it. An example would be in the case of baking soda. For years baking soda was used only for baking and only in small amounts. As the popularity of baking from scratch started to decline, Arm and Hammer began to look for alternative uses for its product. The company began marketing baking soda as an air freshener for refrigerators, opening up a whole new sales category.

Product Improvement You must continually be evaluating how you can improve your existing product, store, or service in order to maintain a competitive edge in an ever changing and increasingly competitive marketplace. Many of these improvements are subtle in nature but over time can totally remake a product. Never change for the sake of change, only to better fill the needs and wants of the target market. Also, test your improved product with the target market before putting it into the marketplace.

Line Extension A line extension is a variation in a family of brands. Coors beer had one premium beer before the line extension of Coors Light. After the introduction, the Coors brand had two beers, a premium and a light. Whereas this was an example of a product line extension, line extensions can also be accomplished through price. In the beer industry there are many examples of premium priced and popular priced beers made by the same brewery.

For retailers, line extensions can mean adding another retail category. A shoe store could add athletic clothing to its athletic shoe department for cross-selling purposes. Sweat pants and other athletic wear could be popular impulse purchases when sold along with the athletic shoes.

New Product This category encompasses the development of new products or innovations not currently available to consumers. The videocassette recorder would be an example of a new product. Prior to the VCR, consumers could watch what was on TV at home or go out to a selected movie. With the development of the VCR, people could watch a selected movie on their TV set at home.

Product Costs

Finally, product costs should be analyzed. If there is a way to manufacture or purchase your product more efficiently, explore it. If you are successful at manufacturing or purchasing your product more efficiently, you will create pricing options such as lowering the cost of an existing product or introducing a line extension at a lower price.

HOW TO DEVELOP A PRODUCT PLAN

A worksheet for developing your product plan is provided in Appendix C.

Step 1

Establish Your Product Objectives

Product objectives will center around one or more of the five following areas:

- Developing new products.
- Developing line extensions for existing brands.

■ Developing new uses for existing products.
■ Product improvement.
■ Finding more efficient ways to produce the product in the case of manufacturers or purchase the product in the case of retailers.

In addition to addressing one or more of the above, the product objectives should incorporate specifics on when the product will be available for distribution or inventory.
An example of a product objective for a manufacturer would be:

> In the upcoming fiscal year, modify the product to reflect the current purchasing habits of consumers interested in low salt foods.

Step 2
Establish Your
Product Strategies

Product strategies define how the product objectives will be accomplished. As an example, the following types of strategies would be developed to meet specific product objectives:

Objective	Strategy Description
Improve the product	(The marketer would list specific product attributes that would be improved and specific innovations that would bring about improvement.)
Find more efficient ways to produce the product	(The marketer would list how that would be accomplished either through a manufacturing technique or a buying practice.)

A specific example of a line extension objective and subsequent strategy for a manufacturer of cross-country skis would be:

Objective

Improve the product to take advantage of the consumer trend toward citizen cross-country ski racing.

Strategy

Develop competitively superior performance skis for both cross-country racing methods, track racing, and the newly developed skating method.

DOS AND DON'TS

Do

■ Review your business review, problems and opportunities, marketing strategies, and positioning statement prior to preparing this section of the marketing plan.
■ Keep an ongoing surveillance of competitive product innovations in your industry.
■ Talk with consumers on an ongoing basis. Find out what they think about your product. Discover which of their needs are not being fulfilled by current products available in the category.
■ Be willing to make product changes, especially if market research discovers a product void or shows your product is not competitive against attributes most important to consumers.
■ Research and test product innovations and changes prior to making them standard.
■ Expect that the vast majority of new product concepts will fail. However, remember that new product *successes* are the lifeblood of most successful organizations.

Don't

- Don't copy every competitive product innovation. Use research to determine consumer likes and dislikes with your product before modifying an existing product or developing a new one.
- Don't change one aspect of your product without considering what the change does to the other attributes. Remember that consumers purchase because of multiple reasons. A cheaper product from a price standpoint may receive less demand if the quality has also diminished. Consumers may like the lower price but may not be willing to sacrifice quality.
- Don't make changes in your product for purely financial reasons. Consumers purchase your product because of its product attributes, not because the product provides a bigger or smaller margin to your company.
- Remember, just as new product development is important to a company so is the divestment or elimination of historically weak products.
- Don't just concentrate on the short-term bottom line while short changing product development and long-term growth and profits.
- Don't overestimate the size of the market for your product. Many products fail because the market is not large enough in terms of sheer numbers of consumers.

BRANDING OVERVIEW

Definition

Branding is the naming of your product, service, or company. A brand or name is with what consumers associate your product. For this reason, a brand or name should help communicate the product's positioning and its inherent drama for the consumer.

HOW TO DEVELOP YOUR BRAND NAME

A worksheet on how to develop your brand name is provided in Appendix C.

Step 1

Establish Your Branding Objectives

Branding objectives should state for what the new name will be used (i.e., existing product, new product, line extension, improved product, repositioned product). Also, the objective should include a final decision date for when the final name will be selected.

Examples of branding objectives are:

Develop a name for the new pizza delivery service by August 1 of this fiscal year.

Develop a new name to replace Big Jake's for the new family apparel store by the end of this fiscal year.

Step 2

Establish Your Branding Strategies

It is important to prepare a branding strategy before developing name alternatives. This greatly increases the probability that you will arrive at a name that is consistent with the product and takes into consideration all of the uses of the name over the short and long term. This strategy should flow from the positioning statement and be followed by a listing of parameters for the new name. The branding strategy should highlight those components that will communicate the key perceptions to the key targets. A branding strategy for the repositioning of Big Jake's from a work clothing store for men to a casual apparel store for families would be:

Rename Big Jake's to describe its *active and casual wear* merchandise, appealing to the woman heavy *purchaser* who is a smart *family* shopper with an appreciation for quality and saving money.

Step 3
Establish Branding Property Parameters

Along with the branding strategy, include branding property parameters. These are an extension of the branding strategy and provide specific guide posts in name development. Potential branding parameters are:

Reflects positioning of the product.

Provides generic identification and clearly identifies with its functional category.

Is preemptive.

Contributes to awareness and knowledge of its purpose.

Is memorable.

Provides potential for growth of other entities/line extensions under its umbrella name.

Possesses a positive connotation—meaning, pronunciation, and visualization.

Reflects the personality of the product.

Has intrinsic meaning of its own (i.e., is not an acronym or set of letters which doesn't signify anything).

Not limited geographically or topically as the organization grows.

Lends itself to/allows for creative development—both visually and in copy.

Must work with current signage/package sizes (the shorter the better).

Is legally acceptable and protectable.

In addition to the actual name, parameters should be set for the name's graphic translation. For example, the name graphically:

Must reproduce in small and large logo form.

Must reproduce in black and white and in color.

Should incorporate colors that reflect the positioning but still are attention getting.

Must have visual impact within both the print and television media.

Step 4
Name Generation and Selection

Using the branding strategy and name property parameters as a guide, begin the name development process by generating a multitude of name alternatives. It is conceivable that the name alternatives could number into the hundreds. Next, using the branding strategy and name parameters as the decision criteria in the screening process, pare back the names in a disciplined manner to approximately ten to twenty names. Then follow with a legal search of these names for trademark availability. Finally, you would be wise to research the remaining name alternatives with the target market(s) before making a final branding decision.

DOS AND DON'TS

Do

- Highlight the key image(s) you wish to communicate to your target market in your branding strategy.

■ Use a disciplined process when developing a name for your product, firm, or store—from what you want the name to accomplish through a thorough name generation process.

■ If possible, use research to test alternative names among the target market. Choose the name which best communicates the branding strategy and has no negatives.

■ Include your employees in the naming process. Have them generate name alternatives and communicate to them the reasons for the final selection before it becomes public.

■ Make sure you have an established plan to communicate your new name to the audience. Acceptance of a new name is often determined by how well the new name is communicated.

■ Have the final list of names go through a legal search to make certain you are not infringing upon someone's trademark. Also consider application of a registered trademark for legal protection.

Don't

■ Don't take the first name that comes to you, particularly if you think it's creative, cool, or cute.

■ Don't complicate your product name. Keep it simple and memorable.

■ If it is a name change, don't expect the new name to be readily accepted. Many people don't like change. However, familiarity breeds acceptability so build high awareness for the new name quickly.

■ Don't go it alone with a name change if your company and agency do not have the time and specific abilities to develop a new name. Consider hiring a consulting firm that specializes in developing new names and brand identity programs.

PACKAGING OVERVIEW

Definition

For manufacturers, packaging protects the product and assists in communicating the product's attributes and image. For retailers and service firms, packaging is the inside and outside environment that houses and dispenses the product/services and helps to communicate the company's attributes and image.

Issues Affecting Packaging

Creating Awareness of the Product

Packaging can help a product stand out at the point of purchase from competing brands. One example of this would be L'eggs hosiery. L'eggs' egg-shaped packaging was unique in two ways. The actual product (hosiery) had few unique qualities from a visual standpoint. Yet L'eggs utilized packaging that created differentiation for a product that was difficult to differentiate. In addition, the eggs were a unique display fixture that could only hold L'eggs hosiery. This meant that the L'eggs brand was guaranteed fairly prominent shelf or floor space wherever it was sold and as long as the display was in the store. In addition, the display was attention getting and created awareness for the product.

Communicating Product Attributes and Product Positioning

The package should provide name or brand identification and communicate product benefits in a clear, memorable fashion. Assume you are selling basketballs and you are positioning them as top quality that professionals would use. A name connoting this positioning such as "Pro Ball" and a testimonial device such as the signature of

NBA players on the packaging helps to communicate this positioning to consumers at the point of purchase. In addition, the quality, color, texture, shape, size, and overall look of the packaging play an important part in selling the product and communicating the positioning.

The simple technique of putting a fine liquor in a silk or cloth bag often serves as a differentiating device to distinguish the liquor from all the other glass bottles on the shelf. This packaging device serves to tell the consumer that there is something a little more special and rich about this liquor than the others.

Retailers use "store packaging," or interior and exterior environment, to communicate an image to their shoppers. They also use store packaging to encourage consumers to walk through their store and make impulse purchases. Many grocers place the meat counter in the back of the store to encourage walk-through traffic. And, point-of-purchase displays of impulse products are located next to the cash registers to encourage last minute purchases of candy, razors, and magazines.

Generating Trial

Packaging can generate trial in two ways. One is through utilizing the package as an incentive carrier. Coupons, bonus packs, and refund offers can be placed on the packaging to encourage trial. These techniques are covered thoroughly in Chapter 12, Promotion. The second way a package can encourage trial is through a device called *implied trial*. Often, actual samples or trial of the product are not possible and creative packaging is used as a substitute. In food stores you see many foods with see-through packaging to reassure the customer that what's inside is truly top quality. Thus packaging can act as a visual surrogate to trial in many situations. The consumer develops a comfort level with the product and gets to know it even though actual use hasn't occurred.

Creative Problem Solving

Creative packaging ideas can help solve many problems which cannot be eliminated by other areas of marketing or through advertising. The size and shape of the packaging may enhance the retailer's propensity to stock the product. The size, shape, and visual appearance can lead to increased awareness and use of the product by consumers due to added convenience, lifestyle association, attention getting graphics or the packaging's overall usefulness in terms of function. Finally, packaging may actually inhibit consumption or use of the product and changes may result in increased sales. For example, the soft drink industry faced the problem presented by the clear plastic, one liter bottles. It was human nature to drink the last quarter of the bottle of soft drink more slowly than the first part of the bottle—consumers would see they were running out and drink the last portion more sparingly. Reportedly, the solution was to put an opaque plastic covering on the bottom part of the bottle. Users couldn't as easily see how empty the bottles were and the consumption rate for the soft drink increased.

The Packaging Basics

When considering your packaging, the following basics must be addressed.

The Packaging's Attention Value If you are a manufacturer your packaging should have a design and colors consistent with the product's positioning which also demands attention on the shelf. If you are a retailer or a service firm, the same holds true. The exterior and interior appearance of the store or office should command attention and communicate a point of difference, but also leave the customer with a lasting, positive impression consistent with the store's positioning.

Dispensing If you are a manufacturer, make sure your packaging allows for consumer convenience. This may pertain to reuseable containers, zip locking for freshness, easy-to-poor spouts, compact containers for storage or any other of the many conveniences the consumer desires. Also, make sure the packaging is convenient to stock and display for the retailer.

For retailers or service firms, make sure your offices/stores are easy to find and have accessible parking. In addition, once in-store, make sure the customers' shopping environment is convenient and is conducive to their needs.

Visual Appearance The package should quickly communicate the positioning of your product. If you are a shoe retailer, your store appearance (both inside and outside) will help communicate whether you sell quality shoes or whether your outlet is a bargain corner because of a carnival type atmosphere promoting low prices.

HOW TO DEVELOP A PACKAGING PLAN

A worksheet for developing your packaging plan is provided in Appendix C.

Step 1

Establish Your Packaging Objectives

Focus packaging objectives on the following:

- *Manufacturer:* Creating awareness for your product at the point-of-purchase.
- *Retailer:* Creating awareness of the retail facility from the outside, and an awareness of the products inside through the internal store environment.
- Communicating product attributes and positioning.
- Generating trial.
- Providing protection for the product.
- Providing easy usage of the product.
- Communicating promotional offerings.
- The time frame for development or when the package design will be ready for production.

Examples of product objectives for the manufacturer are:

Utilize the product's packaging to communicate its family oriented positioning and the extra servings in each container. Final package design and specifications will be available by the end of this fiscal year.

Utilize new packaging by the end of this fiscal year to protect the product on the shelf while still allowing consumers to see the rich, vibrant colors of the product.

Step 2

Develop Your Packaging Strategies

Packaging strategies delineate how the objectives will be accomplished, providing specifics such as shape, size, color, copy, design, and for retailers, overall store environment.

Examples of packaging strategies include:

Develop an unique and colorful package with simplicity in copy and design that will fit into a floor display and stand out from competitive packaging.

Communicate leadership through bold colors and larger than life visuals of the product. Highlight product attributes in benefit oriented sentences.

DOS AND DON'TS

Do

- Review your marketing strategies and problems and opportunities prior to developing your packaging plans. Also, since packaging can be used to execute promotional plans, consider the package as a promotion carrier. If so, address this in your packaging plan.
- Make sure the packaging clearly communicates the name and product benefits of your product.
- Be as creative as possible with your packaging. Make it unique, make it stand out—but keep it simple and functional.
- Think of your package as a billboard—try to quickly communicate and catch people's attention while portraying the intended image.
- If you're a retailer your packaging includes the total store from the parking lot and the exterior of the store to the interior of the store. Utilize the store environment in the same terms as a manufacturer utilizes the package for their products. It should quickly command attention to your product, make a statement about your image and functionally dispense product or provide convenient shopping for your consumers.
- Compare your current package and new prototype to that of the competition in a real store environment prior to and during package development.
- Consider doing research with the target market before finalizing a new package or store design.
- Make sure your packaging meets legal requirements in terms of communication regarding content.

Don't

- Don't view packaging as just a means of product protection or as a way to dispense the product. Use it as a way to create a product difference and as a communication vehicle.
- Don't change your packaging for change's sake, but to increase sales. Like advertising and positioning, you can use familiarity of message to your advantage.
- Don't develop packaging inconsistent with the overall positioning of your firm and your product.
- Don't miss the chance of your packaging plusing your product. The outside of the package usually should enhance the inherent drama of what is inside.

PRICE

T he pricing marketing mix tool is one of the most difficult for which to develop a plan. The pricing of your product is critical yet difficult to determine because it must be high enough to cover costs and make a profit for your company, yet low enough to maximize demand and sales. In addition, the price of a product affects the product's positioning. For example, a high priced product relative to the competition signals quality and is consistent with products which have special benefits. As you will see in this chapter, pricing plans require flexibility, discipline, and judgment to provide for a pricing structure that is competitive, complements the product's positioning, and which maximizes sales *and* profits.

We recommend you apply this pricing chapter by first reviewing the problems and opportunities relating to price from the business review and the marketing strategies that provide pricing direction. Then utilize what is presented in the chapter to help finalize your pricing decisions.

**From This Chapter
You Will Learn**

The definition of price.

The issues affecting your pricing plan.

How to develop your pricing objectives and strategies.

OVERVIEW

Definition

We will define price for purposes of this book as the monetary value of a product.

Issues Affecting Price

Cost

The cost of a product is usually the major factor affecting its selling price. The costs of a product for a manufacturer are often made up of the following:

- The raw material needed to manufacture the product.
- The cost of manufacturing the product (labor and overhead).
- The cost of distributing the product.
- The cost of marketing the product.

 The costs of a product for retailers are often determined by:

- The retailer's purchase price of the products sold in the store.
- The costs of the real estate.

- The costs of selling the product (personnel, marketing, operational overhead).
- In some cases, the cost of preparing and serving the product.

The marketer must determine the total cost of the products and develop prices that will cover the costs and provide a positive return for the business.

Competition

Changes in the competition's price structure often cause reactive price strategies in the marketplace. To a large degree, competitive price information allows you to determine market supply and demand and provides an accurate yardstick with which to gauge your own pricing decisions. Study your business review to determine the price of your product relative to that of your competitors at various times of the year.

Product Type

The type of product makes a big difference in pricing decisions. Products fall into two broad product classifications: differentiated and standardized. Many times a product at introduction is new and differentiated, but once competitors enter the marketplace, the product category becomes standardized, with no real, meaningful differences. The following demonstrates how product classification affects pricing strategies.

Differentiated/Unique Products   Price is not as important in determining purchase behavior. Consumer demand is driven by the product attributes.

Standardized Products   With standardized products, the consumer has many choices among competing products or store concepts. Much of the competition for consumers will be either in price or in service. The importance of customer service versus pure price will be a function of the product—if purchase does not require a great deal of knowledge or education, price will be far more important than customer service. However, if the product is new, if it requires a great deal of education, if it is an important purchase decision, if the consumer's ego is involved with the purchase, or if the consumer is aware he or she can make a mistake in the purchase decision, then service will most likely play a more important role in the consumer's decision of where to buy the product or service.

Product Category Life Cycle

Most products go through a product life cycle. Understanding where your product is in the product category life cycle will help predict the competitive pricing structure. Review Step 5, Product Awareness and Attributes, of your business review to determine where your product is in its product life cycle. Then study the particular stage below that applies to your product to determine the pricing ramifications.

Introductory   Typically during the introduction of a new product category, a company has few competitors and the freedom to set prices based primarily on estimated supply and demand for the product. There are multiple pricing strategies available during this period. Two are at opposite ends of the decision making spectrum.

Premium Pricing Policy   If the product is unique and has little competition, the pricing choice can be one of maximizing profit per unit sold. The strategy involves selling to a narrow group of consumers who are willing to purchase because of unique product attributes. This premium price strategy helps keep the purchaser base smaller than a low price strategy, thus making allowances for limited production capabilities and/or distribution channels. Premium pricing also allows for maximum margins and a potentially quicker payback on the research and development of the new product.

Expanded Market Pricing If one of the marketing strategies is to build the market, then setting a low price will achieve this more quickly than higher prices. Lower prices encourge trial and mass consumption by a broad base of consumers. Thus, lower prices provide an opportunity to quickly establish a loyal consumer franchise before other competitors enter the marketplace. Also keep in mind that competitive pricing will discourage other competitors from entering the marketplace.

Growth The market is still growing with new users purchasing the product for the first time, and the product becoming universally accepted by the public. Now not only are the innovators purchasing, but a wider profile of consumers as well. As product acceptance gains, the number of competitors increases. While competition is focused primarily on product attributes, pricing variations are introduced during this phase, along with diversification and differentiation of the product. Discounters try to steal market share and obtain even a broader customer base by making the product or service more affordable. Higher priced, higher quality positioned products are still viable but hold less potential in this stage.

Maturity In this stage, price becomes very important. Products are often standardized with fewer product innovations and discernible differences. Thus the selling emphasis is on price and service. If at all possible, you should not let your product enter this stage. Attempt to continually improve your product and service for the consumer, providing new consumer benefits that differentiate your product from the competition.

Price Elasticity

As discussed in Step 8, Pricing, of the business review, a price inelastic product is one for which the demand will remain relatively stable when the price is raised or lowered. Usually this is because either there are no substitute products, the product is a luxury good with a loyal following, or it possesses superior product attributes.

Review Step 8 in your business review and your pricing problems and opportunities. You may find that your product is elastic—by lowering the price dramatically you lower your gross margin (selling price less cost of goods sold), but you actually make more profits because of the increased volume. Or you may find that your product is inelastic—higher prices only marginally affect volume, but margins and profits increase substantially. This is useful information in developing your pricing objectives and strategies.

Mathematics of Price Setting

Two types of costs must be considered when establishing prices—variable and fixed.

> Variable costs are costs that vary with the volume of production or sales—for example, costs associated with incremental payroll, new material purchases, etc.

> Fixed costs are costs that do not change with fluctuating sales or production. Fixed costs are usually spread evenly over the company's brands or products, and in this manner are calculated for each individual product along with the variable costs of selling that product. Fixed costs are associated with depreciation on machinery, rent, insurance, real estate taxes, etc.

Also there are two pricing scenarios that the marketer should understand when making pricing decisions.

Short-Run/Excess Capacity Pricing: If there is excess capacity, management needs to set price so that variable costs are covered and there is adequate margin for some contribution to fixed costs or overhead. In the short run, if there is excess capacity, it is far better to take an order with less margin, because total company profit will be greater or profit loss will be less than if the order was not taken and the sale not made.

Long-Run Pricing: In the long run, prices have to be established so that *all* costs (fixed *and* variable) are covered and there is a profit.

The following formula allows you to determine break-even points to help ensure expenditures do not exced sales. The break-even analysis allows the marketer to gain insight into the effect of pricing decisions on income and costs. The analysis enables you to establish a price that will cover all costs.

$$PX = FC + VC(X)$$

Where: P = Price
VC = Variable costs
FC = Fixed costs
X = Volume of units produced at break-even point (the number of units which must be sold)

Assume you are a shoe retailer and the average shoe will be sold at $25, and fixed costs are $10,000 per month, and variable costs are $15 per shoe.

$$\$25X = \$10,000 + 15X$$
$$\$10X = \$10,000$$
$$X = 1,000$$

1,000 shoes must be sold at $25 to cover costs per month.

The break-even chart is shown graphically in Exhibit 9.1. The marketer can also use the break-even chart concept to plot fixed costs, variable costs, and revenues. In this manner, the marketer can usually determine the effect of a drop in price and a resulting increase in sales and potential profits.

Let's assume that the shoe company in the previous example was operating at above break-even, selling 1,500 pairs of shoes per month at $25. As you will recall, fixed costs are $10,000 per month and variable costs are $15 per shoe.

Exhibit 9.1   Break-Even Chart

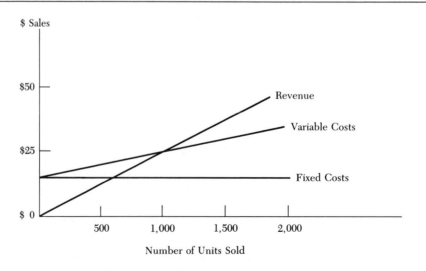

Example A

Number of Shoes Sold	1,500	
Revenue	$1,500 \times \$25 =$	\$37,500
Costs	$\$10,000 + \$15\,(1,500) =$	\$32,500
Profits per Month		\$ 5,000

Now let's assume that the marketer, through past experience, can estimate that a drop in average price per shoe to $23 will result in a 30 percent increase in business.

Example B

Number of shoes sold at 30 percent increase $(1.3 \times 1,500)$	1,950	
Revenue	$\$1,950 \times \$23 =$	\$44,850
Costs	$\$10,000 + \$15\,(1,950) =$	\$39,250
Profits per month		\$ 5,600
Profit difference between Examples A and B		\$ 600

The shoe marketer would make another $600 by lowering the price $2 with an anticipated increase of business of 30 percent. If the increase in volume were only 10 percent, the marketer would make less profit (try the formula to prove this to yourself). Thus, if you can predict your product's elasticity reasonably accurately, you can use the above formula to estimate changes in profitability due to price changes.

HOW TO DEVELOP A PRICING PLAN

A worksheet for developing your pricing plan is provided in Appendix C.

Step 1

Establish Your Price Objectives

Price objectives usually focus on the following issues:

- Lower, higher, or parity pricing.
- Geography of the pricing.
- Timing of the pricing.

Lower, Higher, or Parity Pricing

Reviewing your marketing strategies and your pricing problems and opportunities in the context of the following factors will help you determine whether your company should set a higher, lower, or parity price objective.

Lower Price Objective The reasons for a low price strategy are usually:

- To expand the market, allowing new consumers who couldn't purchase at higher prices to become purchasers.
- To increase trial and/or sales due to price incentives.
- A situation exists with a strong price elastic product where a low price results in increased demand. The result is lower margins but increased profits because of the increased volume.
- To preempt competitive strategies, helping to steal market share. This is often necessary in a mature market.
- To remain competitive with your competition. If a majority of the competitors have reduced their prices, oftentimes you will need to do so, especially if you are in a

price sensitive product category. If a strong competitor is also offering an attribute such as service with which you cannot compete, you may need to lower your price to counter the service offering.

- To keep competitors from entering the marketplace by having a price which is difficult for a new company with high initial investment costs to match. This policy of expanded market pricing allows a company to develop a large, loyal consumer base while keeping competition to a minimum.

Higher Price Objective Several conditions favor a high price objective, where the price of the product will equate to revenues substantially above the break-even point, or the product's price is set above that of the competition.

- A need for a fast recovery of the firm's investment.
- A need for faster accumulation of profits to cover research and development costs. The profits can then be used to improve the product and to sustain competitive marketing tactics once competitors enter the market.
- To substantiate a quality image positioning.
- The product is price inelastic where the demand or sales decrease only marginally with higher pricing.
- The product or service is in the introductory phase of its product life cycle and represents a substantial innovation within the product category. Also, the company may wish to cream profits while there are no substitute products to force competitive pricing.
- The company is stressing profits rather than sales, thus, margins must remain high.
- The product has a short life span. An example would be fad products which last for a relatively short time. This necessitates a high price policy which will help recover the firm's research and development costs in a short time period.
- The product is difficult to copy and reproduce or has patent protection.

Parity Pricing Parity pricing is pricing that is comparable to the competition's. It can be effectively used if your product has superior attributes and it is priced the same as products with inferior product attributes. It can also effectively be used when your product is similar to your competitor's but there are nonproduct advantages that your company can utilize to provide a better overall value to the consumer. Nonproduct advantages, such as service, guarantees, location for retailers, or distribution channel for manufacturers, are often reasons to purchase given a parity pricing structure in the marketplace among similar products.

Geography

Many times a company's pricing structure is not uniform across the country. One market may have much greater competition, necessitating lower prices. Or a lower pricing objective may be required in specific markets to help achieve the marketing strategy of developing trial and placing emphasis on certain markets with greater potential. As a result, your pricing objectives should include a description of how you plan to price by geographic regions.

Timing

Finally, timing should be addressed in your price objectives. Do you plan to use a high price, low price, or parity price objective all year, or only during certain portions of the year? Remember that the pricing is a tool to help implement marketing strategies and also deliver profits. While timing relates to the changing of your price on a seasonal basis, it also relates to the changing of prices in a timely fashion relative to competitive price changes and to addressing increases or decreases in the margin or cost of goods sold.

Writing the Pricing Objective

The following examples of pricing objectives consider higher or lower price, relative to the competition, geography, and timing.

> Utilize a lower price relative to the competition throughout the country for the entire year.

> Increase prices during the strong tourist months of May to September, then lower prices during the off-season.

Step 2
Establish Your Price Strategies

Pricing strategies state how you will achieve your pricing objectives. They provide the specifics you need to finalize your pricing plan. In developing your pricing strategies, the following steps should be taken.

- *Review your marketing strategies:* It is important to focus on the function of price relative to your other marketing mix tools. Remember, pricing is a tool to help implement and achieve marketing strategies.
- *Review your problems and opportunities:* Especially review Steps 8 and 9 on pricing and competitive analysis of your business review and the subsequent problems and opportunities.
- *Review your pricing mathematics:* Determine at what price you break-even. Make certain that if you set a lower price than your competition, it will not cause the company to lose money but hopefully increases sales and profit.

Finally, develop strategies that address how price levels, geography, and timing objectives will be accomplished. Using the information acquired in the three steps above, detail specifics as to your pricing strategy. Consider the following two marketing strategies.

> *Marketing Seasonality Strategy:* Increase sales among current customers during the off-season.

> *Marketing Pricing Strategy:* Maintain a 45 percent margin for the year.

The *pricing objective* might be to utilize a parity pricing structure relative to the competition during the strong selling season nationally and a low price relative to the competition during the off-season nationally. Price then would be one of the tools used to execute the seasonality marketing strategy along with promotion and advertising. And pricing certainly would be used to execute the pricing marketing strategy.

The subsequent pricing strategies might be:

> Utilize a price consistent with the top three market leaders in the northern markets and the top market leader in the southern markets during the months of August through December.

> Utilize a price at 5 percent below the top three market leaders in the northern markets and 7 percent below the market leader in the southern markets during the off-season of January through July.

DOS AND DON'TS

Do

- Review your pricing problems and opportunities and your marketing strategies before developing your pricing plan.
- Closely monitor the competition and keep consistent records of your competition's pricing.

- Be flexible. Be prepared to adjust to competitive pressures and the marketing environment. Be willing to change your price and use it as a tool for achieving marketing strategies.
- Use the pricing tool to communicate the positioning of your product.
- Test your price often. Test higher and lower prices and monitor the response in test markets. Apply what you learn to your total system. Make sure you test your pricing strategies for a long enough period to obtain realistic results.
- Remember, the more intangible (service firms) or unique your product, the more flexibility you will have in setting higher prices.
- Price your product to provide ultimate value to consumers. Remember, you can still give real value through high price (e.g., the product is a little higher priced than the competition, but the customer receives a unique or better service).
- Be aware of the obvious but also the hidden costs when determining your selling price (e.g., shrinkage through employee theft).
- Make sure your pricing policy follows the legal guidelines.

Don't

- Don't look at pricing as static. Your cost of doing business and the competitive activity in your marketplace is not fixed, your pricing shouldn't be either.
- Don't set pricing without first determining how it will affect sales, margins, and the ability of the company to cover variable and fixed costs.
- Don't be afraid to use price to achieve other marketing goals, such as trial. Successful companies often plan for a period of lower prices in an effort to increase trial and build the customer base. Though profitability is reduced temporarily, it is often offset by a sustained period of repeat purchase at full price by the expanded customer base. However, it is a good idea to test this premise to make sure you are receiving adequate repurchase from the new customers to justify a rollout of the program.
- While being flexible, make sure you don't confuse potential purchasers with constantly changing prices.
- Don't over react to the competition. Before you change your *long-run* pricing strategy, wait to see if the competitive price changes are temporary or permanent. At the same time, learn to anticipate and react to *short-run* competitive price changes.
- If you are attempting to build a value image don't lower an already competitive price, put greater emphasis on the quality of your product.

DISTRIBUTION

N ow you need to consider the marketing mix tool of distribution. Up to this point, your efforts have been focused on developing plans to persuade the consumer to purchase your product. Distribution focuses on making sure there is accessible product for the target market to purchase once you have initiated demand.

Begin this chapter by reviewing the distribution issues summarized through your problems and opportunities and the overall distribution direction provided in your marketing strategies developed in Chapter 6. Then utilize the specific information provided in this chapter to develop a comprehensive plan which will allow for effective distribution of your product.

From This Chapter You Will Learn

The definition of distribution.

The issues affecting your distribution plan.

How to develop your distribution objectives and strategies.

OVERVIEW

Definition

In this book, we define distribution as the transmission of goods and services from the producer or seller to the user.

Issues Affecting Distribution

In developing your distribution plan, four main areas should be addressed:

- Penetration (retailers and service firms) or market coverage/shelf space (manufacturers).
- Type of outlet.
- Geography.
- Timing.

Penetration or Market Coverage

Penetration Levels for Retailers and Service Firms Charts completed in the business review will reveal whether your firm has enough penetration to maximize sales, fully utilize the media, and pay out the advertising expenditures in any given market.

If you do not have enough stores to take advantage of the market's sales potential, this market is *underpenetrated*. In this situation, you probably cannot afford broad scale advertising in the market because the expense is too burdensome for a few stores/offices, verus allocating the cost among many. It is important to realize that each store has a natural trading area that can usually be defined in terms of geographical size and number of people. Thus, each market, depending upon its population and the competition, can support a certain number of stores. If, for example, you are underpenetrated and have one store in a city of 300,000 households and the business review determines that there should be one store for every 100,000 households:

> *You will not maximize your sales in the given market.* There are major areas in the market where customers will not be exposed to the store and will not drive out of their way to purchase an item that can be purchased at alternative outlets offering similar merchandise.

> *You will not be able to maximize your media investment.* Instead of leveraging advertising costs across three stores, all expenses are shouldered by the one store. Thus, in order to keep advertising expenses within budget, the store will have limited media support given the size of the market and the cost of the media. And when mass media is purchased, there will be much waste as the communication will be received by consumers outside of the store's trading area. Given this scenario, effective, broad, marketwide media such as television probably cannot be utilized.

Being *overpenetrated*, with too many stores in a trading area, also has negatives associated with it. Too many stores results in inefficiency, with duplication of coverage. Often the effect is cannibalization of one store's customers by another. Accordingly, consideration should also be given not just to opening new outlets, but the need to *eliminate* one or more outlet locations within a market.

Market Coverage for Package Goods Firms and Business-to-Business Firms

Market coverage for *package goods* firms includes three areas:

- The number of potential outlets or distribution centers which carry your product.
- The ACV (All Commodity Volume) of the stores which carry your product.
- The amount of shelf space allocated your product.

The most important distribution measure for manufacturers is not necessarily the number of stores carrying the product, but the ACV of those stores. The percent of total grocery store volume accounted for by the existing stores carrying the manufacturer's product is a critical measure of how much additional market coverage a manufacturer can obtain.

Review Step 7, Distribution, of your business review to determine how many outlets there are in each market with which you do business and the percentage of total business the outlets that carry your product account for. If you are in only three out of ten grocery stores in a given market but those three account for 80 percent of the business, then you don't have to spend a great deal of time trying to expand your market distribution. But, if the three grocery stores account for only 30 percent of the business, an objective should be to increase market coverage.

In addition, review Step 7 of your business review to determine the percent of shelf space your product has relative to the competition. If it is substantially less than the competition, either nationally, in specific markets, or in specific grocery chains, then a distribution objective should address this problem.

For *business-to-business* firms the same process should be undertaken, except the focus of consideration should be intermediate channel targets. And instead of shelf space, the business-to-business marketer should consider the percent of his or her product purchased by each company, distributor, wholesaler, broker, or outlet.

Type of Outlet

In Step 7 of the business review you developed a chart which traces sales by distribution outlet for your product category. Analyze this data for any trends your firm should take advantage of during the next year. We did a business review for a manufacturer of sinks and disposals that had built its business through traditional plumbing channels via wholesalers. However, data showed that due to the advent of the do-it-yourself movement, more sinks and disposals were being sold to do-it-yourselfers through lumber yards and home building centers than to contractors through traditional channels. Thus the company developed a dual channel strategy, using both the wholesale plumbing channels and the consumer home building center channels.

In addition, as with price, the type of product and the product life cycle greatly affect the channel decision. If your product is new and is still being tested, production levels most likely will be relatively small, requiring very specific and limited distribution. In addition, the product may require more in-depth personal selling to the target market because of its complexity and newness. If this situation applies to your firm, determine what type of outlet can provide this service level before establishing distribution objectives.

If your product is already established, production levels will be higher and the product may be more standardized. This would require less demand for a specialized selling effort. Or it may be appropriate to sell your product in a self-service, self-help type of environment.

There are many different types of distribution vehicles or outlet types. Study Step 7 in your business review to determine the different distribution channels for your product category. Note which channels have the most volume and which are a growing influence in your industry. Then list the different attributes of each distribution choice in terms of customer segmentation, customer service provided, price orientation (discount, full price, etc.) to help you make the correct choice for your product.

Geography

The marketer should also consider the BDI (Brand Development Index) developed in Step 6 of the business review. A BDI demonstrates the sales to population ratio relative to other markets in the company's system. For example, if Chicago accounts for 11.2 percent of the population in all the company's markets but only 10.0 percent of a firm's sales, the BDI would be 89 (10/11.2). This is 11 points below the average of 100.

Distribution plans often take BDIs into consideration after they have completed the penetration or coverage analysis detailed earlier. A low BDI in any given market coupled with a penetration or coverage analysis which shows that a firm is underpenetrated points towards potential geographic expansion in those markets.

Also, geographic expansion should be considered for those markets that are underpenetrated and have high CDIs (Consumer Development Index). A high CDI (see Step 6 of the business review) means that consumers in a given market purchase a product at higher rates than the country on a whole. If in the Midwest, purchases of fabric for sewing are at higher rates than the East, then the Midwest should be targeted for future expansion as the chance for success would be greater in this part of the country. Of course the competitive situation would also have to be taken into consideration, but the CDI provides a good benchmark for the success rate potential for different expansion markets.

Thus, distribution objectives should detail penetration/coverage goals and/or use of specific types of outlets on a national, regional, or local basis.

Timing

Finally, timing must be addressed in the distribution objectives. State whether the objectives are to be completed in a matter of months or years. Because distribution involves committing to actual construction or long-term leases in the case of retailers, developing working relationships with wholesalers and brokers by manufacturers, and obtaining valuable shelf space from retailers in the case of consumer goods manufacturing firms, the distribution timing is often longer term than in other sections of the plan. A retail store expansion program is usually not a single but a multi-year, ongoing development. What may be started this year may not be finished until next year and beyond.

Other Miscellaneous Factors

With an increasing number of products available and with limited amount of shelf space, more retailers are requiring up front slotting allowances to carry a product. You must either devise a means to avoid these allowances (sell-in your product to departments of the store which do not require slotting allowances—often times the produce and meat departments) or build them into your cost of distribution.

Finally, note that knowledge pertaining to competitive distribution patterns is helpful when making decisions regarding penetration/market coverage, type of outlet, geography, and timing. Consult Step 7 in your business review to determine competitive distribution patterns. This knowledge is helpful when deciding what markets to further penetrate. If there are two equal markets in terms of potential, the obvious choice for further penetration would be the one with the weakest competitive situation. In another example, if a competitor has shown dramatic sales increases utilizing a new channel of distribution which you do not use, this might provide the rationale to at least test the alternative channel structure for your products.

HOW TO DEVELOP A DISTRIBUTION PLAN

A worksheet for developing your distribution plan is provided in Appendix C.

Step 1

Establish Distribution Objectives

Establish quantifiable distribution objectives for the four categories of:

- Penetration (retailers and service firms) or market coverage/shelf space (manufacturers).
- Type of outlet.
- Geography.
- Timing.

An example for a retail firm would be as follows:

> Fully penetrate the firm's two largest BDI markets (Chicago and Detroit, which account for 25 percent of the firm's business) to equate to the rate of one store

for every 100,000 households within the next two years (8 stores in this plan year and 10 stores the following year).

Continue to utilize strip centers or freestanding units.

Step 2
Establish Distribution Strategies

Your distribution strategies should describe how you will accomplish your distribution objectives. The following should be considered by each business category.

Retail and Service Firms

- Describe the criteria or methodology for penetrating markets or adding new locations. Where will you locate new stores? What demographic, location, cost per square foot, competition, or other criteria will you use to make these decisions?
- If you are expanding geographic penetration, detail if this will be done on a systematic market-by-market basis or wherever the opportunity develops within the total system.
- If a change is warranted, describe how you will make the change from one type of outlet to another.
- Describe your purchase or lease strategies.

Manufacturers

- Describe how you will attain market coverage goals and/or shelf space goals. Some of your strategies to achieve these will be incorporated into your promotional plan. If your business review details that your product does not differ from your competition's, your product is not established with the trade, and your product does not make a large impact on the trade in terms of profits, then you will have to rely more heavily on promotions and trade deals to meet aggressive market coverage and shelf space goals.
- If your objective is to increase market coverage, describe how you will choose the type(s) of channel to target for increased coverage and detail specifically what stores you plan to target.
- Outline whether you are going to use a *push* or *pull* strategy. A push strategy focuses on marketing to the intermediate targets such as distributors and the outlets to obtain distribution and shelf space. A pull strategy involves marketing directly to consumers to build demand, forcing the outlets to stock the product.
- Describe how you will enter new distribution channels if this is an objective. Will you try to place your entire line or one top-selling product in the stores? What kind of merchandising and advertising support will you provide? Will you offer return privileges or lower your minimum order requirements? If storage, display, dispensing, price marking, or accounting specifics are important to the new channel, describe how you will make allowances to gain distribution trial. Will you provide special introductory pricing?

Assume a distribution objective for a package goods firm is to increase market coverage 20 percent among grocery stores in all top 100 markets over the next year. The strategies to achieve this objective might be:

Place additional sales emphasis against large independents with multiple store outlets.

Concentrate on first establishing the top selling line of frozen foods before attempting to gain distribution of the entire line of frozen and canned foods.

Utilize special promotions developed in the promotion plan to help sell-in product via volume trade deals to encourage initial trial and special introductory pricing incentives.

DOS AND DON'TS

Do

- Review your problems and opportunities and your marketing strategies as guidelines for developing distribution objectives and strategies.
- Study your competitors' distribution patterns. Learn from their mistakes and their successes.
- Make sure your distribution structure is consistent with your positioning and your target market's purchasing patterns.
- Be willing to change distribution methods if the marketing environment changes.
- Location of the store and proximity to the consumer must still be considered king in retail.
- Continually test new methods of distribution.

Don't

- Don't make quick decisions. Distribution of your product requires the development of long-term relationships and usually requires a fixed investment of capital. Don't change retail distribution patterns without thoroughly testing alternatives first. If you are going to expand distribution, do it on a market-by-market basis or regional basis in a disciplined roll out fashion.
- Don't remain static in your distribution patterns. Customers change, so must you.
- Don't be inflexible with your distribution policy. There may be regional differences that you should consider.
- Don't expand distribution if you can't fully penetrate markets or consistently deliver product. Retail and package goods firms especially need minimum distribution levels within any given market to leverage advertising and other marketing resources.
- Don't expand your distribution at a rate you cannot effectively support (adequate levels of product, quality service, media weight and support, etc.).

PERSONAL
SELLING/
OPERATIONS

P ersonal selling and operations involve the personal one-on-one contact your company has with the specific target consumer and the day-to-day administration of the selling program, the retail outlet, or the office. Whether it's business-to-business or consumer marketing, personal selling is a very important tool that incorporates the critical human factor into the marketing mix. *It is the one personal and direct link between the target market and your company.*

From This Chapter You Will Learn

The definition of personal selling/operations.

The issues affecting your personal selling/operations plan.

How to develop a personal selling/operations plan.

OVERVIEW

Definition

In this book personal selling for retail and service firms, which is often referred to as operations, involves all functions related to selling in the store, office or other environments such as door-to-door solicitation, in-home selling, and telemarketing. This includes hiring and managing sales personnel, stocking inventory, preparing the product for sale, as well as the presentation and maintenance of the facility.

For business-to-business and package goods firms, personal selling relates to the manufacturers' selling and servicing of its products to the trade and/or intermediate markets (various buyers of the product within the distribution channel from the original producer to the ultimate user).

Issues Affecting Personal Selling/ Operations

Retail and Service Firms

The overriding issue facing retailers and service organizations is to determine a realistic and achievable sales ratio. You must determine a goal for the percentage of individuals walking into the retail outlet that will be persuaded to purchase versus leaving without purchasing. Or, if you are a service organization, a goal must be developed regarding the number of prospects versus the number of converted clients when making sales calls. If you have primary research, you will be able to track your sales ratio and that of your competitors from year to year. This should provide direction when establishing your sales ratio in the marketing plan. If you do not have primary research, we suggest that you initiate an information survey similar to the one in Step 6 of the business review to help guide you.

Whether you have primary research or not, you should analyze the amount of traffic (retailers) or number of sales calls made (service) in daily and weekly increments. Next, estimate your current sales ratio and project what an increase of even 3 to 5 points would do for your sales. Finally, ask yourself, is it realistic to expect a 3 to 5 point increase? In some businesses where there is a lot of competition and consumers shop two or three stores before purchasing, the answer may be no. But in other businesses it may be very realistic to expect a higher sales ratio given the proper selling focus.

In addition, retailers and service organizations must address other *customer behavior goals* when developing personal selling and operation plans. If you determine that customers are more likely to purchase if they have been given a demonstration or tried the merchandise, develop plans that encourage this type of behavior.

Retailers must also consider the in-store selling presentation while service firms must consider their basic selling environment when developing a personal selling and operations plan. The retailer must determine if the store is going to employ a self-service or full-service selling environment. Are you going to employ minimal sales pressure or utilize a harder selling and/or commission based selling structure? In deciding the type of selling environment, you must analyze the needs of the customer and the merchandise being sold.

If the product is extremely technical and/or requires a major dollar outlay, the customer will probably require a great deal of information and a more professional selling technique. If the product is a standardized, utilitarian type of product, there probably is less need for an informational and/or hard sell approach. For example, many self-help or self-service store environments carry less technical and expensive products with which the consumer has had previous experience. This type of selling environment addresses consumers' familiarity with the product(s). The customer can shop and make decisions independently and comfortably without the services of a salesperson.

The discussion regarding the analysis of the consumer's need for information and the technicality of the product is but one portion of the decision making process as to the in-store selling environment. After you have considered these factors, also review the capabilities of your sales staff. It takes a great deal of product knowledge and skill to effectively *sell* potential buyers and not *turn them off*. If you decide upon an aggressive selling philosophy, your company must make the commitment to sales training and ongoing refresher courses.

Finally, the *cost* of selling is another key factor you must consider. A sales or in-store staff is very necessary, but also very expensive to maintain. You must determine the optimum number of salespeople required and the dollar investment to support the selling effort. The cost of selling as a percent of sales will vary depending upon your company, what you are selling, and the needs of the target market. You might want to review industry sources to help you determine what your company's selling/payroll cost should be.

Manufacturers

Package goods manufacturers consider brokers, wholesalers, and outlets while many other business-to-business companies think in terms of intermediate markets when addressing personal selling issues. Like retailers and service organizations, the number one selling issue for manufacturers is the establishment of a sales ratio. A sales ratio for manufacturers is determined by the number of prospects contacted versus the number that actually become customers. In addition to the actual sales ratio figure, other quantifiable objectives should be established to help direct the sales force. The number of sales calls and demonstrations made to wholesalers, outlets, and intermediate markets should be established along with a specific prospect list. These types of parameters provide direction to the sales force and also allow for a measurement tool when analyzing sales personnel results at the end of the year.

Manufacturers must also decide how to sell the product to the outlets, distributors, and other businesses. Manufacturers use three basic methods to sell their product:

- *Direct* to purchasers through an in-house sales force.
- *Indirect* to purchasers through agents (independent sales reps/brokers) or wholesalers/distributors.
- *Mixed* or a combined selling system, which is combination of the two above.

The decision as to which of the above selling methods to use is determined after considering the following factors.[1]

Is the Market Horizontal or Vertical? A vertical market is one that is made up of only one or two industries. It is very specialized. For example, craft manufacturers sell to craft wholesalers or directly to craft retail outlets. The number of wholesalers and retailers in the total industry is very small. Direct distribution is often used because selling is very personal and individual relationships become very important.

However, if the market is horizontal, with the product being sold to buyers in many industries (for example, plastics manufacturers sell to multiple industry types), then the opportunity to reach large numbers of potential purchasers is much better with indirect distribution.

Quality of Product With a direct sales staff you can control the selling effort, since the sales force is made up of your company's employees. For this reason, businesses with rigid quality standards often use a direct sales force.

What Is the Market Potential? Many times a company's only choice is to go through indirect channels. If the firm has only one product with limited sales potential, it is very difficult to generate enough demand to justify the cost of an individual sales force.

Geographic Concentration If the market is geographically concentrated, it is easier to go direct. If clients are dispersed, indirect channels tend to be more favorable, as it becomes very costly to make time consuming sales visits.

Technical Aspects of the Product The more technical the product, the more a direct sales force is favored. The firm needs to supervise the training of the sales force and have a high degree of control over the selling process.

Standardized or Specialized Product If the product is standardized, you can move the product through many different types of channels and selling methods. If it is specialized and requires a high degree of maintenance, specialized care, or instruction, then a direct sales force is often required.

Financial Strength of the Company The manufacturer must consider the cost of each selling method and weigh this against specific market conditions and options

---

[1]The following discussion is based in part on lecture material presented by Dr. Michael Hutt at Miami University.

for selling the product. A direct sales force is far more expensive than utilizing independent representatives. However, there are certain advantages of a direct sales force, as outlined above, that may make the extra cost pay out.

HOW TO DEVELOP A PERSONAL SELLING/ OPERATIONS PLAN

A worksheet for developing your personal selling/operations plan is provided in Appendix C.

Step 1

Establish Selling/ Operations Objectives

Your sales/operations objectives should be as specific as possible and include the following items.

For Retail/Service

- Customer contact—the percent of store visitors having contact and number of contacts with store staff during visit.
- Customer behavior goals such as percentage of customers who are persuaded to try on or experience a demonstration of merchandise.
- The specific sales ratio.

An example of personal selling/operation objectives for a retailer would be:

Establish a minimum of one contact with 90 percent of store visitors and a minimum of two contacts with 50 percent of visitors.

Achieve a 40 percent trial ratio of customers who actually try the merchandise during a hands on demonstration in-store.

Achieve a 60 percent sales ratio (60 percent of the people who visit the store make a purchase) over the next year during the holiday selling season and a 40 percent sales ratio the remaining of the year.

For Manufacturers

- The number and type of companies that must be contacted by the sales force.
- The number of sales calls that must be made to each prospect and/or current customer by company type.
- The sales ratio (number of contacts versus the number of sales).
- The average sales dollar volume and the number of orders per salesperson per year.
- The number of actual product presentations/demonstrations, percentage of product sampling or trial that must be achieved during sales presentations.
- Additional customer behavior goals such as the percentage of customers who are persuaded to sign up for future sales/product information.

Personal selling objective examples for a manufacturer would be:

Contact each current customer twice and make a sales presentation to the top 50 percent of prospect companies in the newly developed construction and manufacturing SIC target markets.

Make full product demonstrations to 75 percent of the prospects.

Obtain a sales ratio of 85 percent among existing customers and 30 percent among new prospects.

Obtain an average dollar sales of $2,500 and generate an average of two hundred sales per salesperson per year.

Step 2
Establish Selling/
Operations Strategies

It will be helpful first to review the questions in Step 7, Distribution, of the business review pertaining to selling. These will help you to form specific selling strategies for your company. In addition, the areas to address when you establish specific selling/ operations strategies to meet your selling/operations objectives follow.

- *The type of selling environment.* A retailer must decide whether the selling environment will be self-service, or whether there will be a full-service sales staff. If there is a full-service sales staff, the decision must be made as to the selling orientation—hard sell or soft sell. A manufacturer must determine whether to use a direct, indirect, or mixed sales staff.
- *The administration parameters of the sales force.* The selling strategies should outline hiring qualifications, salary ranges, payment methods (annual salary, commissions, combination salary and commissions), training and evaluation procedures.
- *Sales incentives.* If they are going to be used, sales incentive programs should be developed in this section of the plan.
- *Seasonal and geographic requirements.* If staffing is a function of seasonal sales or there are different staffing requirements by store or by market, there should be a selling strategy developed to address these issues.
- *Operational requirements.* The selling strategy section should also direct selling technique. For *retailers*, is there a certain selling technique that should be followed to increase the chance of closing a sale? A shoe retailer may require that its sales force initiate as many trial fittings as possible. This might result from data that shows fitting customers and allowing them to try walking in the shoe leads to 25 percent higher sales ratio. Similar selling technique decisions should be considered for *manufacturers*.
- *Store operation guidelines.* Selling and operation strategies should cover:
  Stocking procedures.
  Maintenance considerations.
  Appearance of the store for retailers, office for service, and shelf display for manufacturers.
  Product presentation in-store for retailers, office for service, and display of product for manufacturers.

The following are examples of selling strategies for a ski retailer whose selling objectives were to increase the sale ratio from 30 percent to 45 percent during the next year and to obtain a 35 percent ski equipment demonstration ratio among customers in the store.

Strategies

Develop an aggressive selling environment designed to sell customers during a one-on-one sales presentation in-store.

Develop a program which assures that all customers are greeted upon entry to the store.

Utilize the training hill outside the store as a means to get customers to actually try the equipment and achieve the demonstration goals established in the selling objectives.

Utilize 2 percent commission plus salary to encourage aggressive salespeople.

Establish a bonus system to reward the top producers each week and each month of the year.

Utilize mystery shoppers to rate service and selling effectiveness. Rate each salesperson at least once every six months.

Utilize yearly and semi-yearly reviews of the sales staff to improve performance. Send each salesperson to one selling seminar per year.

Develop quarterly seminars to keep salespeople aware of the latest technology and products in the industry.

DOS AND DON'TS

Do

- Review your marketing strategies and problems and opportunities before developing your selling/operations plan.
- Review your customers' shopping habits and product information requirements before deciding on a selling method.
- If you are a retailer, make sure you plan to train your sales staff properly before you decide to utilize a hard sell approach.
- If you are a manufacturer, review the seven considerations outlined in this chapter before deciding whether to use a direct, indirect, or mixed selling method.
- Have your sales staff reinforce the positioning of your product and your advertising and promotion efforts. Your individual marketing mix tools are far more effective if each one complements and reinforces the other.
- Support your sales staff. They will be more effective salespeople if given the support in terms of brochures, samples, and special offers when interacting with the customer.
- Manufacturers, make sure you are selling to the real decision maker(s) when calling on new prospects.

Don't

- Don't expect your company to change selling methods overnight. It takes a lot of training and the right type of personnel to perfect different selling styles.
- Don't overlook the importance of making sure you have a sound operations system in place to execute your sales plans. This is particularly true in the service industries in which there has *not* been a strong selling orientation, such as healthcare and legal industries. Operations is also important in retail where you have many variables to control in terms of people, product preparation/inventory and presentation, as well as maintenance of the facility. It is our experience that many marketing plans fail, not because they are strategically wrong, but primarily because of poor execution in the field.
- Don't forget the selling function needs on-going attention from management in order to be effective and to show improvement.
- Don't forget, although money motivates, a formalized program to recognize an individual's accomplishment also increases selling effectiveness.
- Retailers, your salespeople can't sell from an empty wagon. You can't sell the product if it is not available for the shopper to purchase. The operations plan has to make sure that there is adequate communication between marketing and the merchandisers so there is adequate inventory stocked in the stores prior to heavy seasonal selling periods and promotions.
- Don't just provide service, use service as a method to *sell* your customers!
- Don't let your sales force forget that while selling new customers is important, the reason for your company's existence is to service and satisfy existing customers.

PROMOTION

P romotion is a powerful short-term marketing tool. Developing a promotional plan requires strategic thinking and creativity. In many instances marketers begin at the execution stage and randomly consider idea after idea without any thought as to the ends they are trying to achieve. The result is usually costly, with time and effort spent on developing promotion ideas that are inappropriate to the current market and the competitive situation. The key is to establish promotion objectives and strategies first and then develop innovative, yet *targeted*, executions.

From This Chapter You Will Learn

The definition of promotion.

The parameters to consider when developing promotion objectives.

How to develop your promotion objectives.

The parameters to consider when developing promotion strategies.

How to develop promotion strategies.

How to develop alternative promotion executions utilizing a promotion format.

How to determine the costs of promotions and analyze promotion payback.

How to select the most appropriate promotion execution alternatives and integrate different executions into a total promotion plan.

The available promotion tools and how they can be delivered.

OVERVIEW

Definition

Promotion provides added incentive, encouraging the target market to perform some incremental behavior. The incremental behavior results in either increased short-term sales and/or an association with the product (e.g., product usage or an event oriented experience). In addition, promotion is more short term in focus. For the purposes of this book, we will define promotion as an activity offering added incentive to stimulate incremental purchase or association with the product over the short run, for a reason other than the product's inherent attributes and benefits.

Consumer and Trade (Business-to-Business) Promotion

There are two broad categories of promotion—consumer and business-to-business or trade. The goal of *consumer promotion* is to influence the end consumer or the ultimate purchaser/user. *Trade or business-to-business promotion* influences the trade or intermediate markets that purchase and resell the product. This chapter discusses both types of promotions.

The major difference between consumer and trade promotion, other than different target markets, is delivery. With consumer promotions, the incentives are delivered either by mass media or through in-store devices. However, because of the relatively narrow customer base for trade promotion, mass communication media are usually not cost efficient—there is too much wasted coverage. Therefore, with trade promotion, added incentives are usually delivered through such targeted media vehicles as direct mail, trade publications, or via the sales force.

Promotion Incentives

Promotion incentives fall into one of four areas:
- *Price incentives*—some form of savings off the original price of the product.
- *Product*—providing a sample of the product.
- *Merchandise or gifts*—giving customers the opportunity to obtain merchandise or premiums with the purchase of the product.
- *An experience*—participation of an individual or a group of individuals in such special events as contests, sweepstakes, parties, or some unique experience. Participation is rewarded either by the chance to win a prize, money, trip, etc., or through the pure enjoyment of the event.

Types of Promotion Categories

There are many different types of promotions. Each has unique advantages and disadvantages that are listed in the Appendix to this chapter. Following are the ten promotion categories commonly used by marketers to communicate or deliver the incentives.

- Price Off/Sale
- Couponing
- Sampling
- On Pack/In Pack
- Refunds
- Premiums
- Sweepstakes/Games
- Packaging
- Trade Allowances
- Events

Timing of the Incentive Payback to the Target Market

The target market receives the incentive for purchase in one of three time periods:

- *Immediate*—the consumer receives the incentive instantly with or without the purchase of, or association[1] with, the product.

---

[1]While in some sweepstakes, games, or events, purchase of the product is not required—association with the product is usually necessary to participate. For example, the law in many states makes purchase an illegal requirement for participation in a sweepstakes game card promotion, where association with the product is often necessary to participate. While the consumer is not forced to purchase to receive a game card, he or she must visit the retail establishment or write the company to receive a game card. And, in the case of mass participation events (e.g., a brand-sponsored concert), association usually equates to attending the event.

- *Delayed*—the consumer receives the incentive at the next purchase or within a specified period after the purchase of, or association with, the product.
- *Chance*—the consumer has the *chance* of receiving the incentive within a specified period of time (immediate or delayed) after the purchase of or association with the product.

In summary, promotions are a behavior oriented, multifaceted marketing tool that provide flexibility to the marketer in terms of the incentive offered, the promotional vehicle used, and the time period in which the incentive is awarded.

ESTABLISHING SHORT-TERM PROMOTION SALES OBJECTIVES

Prior to developing promotion objectives, strategies, and executions, you need to set short-term promotion sales objectives for the promotion time period. In our development of a marketing plan, *promotion is the only marketing mix tool for which we develop specific sales objectives*, because promotion is both exclusively short term in nature and affects customer behavior. Customer behavior is affected through tangible incentives, resulting in incremental sales generation and/or an incremental association with the product. Thus with promotion, the marketer will incur direct short-term expenses in the form of incentives and communication of the incentives in order to achieve the desired short-term consumer response.

The marketer needs to establish promotion sales goals for two reasons. One is so the promotion can be evaluated against projected payback *prior* to and after execution. This will help determine if the expected incremental sales from the promotion are greater than the incremental costs (incentives and marketing costs associated with communicating the incentives). The second reason is to set a definite sales number that the promotion must obtain.

In the sales objective chapter you were urged to develop both yearly and short-term monthly sales goals. *In most cases, your promotion sales goal will be a portion of the corresponding month's or week's sales goal*. This is because promotions are executed to reverse a downward sales trend or provide necessary incremental sales in any given short-term period. The exception is when the promotion is a test. Tests are not used to achieve short-term sales goals but to learn for implementation in future plans. Yet you still must establish sales goals to measure results. In most cases, the sales goals for tests will be above the break-even point or above the sales expectations of existing mainline promotions.

HOW TO DEVELOP YOUR PROMOTION OBJECTIVES

Promotion Objective Parameters

Promotion objectives and marketing objectives are very similar in that both are designed to affect consumer behavior. The difference is that promotion objectives should be designed to affect *specific incremental* behavior over a *short period of time*. Therefore, promotion objectives must:

- *Induce incremental consumer behavior* over what was anticipated with no promotion.
- Be *specific*. The objective should focus on one singular goal.

- Be *measurable*. The results must be able to be quantified.
- Relate to a *specific time period*. However, because promotion objectives are short term in nature, the time period can be from one day to several months.
- Provide direction as to the *geographical* focus of the promotion.
- Include *budget constraints* or *profit parameters*. This is because promotion is a marketing mix tool with its own sales objectives.
- Focus on *affecting target market behavior to*:
  retain current users, increase purchases from current users, increase trial from new users, and obtain repeat usage after initial trial.

Promotions should be viewed as one method to help execute marketing strategies. In order to develop promotion objectives, you must first review the marketing objective and strategy section of your marketing plan and then restate your marketing strategies in quantifiable promotion objectives.

Step 1
Review Your Marketing Strategies

Review your marketing strategies, paying particular attention to those listed under the promotion category and those for which the implementation tool of promotion might be appropriate. A *marketing seasonality strategy* such as, increase sales during the weaker selling months of May through August, could be implemented through promotion. And, obviously, a *marketing promotion strategy* such as, develop in-store promotions during peak selling seasons to encourage purchases of weaker selling product categories, should be addressed in the promotional plan. Thus, the first step requires isolating those marketing strategies you feel promotions can help implement.

Step 2
Review the Selected Marketing Strategies and Their Corresponding Marketing Objectives

This step involves reviewing each marketing strategy selected to be implemented through promotions in Step 1 and its corresponding marketing objective. In order to form promotion objectives, the marketer reviews the marketing objective to determine *what* needs to be accomplished and *who* is being targeted. Then rely on your marketing strategy to guide you on *how* to develop a promotion objective. By linking your promotion objective to your marketing objective and strategy(ies), you insure greater probability of developing promotions that will accomplish your marketing strategies and fulfill the marketing objectives established earlier in the plan.

Assume the following situation:

Marketing Objective: Increase the number of total users / trial among the current target market by 10 percent.

Seasonality Marketing Strategy: Increase the purchasing level during the off-season while maintaining purchasing rates during the peak selling seasons.

Other Marketing Strategies: Note that there would typically be other marketing strategies to achieve the above marketing objective. However, assume that only the seasonality strategy is being implemented through promotion and the other marketing strategies would be accomplished using other marketing mix executional tools.

In this example, the *marketing objective* will provide *what* the promotion objective should achieve and *whom* the promotion should target.

Increase number of users (marketing goal, *what*).

From the current target market (target market goal, *who*).

Continuing, the *market strategy* will help determine *how* the promotion objective is developed.

Increase purchasing during the off-season (method of achievement, *how*).

Step 3

Restate the What and Who Portions of Your Marketing Objective and the How Portion of Your Marketing Strategy in a Quantifiable Promotion Objective

In combining what, who, and how, the marketing objective and strategy can be restated into a quantifiable promotion objective as follows:

Increase the number of users from the current target market 25 percent during the off-season of May and June in all markets, with a positive contribution to overhead.

Note that *geography* and *timing* considerations and a *measurable amount* are incorporated into the objective statement to make it as specific as possible.

Geography and timing in the promotion objective would be consistent with the geography and timing constraints developed in the marketing strategy section of the plan. Also, note that a *budget constraint* is mentioned. In this case, the objective has to be achieved in a manner that contributes positively to fixed overhead. Yet, in a different situation, the objective of new trial might outweigh any short-term profit requirement because the company would be investing in new customers or trial for future profits; however, there would be a budget constraint at the end of the promotion objective to limit the amount of the investment in new trial. The promotion objective might be "increase the number of new users 25 percent during the off-season with a promotion budget not to exceed $500,000." The budget constraint serves to tailor the promotion execution through providing a parameter for how much new trial is required.

The *measurable amount* in the promotion objective (in this example, 25 percent) must be realistic. Past experience provides the best assistance in deciding just how much you will affect target market behavior through promotions. Remember that promotion is just one marketing tool you will be using to achieve your marketing objectives. If promotions were the only implementation tool, then the measurable goal in the promotion objective would have to equal the measurable goal in the marketing objective. In this example, the goal would have to be to add enough incremental new users during May and June to increase the total new user base for the year 10 percent above last year's results. This is highly unrealistic and points out why there are usually multiple marketing strategies for any given marketing objective. In addition, promotion is most often only *partially* responsible for the implementation of any given marketing strategy. Other marketing tools, such as advertising, distribution, pricing, merchandising, etc., might also be used in conjunction with promotion to implement a specific marketing strategy.

In going through the above process, you may develop several promotion objectives, as there may be several marketing strategies that can be implemented and accomplished through the use of promotions. Each promotion objective will require one or more promotional strategies.

PROMOTION STRATEGY AND EXECUTION CONSIDERATIONS

Promotion Strategy Parameters

Once the promotional objectives are established, promotion strategies must be formulated demonstrating how to accomplish the promotion objectives. Promotion strategies should include:

- Type of promotion device.
- The promotion incentive.
- Whether to implement a closed or open promotion.
- The delivery method.

Type of Promotion Device

The marketer has to determine which promotional device (sampling, premiums, etc.) will best meet the promotion objective. The ten most common promotion categories were listed earlier in this chapter. Further details and the advantages and disadvantages of each of these promotion vehicles is presented in the Appendix to this chapter.

The Promotion Incentive

The promotion incentive must include a *basic reward* for the consumer. Since promotions are responsible for affecting target market behavior, the incentive needs to stimulate demand. The promotion incentive must be strong enough to move the market to participate in the promotion and purchase the product.

Keeping in mind profitability goals, in most instances, the promotion incentive should be *broad in scope*. This means that the incentive must appeal to a broad category of consumers. One mistake to *avoid* is spending substantial promotion dollars on promotion incentives that affect only small segments of the target market and thus have limited payback potential. A footwear retailer found that it was much more effective to promote 20 percent off all athletic shoes than to promote price reductions on five individual running shoes. The broader nature of the 20 percent off all athletic shoes (court, running, fitness, walking) appeals to a much larger cross section of consumers. The result is more interest and trial of the store, greater sales of athletic shoes, and ultimately more sales in nonathletic departments because of the increased traffic.

One exception is when an individual product or narrow group of products are promoted with substantial incentives. The larger the individual incentive the greater the impact of the promotion. The strongly promoted individual product often acts as a loss leader. A loss leader is a product intended to build trial for the product or traffic for a store. Another exception to the principle of developing broad targeted promotion incentives is when the marketer is targeting a narrow target market. In this situation, an incentive that appeals to a select group of consumers might be very appropriate. Accordingly, you should expect a more limited response.

Finally, as a counter to the above broad scope incentive parameter, the *cost of the incentive* must also be considered in conjunction with the promotion budget parameter. A half-price sale or a free premium would certainly be broad and appeal to a large cross section of consumers, but the cost in terms of reduced margins must also be considered and weighed against the anticipated increase in sales generated from the promotion. The key is to develop promotion rewards that are perceived to have high value by the consumer but do not cause major erosion to the margins, thus ensuring profitability.

The end result is that the promotion incentive must achieve the promotion objective. If the promotion objective is to increase purchases among existing customers nationally by 20 percent over the first quarter with a positive contribution to profits, then the promotion can't just generate additional purchases; it must do so profitably. The incentive must be enough to generate additional purchases, yet it cannot be too costly or the promotion will not be profitable. However, if the promotion objective is to increase new trial nationally by 20 percent among the target market with a budget of $500,000, then the strategy doesn't need to address a profit constraint, only a budget parameter. This promotion objective might be used by a company concerned with generating new trial as an investment for future profits. Yet in this example, the budget constraint makes certain that a realistic investment is made and that the promotion is developed in a fiscally responsible manner.

Closed versus Open Promotions

A promotion can be open or closed. There are also degrees between these two extremes. An *open promotion* is one where the company offers an added incentive to purchase with no specific behavior required to take advantage of the offer. A good example of this would be a 20 percent off sale at the retail level. In order to take advantage of this incentive or offer, consumers merely have to shop at the store. Anyone can participate, with no restrictions.

Open promotions have the ability to generate maximum participation. Our experience shows us that any restriction will reduce the consumer's interest, propensity to respond, and ultimately the effectiveness of the promotion. In retail the sales results between an open sale (one where 20 percent off is advertised with no restrictions) and a closed sale (one where consumers are required to bring a coupon to receive 20 percent off) is substantial. However, because of the increased potential participation, open promotions are more costly, since consumers who were going to purchase at regular price will also receive the discount. But remember, greater promotional cost doesn't necessarily mean less profit; greater sales can make up for a loss in margin. We ran a promotion for a client that reduced overall margin by six points, but added $500,000 to the bottom line. An open promotion also means greater trial and potentially more repeat purchases in the future.

With a *closed promotion*, an added incentive to purchase is offered to consumers, but they are required to do something in order to take advantage of the offer. An example would be a coupon that must be redeemed at purchase or a refund that requires ten proof-of-purchase validations.

There are degrees to the extent that a promotion is open or closed. Consider the example of instant coupons: the requirement of the individual consumer, beyond simply shopping, is very minimal. The customer has to tear a coupon off the package and present it at the checkout counter. However, a promotion such as a refund requiring multiple proofs-of-purchase may prove to be very restrictive. This type of promotion requires a great deal of purchase commitment on the part of the consumer before the incentive is received.

Closed promotions are used when the marketer wants to target a specific target market group or limit the cost of the promotion. When Chalet Ski entered the Twin Cities market, it staged a grand opening promotion offering a free pair of ski goggles to shoppers who redeemed a coupon at either one of their two new stores. The ski shop wanted to limit the cost of the promotion, and it wanted to make sure that the people who visited the shops and received the goggles were skiers who would be potential future customers. The promotion was delivered via direct mail coupon to a targeted list of skiers in the Twin Cities area. The closed promotion allowed Chalet Ski to achieve its objective of developing trial of the two new ski shops among existing skiers.

Delivery Method

Promotions can be delivered by three basic methods or combination thereof:

- *Media*—there are multiple forms of media delivered promotions. Direct mail, magazines, and newspapers are the most common media delivery methods for package goods and business-to-business firms, while television, newspaper, direct mail, and radio are the most common media delivery methods for retail firms.
- *On, in, or near package*—for manufacturers, promotions can be delivered on the

package itself, in the package, or near the package via a point-of-purchase display. For retailers, the promotions can be delivered in-store through signage and point-of-purchase displays.

■ *Salespeople*—many companies, especially manufacturers, such as package good or business-to-business firms that sell to intermediate markets, use salespeople to deliver a promotional offer. If the target market is not a major consumer group but a more limited purchasing group, direct personal communication of an offer can be efficient and very effective.

HOW TO DEVELOP PROMOTION STRATEGIES AND PROGRAMS

Now comes the fun part, the process of actually establishing promotion strategies is fairly simple and allows for a great deal of creative flexibility.

Step 1
Review Your Promotion Objective(s)

Review your promotion objective(s) to make certain you are focused on what you are trying to accomplish. Be particularly cognizant of who you are targeting and the measurable result that is expected.

Step 2
Review Your Problems and Opportunities

Review the listing of your problems and opportunities, as these are your knowledge base and will provide insights and ideas on what direction you should pursue in developing your promotion strategies. As you are reviewing your problems and opportunities, refer to your idea page (discussed in the Introduction of this book) where you can write down any ideas you may have. Refer to this later when you are actually formulating your strategies.

Two purchase rate/buying habit problems might be:

The average shopper is extremely brand loyal.

The Southwest consumes the product category at below average rates on a per capita basis, and your company has poor sales in this region of the country.

These two problems will affect your promotional strategies in the area of what incentive to offer. Knowing that the category is extremely brand loyal means that it will be very difficult to induce trial, so the incentive will have to be greater. And if you are going to target the Southwest, the challenge will be even greater, since it is a low consumption area where your company has poor sales.

These are examples of how your problems and opportunities will provide direction and insights concerning development of your promotion strategies. Study your problems and opportunities very carefully. They will help you in developing intelligent, databased promotion strategies.

Step 3
Finalize Your Promotion Strategies

A promotion strategy must incorporate each of the issues outlined in the section on strategy parameters:

■ Type of promotion device.
■ Promotion incentive.
■ Closed or open promotion.
■ Delivery method.

Assume the following situation:

Marketing Objective: Increase usage rates among the target market nationally over the next year by 20 percent.

Marketing Strategy: Expand alternative uses of the product from exclusively a hot drink to include acceptance as a cold served beverage.

Promotion Objective: Obtain initial trial of 100,000 *new customers* nationally for the product as a cold beverage during the months of April and May. Achieve initial trial with a budget of $2,000,000.

Note that with this situation there would probably be an alternative promotion objective aimed at stimulating trial from among the existing customer base. This objective would have separate promotion strategies and executions.

The following promotion strategies could be utilized to accomplish the promotion objective. (A worksheet is provided in Appendix C.) Each of four strategy parameters will be addressed. The cost parameter is addressed only indirectly through the choice of an incentive amount. It will be covered in more detail in Step 5.

Promotional Strategy Examples

Utilize sampling of the product in-store to soft drink purchasers.

Provide coupons to potential customers in-store worth 50 cents off the purchase price the day of the sampling.

Incorporate a trade program offering price incentives as a way to induce shelf space and merchandising support.

Step 4

Develop Alternative Promotion Program Executions

The next step is to develop alternative executions for each promotion strategy. Then choose the most appropriate execution for inclusion in your program. Multiple executions can be developed for each promotion strategy. Be creative and think of as many as you can. Some alternative promotion executions are presented in Exhibit 12.1. These alternatives were developed to meet two of the strategies of: "Utilize sampling of the product in-store," and "Provide 50 cents coupons to potential customers in-store." A worksheet to help you channel your thinking and stay consistent from one execution to another is provided in Appendix C.

Note that there is a sales objective included. Since promotions are a short-term marketing tool affecting customer behavior, there will be short-term sales results generated by the promotion. Thus it is a good idea to establish a sales goal along with the promotion objectives, strategies, and executions. Then when you analyze your promotion results, you will have two results to gauge your success against— the sales goal and the quantitative promotion objective.

Step 5

Calculate the Cost and Payback Potential of Your Promotions

Expenses must be projected for each promotion in your promotional plan. Included should be all costs associated with communicating and delivering the promotion to the target market. This includes media costs associated with delivering the promotion. (This does *not* include the media costs associated with your normal nonpromotion/ image advertising.) In addition, you must also estimate the cost of the offer or incentive. If you use 25 cent coupons, you must estimate the redemption number and multiply this by 25 cents plus handling costs to calculate a dollar cost of the coupon incentive.

Cost Calculation for Closed Promotion

In order to calculate the cost and potential payback of closed promotions, you need to accurately project participation of redemption rates for your offer.

Exhibit 12.1   Alternative Promotion Program Execution

Program Theme

"Have one on us."

Sales Objective

Develop sales of $20,000,000 over a two month period.

Promotion Objective

Obtain initial trial of 100,000 new customers nationally for the product as a cold beverage during the months of April and May. Achieve the initial trial with a budget of $2,000,000.

Promotion Strategies

Utilize sampling of the product in-store to soft drink purchasers.

Provide coupons to potential customers in-store worth 50 cents off the purchase price wherever the product is sampled.

Description

Display a giant, self serve beverage bottle with product being served hot from one side and cold from the other in grocery stores carrying the product.

Offer free samples in paper cups to all shoppers during four weeks in April and May, effectively leading the summer selling period.

Provide a 50 cents instant coupon to all consumers who sample the product.

Support

In-store signage and display.

Rationale

The promotion will build trial and exposure for the new cold drink. Serving the cold drink with the established hot drink will show customers alternative uses for the product and link the new brand to an established and accepted product. April and May were chosen as the time to sample because the time period effectively bridges cold and warm weather months.

The instant coupon will encourage immediate purchase after trial. The 50 cents incentive will be a strong inducement, and along with the sampling, will lower the risk of trying an unknown product.

Note: Alternate executions would be developed for the same objectives and strategies. You could then choose the execution that most effectively and efficiently meets the objectives.

The following will provide you with ballpark estimates for participation or redemption rates using different closed promotion vehicles. Actual participation rates should be individually adjusted as they are a function of:

> *The offer*—greater incentive, less restrictions equals greater participation.

> *The product category*—for example, health and beauty aids have average redemption rates lower than those of household products or beverages.

> *Total cost of product*—the higher the cost of the product, the less the participation.

The participation estimates shown in Exhibit 12.2 are based upon a combination of our client experience and redemption averages published by industry sources.

Exhibit 12.3 demonstrates how to calculate the cost of a promotion. A worksheet is provided in Appendix C. We used a coupon promotion as an example because it has applications to retail, package good, and business-to-business firms. Three different redemption rates were used, to provide the marketer with a range of expected responses. The cost of this promotion would be somewhere between $110,000 and $101,250 with a medium estimate of $105,000. This cost will be used along with incremental sales and profits when calculating potential payback for a closed promotion.

In addition, if you are a package good firm with coupon redemption in grocery

Exhibit 12.2   Estimated Participation and Redemption Rates

Promotion Technique	Average Redemption Range	
	Low	High
Newspaper (Run Of Paper—ROP)	0.5%	3.5%
Newspaper co-op (multiple coupons from different companies in one promotion piece)	0.8	3.4
Free standing insert (FSI)	2.5	6.0
Magazine on page	0.8	2.6
Magazine pop up	2.5	6.5
Direct mail	0.5	10.0
In product	10.0	15.0
On product	8.0	12.0
Cross-ruff or cross-pack	4.0	8.0
Selfliquidating point-of-sales premium	0.3	1.0
Refunds	0.5	3.5
Instant coupon on pack	15.0	25.0

Exhibit 12.3   Calculating Cost of a Coupon Promotion

	High	Medium	Low
Redemption Costs			
Value of coupon	50¢	50¢	50¢
Number of coupons distributed	500,000	500,000	500,000
Estimated redemption rate	4.0%	2.0%	0.5%
Number redeemed	20,000	10,000	2,500
Dollar value or offer (number redeemed × value of coupon)	$ 10,000	$ 5,000	$ 1,250
Advertising and Media Costs			
Printing of coupons (500,000 × 0.01)	$ 5,000	$ 5,000	$ 5,000
Mailing cost/envelopes (500,000 × 0.19)	$ 95,000	$ 95,000	$ 95,000
Total cost of promotion	$110,000	$105,000	$101,250

stores, there are handling charges to be included. If you are utilizing a clearinghouse, you must pay a charge for each coupon handled. Also, the grocer charges for each coupon handled. At press time of this book, the average total cost was approximately 10 to 12 cents per coupon redeemed.

Finally, the cost of the promotion must be compared to the incremental sales the promotion is expected to generate. This can be determined through a payback analysis.

Payback Analysis

Before you execute any planned promotion, you should make sure to review the numbers to determine if the promotion makes sense from a payback analysis standpoint. We recommend calculating the contribution to fixed costs,[2] as this method isolates the promotion and takes into account any incremental variable cost associated

---

[2]This method is commonly used by retailers, service firms, and manufacturers. However, manufacturers also utilize a gross margin to net sales method that is detailed in Chapter 17, Marketing Budget, Payback Analysis, and Marketing Calendar.

with the promotion. In using this method, incremental costs of the promotion (communication of the promotion and incentive costs) are subtracted from incremental sales generated from the promotion.

Exhibit 12.4 presents an example for a retailer considering a 20 percent off sale as an open promotion. A worksheet is provided in Appendix C. The retailer had experience with similar sales in the past and had a rough estimate on the incremental sales which could be generated by the promotional offer. This method looks at incremental sales and costs to calculate what the promotion will generate in terms of a contribution to fixed overhead. The incremental margin sales are sales above and beyond what would normally be expected for the time period. In this case, the retailer had a good idea of what to expect. If you haven't run the promotion before, make a high, medium, and low estimate based upon similar promotions in the past. This provides best, most likely, and worst case estimates.

Note that the *cost of the promotion* (reduction in gross margin dollars) was calculated directly into the projected incremental sales figure. In some cases you may want to break this step out to show what the promotion costs were, particularly if you are a package goods marketer and you wish to show redemption projections.

Remember, the promotion must stand on its own. The only way to determine its potential success or failure is to weigh the projected incremental sales against the expected incremental expenses of the promotion. If the promotion contributes a meaningful positive dollar figure to fixed overhead (expenses that occur no matter what happens—e.g., rent) and meets the promotion sales goals, then the promotion should be executed. If the payback analysis shows that there is a negative contribution to fixed overhead, then you should consider another promotion, or rework the promotion with less incentive or a different product mix. The exception to this is if there is no budget parameter specifying that the promotion must contribute to

Exhibit 12.4   Payback Calculation Example for Open Promotion

Situation
Promotion: 20 percent off women's department merchandise.
Estimated storewide margin decrease from 50 percent to 45 percent during promotion.
Time period: First three weeks of March.
Geography: All three stores in Madison, WI.

Sales

Estimated sales for period without promotion	$300,000
Estimated gross margin dollars for period without promotion ($300,00 × .50)	150,000
Estimated sales with promotion	360,000
Estimated gross margin dollars with promotion ($360,000 × .45)	162,000
Estimated net margin dollar increase with promotion ($162,000 − $150,000)	12,000

Media and Advertisting Cost

Estimated ongoing advertising and media costs with or without promotion*	15,000
Total advertising and media costs with promotion	20,000
Incremental advertising and media costs due to promotion	5,000

Payout

Incremental margin sales	12,000
Incremental advertising and media expenditures	5,000
Contribution to fixed overhead	7,000

*What would have been spent in regular mainline advertising and media.

profits. If the firm is simply trying to gain trial, which it feels will translate into future profits, then the major constraints will be the budget parameter and the amount of desired trial.

Step 6

Select the Most Appropriate Promotion Executions

You have developed promotion objectives and strategies, created promotion execution alternatives, and analyzed costs and paybacks for each execution. Now it is time to select those executions that will best achieve the promotion objectives within the budget constraints established. When choosing your promotion executions, try to make sure the executions complement each other and work together through the year. Two premium offers back-to-back would probably be ineffective compared to other combinations of promotions. The best method to determine if your promotions properly interface with each other is to list the promotions in calendar form according to when they will be executed. This will allow you to make judgments on whether you have selected promotions that complement each other. It will also be useful when you are transferring your marketing tool executions to one master calendar as is detailed in Chapter 17, Marketing Budget, Payback Analysis, and Marketing Calendar.

HOW TO DEVELOP A LONG-TERM PROMOTION PROGRAM

Promotion plans should be developed from the standpoint that achieving promotion objectives are not the end result, but rather the means to implementing marketing strategies and helping to fulfill marketing objectives. With this in mind, promotions can be successfully integrated into a year-long marketing plan. They can serve as *intermediate tools* or means of achieving specific requirements necessary to achieve longer-term goals.

One method of incorporating promotions into a long-term plan is through a trial-to-loyalty promotion program. This is a method through which a marketer can take the consumer through successive steps from trial to repeat buying by using a disciplined promotional program. With each step the consumer is asked to perform a stronger behavior and is given less reinforcement to purchase the product, until finally purchase is at full price and the consumer is a brand loyal, long-term customer.

The trial-to-loyalty promtion program[3] occurs by using primary reinforcers to stimulate initial trial and secondary reinforcers to encourage repeat purchase. The primary reinforcers provide strong promotional incentives while the secondary reinforcers have weaker incentive properties—the reason being that in order to attract new customers, there is usually a need for greater incentive to initiate trial. However, once the consumer has tried the product, each successive trial should be more and more due to the product's attributes rather than the incentive, until finally the consumer purchases at full price because of the product's attributes.

Thus, there is need to educate the consumer during the initial trial stages on why the product is superior or is consistent with the image the consumer wants to portray. Education is achieved within the promotion communication. A package good could develop the following promotional schedule to achieve a trial-to-loyalty promotion program.

---

[3]This program is similar in theory to the one discussed by one of our partners Michael L. Rothschild in his text *Advertising: From Fundamentals to Strategies*, D.C. Heath and Company, 1987.

Step 1 **Trial Stage**	Utilize the primary reinforcer of a free sample of the product. A sample of the product is delivered either by mail or in-store to the target market. Included in the package is a half-price coupon good for the next purchase. In doing this, trial is encouraged with no commitment from the consumer. Repeat purchase is encouraged; however, there is a large inducement so the consumer does not have to fully commit to purchase but is essentially subsidized by the company.

Step 2
Brand Conscious Stage

Phase 1

Utilize the secondary reinforcer of proof-of-purchase premiums or refunds. Have the company promote continuity of purchase through a proof-of-purchase premium or refund incentive. The consumer is asked to purchase three packages at full price prior to receiving a reinforcer in the form of a refund or premium. During this sequence, the consumer has actually purchased the product at full price for its inherent value with the promise of a future reward.

Phase 2

Utilize a sweepstakes to communicate the product's attributes and benefits. The sweepstakes would offer a prize consistent with the product's positioning. Entry would be qualified by having the entrant answer questions about the product that can be found on the product's packaging. This makes each entrant pick up the package, think about the product's name, and answer questions about the product's benefits. A soft-drink product might have a line under the product name that says, "It's the fruit juice that counts." A question on the sweepstakes entry card might read, "What counts most in a soft drink?" One of the answers would be, "It's the fruit juice that counts." Correctly answering the questions would qualify entrants for a drawing to determine the winner. Ideally, the sweepstakes display would be in-store next to the soft drink display, providing point-of-purchase identification for the soft drink.

Step 3
Loyalty Stage

Purchase at full price. During this phase the product would be sold through just advertising and/or only P.O.P. merchandising.

DOS AND DON'TS

Dos

- Utilize promotions to encourage *incremental* target market behavior.
- Make sure promotions are measurable.
- Utilize specific promotions for short-term durations.
- While promotions are effective in increasing sales in the short-term, remember that they also can have long-term attitudinal and behavior consequences.
- Try to utilize promotions that are consistent with and will enhance your positioning.
- Plan your promotions so they complement the use of the other marketing mix tools. (An example of this would be national image advertising complemented with co-op in ad features of the product and point-of-sale displays in the stores. All advertising would also incorporate the same basic selling theme and tone.)
- Make sure you determine the cost and the potential payback of your promotions before implementing them.
- Evaluate the success or failure of each promotion to help in developing stronger promotions in the future.

- Promotion can be a very powerful but expensive marketing tool. Plan and evaluate carefully.
- Whenever possible, test new promotions before making a major investment and using them on a broader scale.
- Use incentives that appeal to your target market and that are realistic for a vast majority of the target market to obtain. A sweepstake will not pull as strongly as a percent off coupon because the reward is not as obtainable. Only a few lucky people win the sweepstakes where everyone is eligible for the coupon.
- To have a successful promotion, remember that you need broad target market appeal, a strong promotion incentive, high promotion awareness, and minimum restrictions for participation.

Don'ts

- Don't expect promotions to solve long-term sales declines or create a loyal consumer franchise among those who purchase the product for its inherent benefits—leave that to such other marketing tools, as packaging, product improvements, and image advertising.
- Don't rely on only a few promotional devices. Consider all the promotional tools available to you but only use those that are appropriate to your product.
- Don't overuse or develop a dependance on promotions. This may cause an erosion of value and image.
- Don't schedule promotions without reviewing the whole marketing and promotion schedule. Very similar promotions, such as two "20 percent off" promotions in a row, will diminish the success of the second promotion.
- Don't run promotions just because you ran them last year. Think strategically.
- Don't give deals unless you can document that it builds the business.
- A promotion should not replace other tools of the marketing mix, use this marketing tool for its inherent strengths.

APPENDIX OF
PROMOTION
VEHICLES

Definition of Promotional Vehicles

Couponing	A type of promotion involving the distribution of a coupon which has a value upon redemption.
Newspaper ROP (run of press)	A method for delivering promotion incentives, ROP involves the printing of an incentive in the newspaper, usually in an ad, on regular newsprint, with no special paper or inserts.
Magazines and supplements	A method for delivering promotion incentives, most commonly coupons, printed on the page as part of an ad. Two variations are the pop-up coupon, printed on separate card stock and inserted into the magazine's binding, and tip-on coupons, which are glued to supplement inserts.
Cross-ruff coupons	An execution method for couponing, this involves taking the consumer from one product, store, or department carrying the coupon to a different product, store, or department for which the coupon is redeemable.
Sampling	A type of promotion that involves the free trial of a product.
Premiums	A type of promotion involving a product (gift) of perceived value which is given away, or made available, with the purchase of the product.
Selfliquidating premiums	An execution method for premiums, where the customer is required to cover the cost of the premium via payment.
Proof-of-purchase	An execution method for premiums, where the premium is sent to the customer in return for proof of one or more purchases.
Sale priced reduction or cents off label	A method for executing the price reduction promotion; it can be in the form of advertised sales prices, prepriced goods, labels on the product that flag the price reduction, or price packs, which are specially priced make ups of different size than the regular package.
Free standing insert (FSI)	An insert with coupons or other promotional offers that are loosely inserted in a carrier such as the newspaper. Co-op FSI's carry mutiple coupons for different product categories.
Instant coupon	A method of coupon delivery where the coupon is attached to the outside of the package. The consumer can pull it off in-store and utilize it during purchase.
Bonus pack	A method for executing the price reduction promotion. It involves providing bonus product for the price or close to the price of the original product.
Refunds	A type of promotion offering money back after the purchase and usually requiring some proof of purchase.
On pack/in pack	A method of promotion delivery where the offer is either flagged on the package or included in the package.
Stamps	Stamps may be redeemed for some item of value once specific levels have been accumulated.
Contests and sweepstakes	Games and events where customers participate for the chance of winning a prize.

Evaluation of Promotional Vehicles

Promotion	Objectives	Execution/ Delivery Methods	Advantages	Disadvantages
Couponing	Stimulate trial	Sales force	1 Allows pinpoint targeting of customers 2 Creates a value added sales call	1 Very high delivery costs per coupon 2 Distribution of coupons limited
	Increase frequency of purchase	Direct mail	1 Higher redemption rates 2 Permits selective customer targeting	1 High delivery costs per coupon
	Increase multiple purchase	Newspaper ROP	1 Low delivery cost per coupon 2 Permits limited geographic distribution 3 Offers flexibility in timing, size, and layout of coupon ad	1 Lower redemption rates 2 Clutter and competitive advertising 3 High potential for misredemptions
		Magazines and supplements	1 Low delivery cost per coupon 2 Permits mass distribution to segmented audience 3 Allows some geographic selectivity through regional editions of national magazines 4 Allows high quality reproductions for creative appeal	1 Loss of flexibility in timing due to long lead times for insertion 2 Lower redemption rates relative to other vehicles
		Free standing inserts (FSI)	1 Higher redemption rates than ROP coupons 2 Lower delivery cost per coupon than direct mail 3 Permits limited geographic mass distribution 4 Permits more creativity than with ROP	1 High potential for misredemptions 2 Needs longer lead time to print and insert than with ROP
		In package/on package coupons	1 Draws attention to package at P-O-P 2 Higher redemption rates 3 Lower delivery cost per coupon 4 Effective stimulant of repeat purchase	1 Limited stimulus for trial by new category users 2 Customer may seek simultaneous redemption of coupon on package and previously distributed coupon 3 Distribution limited to users of the product category
		Cross-ruff coupons	1 The product the coupon is promoting receives implied endorsement from brand carrying coupon 2 Package with coupon perceived as value added 3 Can obtain trial of promoted brand by new users with demographics similar to carrier brand 4 Strong selling brand can cross-sell for weaker selling brand 5 High redemption rate if promoted brand has natural relationship to carrier brand 6 Low delivery cost of coupon	1 Effectiveness of coupon is a function of the effectiveness of carrier product 2 Limited distribution and target market reach
		Instant coupon	1 Very high redemption rate 2 Very low distribution cost per coupon	1 More likely to appeal to current users rather than creating new trial 2 High gross redemption rates
Sampling	Develop initial trial of new products	In pack or on pack	1 Low distribution costs 2 Sample receives implied endorsement of carrier brand 3 Pack with sample increases trial of carrier brand 4 Selective distribution of pack with sample permits testing of sample's promotional effectiveness	1 Distribution limited to buyers of carrier brand 2 Trade may reject package if unusual size creates special handling requirements 3 Expensive because of cost of the sample and delivery of product

continued

Evaluation of Promotional Vehicles—*continued*

Promotion	Objectives	Execution/ Delivery Methods	Advantages	Disadvantages
Sampling *continued*		Direct mail	1 Selective customer permits a variety of creative and product presentations 2 Delivery may be timed to tie in with other promotions and advertising 3 May create consumer interest forcing the trade to carry the product 4 Permits mass distribution	1 Some product's size, weight, or fragility prevents mailing 2 High delivery costs per sample 3 Any wasted coverage due to inaccuracies in mailing list is very expensive 4 High cost of sample
Premiums	Provide added value to the purchase of your product thus increasing trial Create impulse trial	Self-liquidating premiums	1 Potential value added to product at minimum cost to the marketer 2 Premiums of value often get trade display 3 Image of brand may be enhanced through association with quality premium or premium consistent with brand's positioning 4 Repeat purchases can be increased by requiring multiple purchases for premium eligibility 5 Permits geographic and creative flexibility	1 Typically unused premiums cannot be returned forcing testing of consumer response rates. Even then an unpopular premium may result in an inventory of costly and unwanted premiums 2 Stimulates sales less than free premiums because consumer must make cash outlay
	Develop continuity of purchases and multiple purchases	In pack or on pack	1 May force increased shelf space and merchandising support from the trade 2 Provides added value to the consumer 3 Premiums can be targeted to specific consumer segments 4 Promotes trial and repeat purchase 5 Permits geographic selectivity	1 Premium should be tested to accurately predict consumer response 2 Physical size of premium may cause trade to refuse to handle product due to space limitations 3 Poor quality or inappropriate premium may detract from brand's image
		Proof-of-purchase	1 Encourages multiple purchases and continuity of purchases 2 Low redemption rate permits use of higher value premium 3 Consumer can be encouraged to trade up to larger size or more expensive item	1 Lack of immediate reinforcement reduces consumer interest 2 Impulse sales weaker than with instant premium 3 Supporting advertising often needed to promote longer-term purchasing commitment
Price reductions	Stimulate incremental purchase/trial Influence purchase decision/increase purchase ratio at P-O-P Increase purchases per transaction Increase dollar amount per transaction	Sale price reduction	1 Greater profits may result if expected increase in sales exceeds effects from margin decrease 2 Can counter competitors' activities encouraging repeat purchases by current users	1 Continued price reductions can erode brand image over time 2 Potential for price wars 3 Too frequent price reductions makes reduced price the expected norm and consumers won't purchase at full price
		Cents off label	1 Increased attention from flagging of package can influence purchase decisions at P-O-P 2 Increased trade support results from anticipated increase in product demand 3 Sales force provided with opportunity to increase sales to the trade	1 Some stores will not accept flagged prepriced packaging
		Bonus pack	1 Increases perceived value at a P-O-P 2 Stocking up takes customers out of market for competitors' products and habituates them to using your product	1 Potential trade resistance to larger pack without profit incentives 2 Customers may feel cheated when package returns to original size

Evaluation of Promotional Vehicles

Promotion	Objectives	Execution/ Delivery Methods	Advantages	Disadvantages
Refunds	Develop trial and continuity of purchase Encourage multiple purchases (where multiple proof of purchase required)	Same methods as for couponing	1 High perceived value by consumers 2 Relatively low cost promotion because large percentage of nonredemption 3 Can extend buying period of seasonal products with multiple purchase requirement 4 Flagging package with refund offer increases P-O-P and impulse sales 5 Multiple purchase requirement limits number of successful redemptions	1 Lack of immediate gratification reduces incentive to buy 2 Tends to reward current users rather than creating new trial
Repeat purchase offers	Develop repeat and continuity of purchases Increase purchases per transaction Encourage seasonal purchases Reduce competitive purchases	Refund program On pack or in pack premium program Stamps	1 Continuity programs help to create brand loyalty and establish consumer purchasing habits 2 Repeat purchase requirement often creates multiple purchases temporarily taking the consumer out of the market for the product class. This reduces chances of success for competitors' programs	1 Requires consumers to make a long-term commitment to the product 2 Thrust of repeat purchase program is maintaining current users not developing new trial
Contests, games, and sweepstakes	Develop multiple purchases Enhance brand image and develop attention through excitement of contest	Product in store, P-O-P media	1 Contest can be built around inherent drama of the product and communicate specific product attributes 2 Contests can be directed to specific target audiences 3 Contests' excitement can help generate trade support and P-O-P displays	1 Impact is limited since there is no guarantee of reward. Participation is less than that of price incentives, bonus packs, and other instant gratification promotions 2 Contests target current users more than they develop new trial 3 There are many legal issues which must be considered before execution
Trade promotions	Increase trial by new customers Create multiple purchases Increase distribution Increase shelf space Obtain P-O-P merchandising support Introduce new or improved products to the trade	Price reductions or incentives Refunds Contest aimed at the trade P-O-P displays	1 Promotions to the trade help insure the product's availability for consumers and results in favorable merchandising 2 Limited target market for promotion makes it easier to implement 3 Promotion easily tailored to meet specific needs	1 Trade can come to expect deals 2 Can take away funds from consumer advertising and promotions so that even if the trade stocks the product the ability to generate consumer demand is diminished

13

ADVERTISING
MESSAGE

N ow that you have decided how to market, position, price, distribute, sell, and promote your product, you are ready to write the advertising section of your marketing plan. This is another key learning chapter because it deals with the translation of marketing into advertising, which is usually the most visible communication to your external and internal targets. While developing the advertising message portion of your plan requires strategic and innovative thinking, the most fun will come when you and/or your agency actually get into developing the advertising executions. Because this is a how to for marketing plan preparation, this chapter will *not* review how to develop the advertising executions.

From This Chapter You Will Learn

The definition of advertising.

The difference between advertising and the other communication elements of the marketing mix.

The role of advertising to help make the sale.

How to use a disciplined process that will lead to creative advertising that sells.

How to arrive at and write advertising objectives.

How to develop an advertising strategy that will be a catalyst for attention getting advertising that clearly communicates and sells.

Executional elements to consider before preparing the actual advertising.

How to select an advertising agency that will best execute the advertising program and your marketing plan.

OVERVIEW

Definition

Before discussing how the communication elements are factored into a marketing plan, it is necessary to understand the differences between these communication elements. It is a common error to bunch advertising, public relations or publicity, promotion, and merchandising together as one and the same. In fact, all these forms of communication are very different from each other in terms of what they are capable of doing and what role they each play in the marketing plan. For this marketing plan discussion, we will define advertising as that which informs and persuades through *paid* media (television, radio, magazine, newspaper, outdoor, and direct mail).

Advertising versus Other Forms of Communication

In order to prepare an effective marketing plan, it is important that you do not confuse advertising with other communication tools in the marketing mix.

While advertising informs and communicates through paid media, *publicity*, though it informs and can affect attitude, is not paid. Its messages sometimes reach the target market through personal contact and presentations, but primarily through the news and editorial departments of the various media. These news departments have control over the information you give them. The news media, acting as a gatekeeper, constricts and conforms the communication it receives and then disseminates. While advertising is considerably more costly, it most often is much more effective, because you as the advertiser have total control over what is communicated and when and how often it is communicated.

While advertising is informational and image oriented, *promotion* is a marketing tool used to provide extra value to the product and/or added incentive (cents-off coupons, free goods, etc.) directly to the ultimate user of the product or to various links throughout the distribution channel, such as distributors and retailers.

While product promotion can be implemented with or without media support, *merchandising* (sales brochures, audiovisual presentations, product displays) is a pure nonmedia tool. It is used specifically to sell the idea of the product concept or the promotion, as well as reinforce the advertising.

Now that you have an understanding of what advertising is and is not, this chapter will discuss how to provide the direction for the advertising message for both consumer advertising and business-to-business advertising. In most cases the major strategic differences between the two types of advertising occur not in the message but in terms of medium used to deliver the message. In this book, advertising will refer to the message and media will refer to how it is delivered.

HOW ADVERTISING HELPS TO SELL

Build Awareness

At the minimum, in order to help sell the product, advertising must first attract attention, building awareness for your product. If your target market is not aware of what you're selling, they cannot buy it. It has been proven over and over again that the reason many quality products don't become sales successes is because the majority of the target market is virtually unaware of their existence. Accordingly, you must build unaided awareness for your product. The higher the percentage of the target market that can remember your product on their own while in the purchasing mode, the greater the chance of selling your product. Stated very simply, yet so important, *you must increase share of mind before you can increase share of market*.

Positively Affect Attitudes

While just having awareness will help sell some product, in most cases the target market must also have a positive attitude toward what you are selling, particularly beyond what is being marketed by the competition. Further, as we discussed in Chapter 7, Positioning , you want the target market to think most positively about your product regarding those attributes they consider most important.

Initiate Behavior

With unaided awareness and a positive attitude toward your product, the final step is to move the target to action and buy your product. Sometimes advertising alone can accomplish this important task—through direct response advertising. Direct mail is a good example of this. However, in the majority of situations, advertising cannot make the sale unless the product is on the shelf, there is a conveniently located store to visit, the wholesaler carries your product line, and/or a sales call is made to detail the product and close the sale. Because advertising usually cannot alone initiate behavior the behavior element should be included as a marketing objective previously presented in the plan.

What Is Expected of Your Advertising?

Before you begin developing the advertising section of your marketing plan, you must decide what your advertising can realistically accomplish. For your product, advertising can build recognition, help create a positive image, and differentiate it from the competition. Advertising can also build store traffic, assist in introducing new products and line extensions, feature products improvements, and announce promotions. Specifically, in the business-to-business category, advertising can also generate customer leads ("please send me more information"), and open doors for the sales force. You must make sure you know what you expect advertising to accomplish for your product.

THE DISCIPLINED PROCESS FOR ADVERTISING

Because of its tremendous attention getting power and inherent creativity, advertising is continually on stage for everyone to critique. Accordingly, nearly everyone thinks they are experts on advertising because it is a marketing tool that has much subjectivity associated with it. Therefore, it stands to reason that the more subjective it is as a marketing tool, the more necessary it is to use a disciplined process to arrive at advertising that sells. This is basically a 1-2-3 process:

- Define your advertising objectives.
- Write your advertising strategy.
- Detail what will go into the execution.

No doubt by now you have come up with a number of advertising ideas. However, before going ahead and actually executing your creative ideas, go through this disciplined process. Using this disciplined approach will assure that the final advertising will be effective, or at least more effective than if you had gone with the first ad idea that came to mind. Also, it should be pointed out that given the choice between nonmarketing based advertising and advertising based on sound marketing, the latter will win most often. It will win because it is databased and relates to the real marketplace communicating to the right target market the meaningful product attributes. Accordingly, great advertising is usually based on great marketing.

Further, bear in mind that your market positioning is the key to effective advertising. It is in essence the bridge from the more objective marketing to the more subjective advertising.

Step 1

Advertising Objectives

Advertising Awareness and Attitude Objectives

Advertising objectives deal with what you want your advertising to accomplish. The objectives are quantifiable while the advertising strategy is not. The strategy deals primarily with describing the necessary message communication to fulfill the advertising objectives. Your advertising objectives nearly always will define awareness and attitude goals as they relate to the target market.

Exhibit 13.1   How to Write Advertising Objectives

Awareness Objectives

Increase unaided awareness among the target market from 18 percent to 25 percent.

Establish among the target market an unaided awareness percentage twice that of the product's current share of market.

Attitudinal Objectives

Move the product *quality* attitude ranking among the target market from fourth to third place.

Establish a leadership image with 25 percent of the target market.

Before you begin, check that you did *not* include advertising objectives in your marketing objectives and strategies section. The tendency is to deal with such communication issues as recall and understanding under marketing, but they belong under advertising.

Measurable Advertising Objectives

When setting the advertising objectives, remember to make them measurable. Even if you are not planning or cannot afford to implement a research program to measure the effectiveness of the advertising, setting measurable advertising objectives will force you to objectively evaluate the advertising challenge. Further, if your time period to achieve the advertising objectives differs from the time period set for the marketing objectives, indicate the time period with the advertising objectives.

Exhibit 13.1 presents some examples of how to define your advertising objectives. It is easier to set your advertising objectives if you have primary research. However, in many cases you will not have done market research that establishes a benchmark from which to measure awareness and attitude changes. Nevertheless, it is a good learning process to estimate (even if you can only make educated guesses) what percent of unaided awareness is necessary to affect a predisposed attitude to buy that then translates to a specific percent of the target market that will purchase stated as a marketing objective. For example:

	Percent	Number
Total target market	100%	100,000
Unaided awareness	40	40,000
Probably/definitely will purchase	10	10,000
Purchasers	5	5,000

You should also include a rationale for the advertising awareness and attitude objectives based on available awareness and attitude research. With or without this type of research, your rationale should include a discussion of the competitive share of market, and the strength of your communications program versus that of the competition's past and anticipated marketing activity, particularly their advertising program.

Step 2
Advertising Strategy

The advertising strategy, also referred to as the creative strategy, is the catalyst of effective advertising. It provides direction on what should be communicated in the advertising message and how it should be communicated. It is a big part of the *means* that gets the desired product perception into the mind of the consumer. This strategy is the guide for development of creative and communicative advertising; the goals are to gain attention, be remembered, positively affect attitudes, and help move the target market to purchase your product. It becomes a guide for those (possibly yourself) who will actually create the advertising. Further, the advertising strategy describes the personality of the advertising and the parameters of the creative environment in which the advertising must perform. Without this guide, the final advertising could very well be exceptionally entertaining but not necessarily effective. Although we may like the advertising, it might not communicate the benefits of your product that will fulfill the needs and wants of the specified target market.

The advertising strategy is not only a guide for creative development, but is also the basis against which creative work is evaluated to make sure that advertising communicates effectively. Usually you want to develop alternative creative approaches against the agreed upon advertising strategy and then judge the best approach to execute the strategy. Also, if you are having an advertising agency execute the creative, both the client and the agency should have input into and mutually agree to the written strategy before it is executed. This strategy agreement is necessary so that when the advertising work is presented, there is no confusion or disagreement in terms of the description of the product, specific benefits, claims made, and feeling of the advertising. Further, having an agreed upon strategy up front will save time in creative development and help eliminate frustration for all involved.

The advertising strategy should include:

- *Key Target Market Identifier:* Insert the key purchaser/user description; however, make sure whoever develops the creative execution has reviewed your total target market description so they thoroughly understand for whom they are creating the advertising.
- *Promise:* Define the reward/benefit for the target market in solving a problem or taking advantage of an opportunity.
- *Support for This Promise:* Give substantiation for the promise or reasons to believe.
- *Tone:* Describe the feeling of the planned advertising that is consistent with the personality of the product. The tone must be appropriate not only for your product, but also for the target market of the advertising.

Look to your positioning statement for direction in writing the advertising strategy, because it will be the key in developing an advertising strategy to differentiate your product from the competition. Make sure your advertising strategy speaks directly to conveying the image you want to instill in the minds of the target market.

Don't expect to complete an advertising strategy on the first attempt. Plan to rewrite each segment of the advertising strategy a number of times until you arrive at a strategy that clearly states what you want your final advertising to communicate. Each word in your advertising strategy is critical; therefore, make sure it communicates the intended meaning. However, do not expect to see a *lift* of the strategy wording in the finished advertising. Keep the strategy simple for clarity and single minded for focus. Make sure your strategy conveys the inherent personality of your product that can come alive in your advertising.

The advertising strategy that has been reworked and included in your marketing plan should be the strategy that reflects the positioning and provides the *overall direction* for a *unified advertising campaign*. However, it might be that your marketing plan calls for additional but separate advertising strategies, such as for specific products within a company line. An advertising strategy for Green Giant Corn would be a modification of the overall campaign strategy for Green Giant Canned Vegetables. Or you may need separate strategies for special geographic and demographic markets, promotions, or trade advertising.

Although it is likely you will need substrategies, it is important that your overall advertising strategy is written to be a *campaign strategy to guide all your adver-*

Exhibit 13.2   How to Write Advertising Strategies

Promise

Convince the married woman 18 to 34 that General Hospital is the special place to give birth to her
    child because it is the only *hospital* that provides *both* the best personal and professional care for
    baby *and* mother.

Support for This Promise

Mothers have rated General Hospital's OB Department the best in providing personal care when
    having a baby, and it has been officially designated as the area's referral hospital for high risk
    expectant mothers and newborn babies.

Tone of the Advertising

The tone of the advertising will be preemptive and professional, but personal, conveying a warm and
    enduring feeling consistent with individual care and safety provided to baby and mother.

Rationale

Expectant women are most concerned about personal care and safety for their babies and themselves.
Competitors have not placed major emphasis on these two very important attributes.

---

tising—consumer and/or business-to-business as well as promotional and institutional, and subset geographic or demographic targets. Your primary strategy
should lead to an advertising campaign in which all the individual advertisements
contintually reinforce your positioning. This is very important, because an
advertising campaign will create a unified image and will provide a consistency
for all your creative executions. Obviously there are always exceptions to this, particularly if you are marketing very different products to very different target
markets.

An effective selling, strategic advertising campaign will incorporate similarities.
The advertising within a campaign should include as many common properties as
possible, such as a similar look, sound, and/or feel/tonality that conveys a consistent
personality. Further, in most cases, each advertisement will include a unified basic
selling idea (theme line) such as "Fly the Friendly Skies" or "Marlboro Country."

The rewards of developing a campaign are many. It will become cumulative in
scope, with each advertisement reinforcing the others for a multiple effect, making
your advertising work harder and maximizing your advertising investment.

Remember, before moving on to execution, include a brief rationale for the advertising objectives and advertising strategy(ies), defining why the objectives are
attainable and the strategies are appropriate. The rationale should include specific
reasons for what is included in the strategy.

Exhibit 13.2 presents an example of an advertising strategy for a hospital marketing
its obstetrics department.

Step 3

Consideration of Executional Elements

The execution portion of your advertising section outlines those specifics that must
be included in the advertising.

Most often the execution segment of the advertising section is not included in
the marketing plan but is detailed in what is sometimes referred to as an advertising
implementation plan. This plan includes all the information necessary for those
responsible to create the advertising. An example of an implementation plan format
is provided in Appendix C.

Under execution, you might want to include additional copy or product information that is important to know, but, in order to maintain strategic focus, is not
included in the advertising strategy. This additional product information will provide

**Exhibit 13.3   How to Write the Advertising Executional
Considerations (If no separate advertising
implementation plan is prepared)**

Additional/Key Strategy Information
More babies have been delivered at General Hospital than any other hospital in the area.
General Hospital has the most experienced physician and nursing staff.

Specific Legal Considerations
Include title of research study as disclaimer in the advertising as support for superiority claim

Advertising Requirements
Include advertising theme "We care . . . A lot" in all advertising.
List both site locations in all advertising.

for creative enhancement and increased understanding when developing the actual
advertising.

Another executional consideration is the legality of the advertising. Make sure
everything you include in the advertising is truthful and can be documented. In this
section or in a separate implementation plan, list any legal restrictions/considerations
you are aware of for your product, the target market, and the geographic area that
will receive the advertising.

Many times in advertising, you are walking a fine line between what is legally
acceptable and what is not. You should have written support for any specific claims
made in the advertising. With this support in mind, make sure your advertising
execution is truthful and legal yet fully exploits the advantages of your product.

Along with legal considerations (if not included in a separate implementation plan),
list any advertising requirements. For example:

- How the company and product name/logo must be used in the advertising.
- How the theme line must be used in all advertising.
- Product line/store locations to be included.
- Preproduction copy test requirements, production cost parameters, ad size, etc.

Exhibit 13.3 presents an example of items in the advertising execution section.
Formats to use for preparing the advertising message and for implementing the
advertising plan are provided in Appendix C.

Helpful Hint

With this creative section written, you are halfway to achieving creative advertising
that will motivate. This book's aim is to show how to write a marketing plan, not
how to create advertising, therefore you may want to refer to a number of how to
advertise books. These books are available in your local library or nearby book store
and are useful even if you do retain an advertising agency.

HOW TO SELECT AN ADVERTISING AGENCY

Once you have completed your marketing plan, you might find you need additional
expertise to help in the execution of the advertising and other elements of the
marketing plan. If this is the case, here are some things to keep in mind when
selecting an advertising agency.

Screening Process

1. Do not select an advertising agency before comparing a number of different agencies.

2. In order to arrive at a number of different agencies to evaluate you can:
   - Solicit agency referrals from fellow business associates.
   - Review advertising in various media and ask the management of the particular media vehicle (magazine, newspaper, station, etc.) for the name of the agency that placed the specific advertisement(s) that impressed you. Also, ask the media management for their agency recommendations.
   - Check out the *Standard Director of Advertising Agencies* (referred to as the Red Book). It is most likely available in your local library and lists agencies by geographic areas along with each agency's clients, size, and key personnel.

3. Once you have arrived at a number of agencies to evaluate, interview them and make a selection. Or if you have a large list of agencies (five or more) to evaluate, have each agency complete a questionnaire. An advertising agency questionnaire is shown in Exhibit 13.4. After reviewing the completed questionnaires, select three or four agencies for personal presentations. Involve others in your company when reviewing the agencies, both for more perspective and consensus.

4. The agency you select should:
   - Be genuinely honest and not promise miracles.
   - Sincerely care about you and your business, working with you as a partner, not just a vendor.
   - Provide the optimum in personal attention, experience, and expertise. The agency people must have real credentials.
   - Be a leader and not a follower. You should not have to tell the agency what to do with your advertising; they should provide sound recommendations.
   - Not consistently turn over staff people and clients.
   - Be looking for a long relationship, not quick fixes.
   - Develop good advertising, but also thoroughly understand good marketing.
   - Provide a real value (good advertising at competitive rates) and can document it; not provide the cheapest rates in town.
   - Have financial strength, accurate accounting systems, and a billing program to fit your needs.
   - Have full-service capability—can provide real expertise in assisting you with your creative (including campaign development) and media needs along with assistance in marketing, promotion, merchandising, and perhaps even research.
   - Have the right ingredients to match your organization's needs in terms of size, consumer/business-to-business experience, staff personalities, and level of expertise. Is your advertising account/budget too small/big for them? There must be a match between agency ingredients and client needs in order for both to find the right chemistry for a mutually rewarding relationship.

5. It is also a good idea before making a selection decision to give the agency finalists a real product problem to solve in order to assess their strategic thinking and executing abilities.

6. Before making the final decision on an agency, actually visit their offices and check with a few of their current and past clients. It's amazing what you will learn. How many quality people does the agency really have? Do clients receive the agency's account supervisor's personal involvement? Does the agency come up with big ideas that can affordably be implemented? Does the agency pay attention to details?

Exhibit 13.4   Advertising Agency Questionnaire

Your Business Strategy
1. What are the objectives your agency, as a business enterprise, is pursuing?
2. What business strategy has your agency adopted for achieving these objectives.
3. What do you consider to be the principal product your agency sells? What is the main competitive advantage it has over that of other agencies?
4. What method do you have for controlling the quality of your agency's service (specifically in the areas of marketing counsel and creative development/execution)?

Your Marketing and Advertising Philosophy and Practice
1. What is good marketing?
2. Do you prepare marketing plans and, if so, what is your approach?
3. What makes advertising effective? Include three examples of your most effective advertising.
4. How do you measure the effectiveness of advertising?
5. What is the method you use for developing effective advertising?
6. What are your attitudes/opinions on the role of research in advertising?
7. To what extent do you feel an advertising agency should or could act as a marketing support function?
8. What consumer/business-to-business marketing successes has your agency recently contributed to in a major way? When were they? On what basis do you judge them successful? Please limit your examples to no more than three.

Factual Information about Your Agency and Its Services
1. What was the total billing of your agency office (and of the entire agency if applicable) for each of the previous five fiscal years?
2. Which 12 months make up your fiscal year?
3. What percent of your billing is in each of the major media?
4. What is the amount of your largest account billing? Your smallest? Please submit a list of your current clients.
5. Describe the stability/longevity of your relationships with your clients in some way that will be more meaningful than a single average number of years figure.
6. What accounts have you added and what accounts have you lost in the past three years? Why? What is/was their approximate annual billing? (This can be a total figure if confidentiality is required.)
7. What experience does your agency have with consumer goods/retail/service/business-to-business, and which of these accounts do you believe would be of distinct value to our business?
8. Who are the senior general management and department management executives in your office? *Briefly*, what is the background of each one, including length of service and experience with your agency and other agencies or client organizations?
9. To what extent, if any, would these key executives participate in work on our business?
10. Does your agency have a good history of profitability? Are you currently financially sound?
11. Briefly describe your standard billing policies. What services would be covered by commissions earned. What would be billed net (and at what rate). What would be marked up? Etc.
12. If your prefer fee, how do you compute the fee?
13. Are you willing to negotiate a compensation plan?
14. Describe your agency's research capabilities and how they have contributed to one or more of your client's successes.
15. Describe the interaction of the research department with the account service, creative, and media departments.
16. Describe your agency's media capabilities.
    Planning, execution, and post analysis for national and local broadcast and print media.
    Marketing and media measurement/planning sources.
    Media planning and experience.
17. Briefly discuss how the agency's media expertise has contributed to the successful marketing of one or more of your client's products.
18. Include a brief discussion of your media department's organization/operational structure.
19. If available, describe your promotion, merchandising and publicity capabilities and experience.

New Product/Concept Development
1. What role do you think your agency could play in the development of new product ideas?
2. Do you have a specific system for product idea generation? Please describe.
3. What are some of the major contributions you have made to the development of new products for your clients? Have these new products been successful?

DOS AND DON'TS

Do

- Make sure marketing leads the advertising.
- Use positioning as the bridge to effective advertising.
- Use the disciplined step-by-step process in developing creative advertising.
- Remember the awareness, attitude, action sequence as you are developing your advertising program.
- Make sure your advertising objectives are measurable.
- Make sure your advertising strategy has focus.
- Develop and evaluate alternative creative executions against the agreed upon advertising strategy.
- Develop specific advertising objectives and strategies for each target market if you are advertising to more than one.
- Develop campaigns, not just ads.
- Make sure your advertising communicates and is creative.
- Before producing the final advertising, ask others not directly involved with developing the advertising executions what the advertising says to them and what feeling they get from it.
- If you plan to use an advertising agency, do a thorough agency search and screen.

Don't

- Don't confuse advertising with other communication tools.
- Don't expect advertising to make the sale by itself.
- Don't advertise if you cannot deliver the product as advertised.
- Don't expect to sell anything without first making the target market aware of what you're selling.
- Don't begin creating any advertising until you have agreed upon a written objective and strategy.
- Don't accept any creative approach (whether your idea or the agency's) unless it is on strategy.
- Don't create advertising that you cannot afford to produce.
- Don't create advertising that is so expensive to develop that you can't afford adequate media to deliver the message.
- Don't make your advertising different just to be different, but to better sell your product.
- Don't drop a campaign because you and/or your agency become tired of it; do this only if it doesn't communicate and motivate. Most likely your target market has not tired of the advertising.
- Don't create advertising that pleases a boss or committee. Create advertising that you believe will sell.
- Don't begin creating an advertisement until all the executional details are clearly spelled out.

ADVERTISING

MEDIA

N ow that you have an understanding of what promotional and/or image messages need to be externally communicated, the next step is to prepare a media plan that will most effectively and efficiently deliver these messages. This is a very important element of the marketing plan, because media most often represent the largest single dollar marketing investment. It is also the marketing mix tool that is probably the least understood from the technical standpoint. Accordingly, you will find that learning how to plan media is one of the most challenging, complex experiences you will encounter as you write your marketing plan. Finally, as you make your media plan decisions, keep in mind that you use hard data whenever possible, but that you also apply basic common sense as well.

From This Chapter You Will Learn

The marketing and media background data needed to prepare a media plan.

What media objectives are and how to set them, particularly in determining "how much media is enough."

How to develop media strategies that meet the objectives.

How to evaluate specific media and media vehicles, as well as overall plans.

How to construct a media plan in written and graphic form.

How to summarize a media budget.

OVERVIEW

Media can be divided into two parts: planning and execution. The overall goal of media planning and execution is to deliver the optimum number of impressions (messages) to the target audience at the lowest cost within the most suitable environment for the message.

Planning consists of arranging the various media in combinations and support levels designed to most effectively and efficiently help fulfill the marketing, advertising, and promotion objectives and strategies. It is in essence the process of refining probabilities in a step-by-step, disciplined manner.

Execution, on the other hand, encompasses negotiating, purchasing, and placing the media once the media weights, types, and budgets have been determined. Another part of media execution is the evaluation of the purchased media's performance once it has run, which is referred to as the postbuy. Depending upon the size and structure of your organization, you may have an outside agency assist in both planning and execution. This chapter concentrates only on media planning. Refer to a text on media buying if you intend to purchase your own media.

The actual media plan included in the marketing plan consists of three basic elements:

- Media objectives
- Media strategies
- Media plan calendar and budget summary

Because preparing a media plan is a long, complex process, and because this chapter will be challenging to grasp, it is wise to review an outline of the step-by-step media planning process and then refer to it as you work through this chapter. A format to use in developing your media plan is provided in Appendix C.

Step 1. Review of information needed to write a media plan

    A. The marketplace

    B. Competitive activity

    C. Your product's marketing history

    D. The problems and opportunities section

    E. The sections of this marketing plan that have been prepared

Step 2. Set the media objectives

    A. Target market

    B. Geography

    C. Seasonality

    D. Communication goals

        1. Review of rating points, reach, frequency, and GRPs

        2. Quantitative media goals

            a. Macro methods of determining media weight goals

                i. Advertising as a percent of sales

                ii. Share of media voice versus share of market

            b. Micro target market method

                i. Determination of required reach of your target market

                ii. Determination of necessary frequency of message to your target market

                iii. Determination of necessary media weight goals

            c. Examples of media weight goals

        3. Qualitative media goals based on the optimum media environment for the message

    E. Optional media objectives

        1. Media budget

        2. Media testing

Step 3. Prepare the media strategy

    A. Determining your mix of the various media

        1. Description and value of each medium

2. Arriving at the right media mix
   a. Screen out inappropriate media
   b. Evaluate on a quantitative cost per thousand (CPM) basis
   c. Evaluation on a qualitative basis
   d. Consider the competition's media mix
3. Media mix strategy examples

B. Specific usage of each medium
   1. Daypart mix, length/size of message, and tactics of each medium
   2. Examples of medium usage strategies

C. Scheduling of the media
   1. Scheduling approaches: Continuity, heavy-up, pulsing, flighting, and front-loading
   2. Examples of scheduling strategies

D. Media testing strategies

Step 4. Development of final media plan and budget summary
   A. Prepare and review alternative media plans
   B. How to prepare a media flow chart calendar
   C. How to summarize a media budget
   D. Questions to ask yourself as a final check of the media plan that has been prepared

DISCIPLINED APPROACH TO MEDIA PLANNING

Step 1

Review of Information Needed to Write a Media Plan

Before you can begin to prepare your media plan, you must first review all the pertinent marketing and media data. Most of this information should be included in your business review. Below is a list of marketing and media data to be reviewed over a three to five year period with five years of history preferred. Attempt to gather and review all of the items, depending on the data and time available to you.

- Review the size and growth of the marketplace in dollars and units.
- Analysis of the competitive market (including your product):
  If available, sales history of each major competitor by size, share, and growth.
  If available, competitive media review of each major competitor.
    Level and share of media spending/weight.
    Spending and weight levels by medium, seasonality (quarterly if possible), and market.
    Determine media spending as a percentage of sales.
  If available, review unaided awareness, advertising awareness, and attitudes of the potential users/purchasers, on both a national/system wide and market-by-market basis.
- Analysis of your product(s)'s sales, marketing, and media history.
  Sales history by product, market, and store/distribution channel.
  Your media target market.
  If available, unaided awareness, advertising awareness, attitudes, and behavior/usage.
  Historical media review of your product.
    Overall media weight delivery and spending.
    Spending and weight levels by medium (quarterly) and market.
    Media spending as percentage of sales.

Results of media schedules run.

Changes in awareness, attitudes, and behavior.

Impact on overall sales, promotions, events, and media tests.

Review the dollars allocated to media versus the other marketing mix tools.

- Review of the problems and opportunities section.
- Review this marketing plan again, from sales objectives through advertising message. This information will point out what the media plan must accomplish and provide directions for the development of the media plan.

Step 2
Set the Media Objectives

Your media objectives must provide a clear and definitive direction in the following critical areas:

- To whom the advertising is to be directed (target audience).
- Where the advertising is to go (geography).
- When the advertising is to appear (seasonality).
- What the communication goals are.
  How much advertising is deemed sufficient to achieve the advertising objectives?
  What media environment will meet the advertising strategies in helping to communicate the message?
- Determination of whether there is a going-in set budget allocated for media spending or if a task method approach will be applied to arrive at a media budget. If there is a set going-in media budget allocation, it should be included up front in the media plan as a media objective. A task derived media budget is dependent on the media support necessary to meet the awareness and attitude levels that will stimulate adequate usage to meet the sales objectives. In this case, the media budget is finalized and presented at the end of the media plan.
- Determination if your marketing plan calls for testing of media. If so, you will include media test objectives in this section of the media plan.

Target Audience

To arrive at a target audience, simplify the target market you have already detailed by listing the key strategic and demographic descriptors.

The *strategic target* relates to purchasing and usage. Mothers *purchase* powdered soft drinks for their children while their children who consume powdered soft drinks are the *users*. The *demographic target* audience should parallel the media demographic breakouts provided by syndicated media services that measure audience media habits and such media vendors as direct mail houses, broadcasting stations, and catalog publishers. If you have key submarkets, such as the trade (wholesalers, retailers, etc.) for a package goods product, that cannot be accommodated in one media plan, a separate media plan should be prepared for these target markets.

The media target audience should be limited to those descriptors that can be readily and effectively used in the planning, measurement, and evaluation of the various media. Review your target market sections in the business review and the audience sources listed in Exhibit 14.1 to arrive at meaningful descriptors. Also included in this exhibit are sources for the current media costs needed eventually to complete your media plan.

Some target audience examples:

For a CPA firm

Companies that do not use a CPA firm

Businesses less than $3MM in revenues

President, owner, and treasurer/financial officer

Exhibit 14.1   Media Audience and Cost Sources*

Medium	Audience Data	Cost Data
Television	Nielsen Research Services (NTI, NSI) Arbitron Research	Network/Station representatives Media Market Guide Spot Quotations and Data, Inc. (costs are negotiable)
Radio	RADAR—Network Arbitron Research—Spot Birch Research—Spot	Network/Station representatives Media Market Guide Radio SRDS (costs are negotiable)
Magazines	Audit Bureau of Circulation (ABC) Simmons Market Research Bureau (SMRB) Mediamark Research Inc. (MRI) Individual magazine representative	Magazine SRDS Magazine representatives (ad position is usually negotiable, but cost usually is not)
Newspapers	Simmons/Scarborough Report Newspaper Advertising Bureau (NAB) Local newspaper representative	Newspaper SRDS (space costs for national products) Local rate cards via newspaper representatives (lower cost for local business advertising than national products; costs are not negotiable; sometimes ad placement can be negotiable)
Outdoor	Traffic Audit Bureau (TAB) Local representative	Outdoor SRDS Outdoor representatives (costs are sometimes negotiable while board position is usually negotiable depending on availability)
Direct Mail	Direct Mail SRDS Dun's Marketing Services	Direct mail SRDS Dun's Marketing Services

*A handy and portable reference to current media rates, data, and demographics for most consumer media updated quarterly is *Adweek's* "Marketer's Guide to Media."

For a company selling hot dogs

Heavy purchasers of hot dogs for the family

Women 18 to 49

Household income of $15 to 30MM

Household size of 3+

Geography

Once you have determined your specific media target audience, you must decide where and with what emphasis you want to place your media. Geographic media variation depends on the marketing strategies, as well as sales potential and profitability differences on a market-by-market basis or within a market.

Geographic weighting of media levels by market is based on many factors. A number of these geographic factors to be taken into consideration when developing geography media objectives are:

Sheer geographic size and physical makeup of your trading area.

Competitive media activity.

Media available to support your product.

Concentration of potential users of your product.

Concentration and trending of your product sales.

The last two of these geographic factors can be taken into account by evaluating on a market-by-market basis the sales of the product category and the sales of your product. The market-by-market variations should have been detailed in your business review as a comparison of markets in two ways: category development index (CDI = percent category sales/percent households in a given market) and brand development index (BDI = percent product sales/percent households in a given market). You most likely will place some media weight where you have a set minimum level of sales and even greater weight where there is an above average concentration of category sales and very importantly an above average concentration of sales for your product. Accordingly, you will develop a media objective that takes into consideration the CDI, the BDI, and the relationship between the two. (For more detail on CDI and BDI analysis, see Step 6 of your business review.)

Before finalizing your geographic media objectives, you should decide, on a market-by-market basis, whether your strategic marketing thrust is defensive (spend in markets to protect your business) or offensive (spend where there is potential but where sales have not been solidly built). This offensive strategy is also referred to as investment spending.

A beginning BDI/CDI guide for a defensive versus offensive approach might be:

High BDI/High CDI = Higher media spending to protect share.

High BDI/Low CDI = Media maintenance unless competition increases media weight.

Low BDI/High CDI = Investment media spending to capitalize on opportunity markets via new advertising, additional promotion, improved product/distribution/store penetration, etc.

Low BDI/Low CDI = Limited, if any, media support.

In addition to BDI/CDI considerations, you must also consider the trending of sales on a market-by-market basis. You might place additional media weight in markets with positive sales trends, while in markets with negative sales trends you might reduce the weight until a nonadvertising problem is fixed, or add media weight to support promotional advertising to reverse the sales trend. Some examples are:

For a national package goods product:

Provide national media support.

Provide incremental local media weight in high BDI markets that cumulatively account for a minimum of one third of sales.

	Percent Volume	BDI
Los Angeles	8.3%	119
New York	8.0	123
Chicago	7.7	125
Philadelphia	6.5	121
San Francisco	4.4	118
	34.9%	

For a business-to-business company:

Provide broad based media support of the full line of existing equipment.

Provide full introductory media support in addition to base support of the east, north, and central divisions for the new equipment introduction as soon as service commitment has been confirmed.

For a local retailer:

Provide marketwide media coverage.

Provide incremental media weight within one mile of store that accounts for 50 percent of current customers.

Seasonality

As important as it is to advertise to the right person in the right place, it is also important to advertise at the right time. Accordingly, to arrive at the right seasonality media objective(s), you must review the seasonality of your product sales, as well as of the category, to determine when sales for your product and the category are at their highest levels. A normal media practice is to plan your greatest media weight support for periods of high sales volume.

Most products have sales skews. When monthly sales index near 110 or greater, you would most likely heavy-up (increase) your weight levels. Sometimes the seasonality of your product might differ from that of the category, with the category's heavy sales season beginning earlier or later than that of your product. After reviewing the reason(s) for this seasonal sales difference (e.g., special promotion or different competitive weight levels), you will probably want to concentrate your media weight when the target market is most likely to purchase. However, you must still support with media a successful sales period that might have been self-created and/or when customers have been conditioned to purchase.

Also a key point is to *lead* the natural buying season, placing higher levels of media just prior to heavier sales periods. This is done to presell the consumer, building awareness and putting the consumer in a positive mode to purchase your product when the natural buying season arrives. With minimal media dollars, concentrate media weight at the beginning of the heavy buying season. It is most efficient to reduce your media weight just before the end of the increased sales period so that you are not investing media dollars against a diminishing market; let the established awareness you built carry the latter portion of the sales period.

Another factor to consider in setting a media seasonality objective is what the competition has done in the past and what you anticipate they will do in the coming year. You may want not only to lead the peak selling season but also to be the first into the media arena, preempting the competition.

Some examples of seasonality objectives:

For a public transit company

Concentrate media in the adverse winter weather (highest usage) months of January/February/March and the back-to-school period of August/September while maintaining a media continuity throughout the year.

For a retail fabric chain

Provide media continuity support throughout the year with a concentration of media effort in the heavy selling seasons of August through October and February through April.

Communication Goals

Having determined your media objectives of target audience, geography, and seasonality, you must next determine what your communication goals will be in terms of the quantitative and qualitative media delivery necessary to meet the awareness and attitude goals that will lead to projected sales.

Review of Rating Points, Reach, Frequency, and GRPs Determining quantitative communications goals is very difficult even for the most experienced media planner because of the ever changing marketing environment in which there are no real definitive benchmarks, an uncontrollable competitive marketplace and the continually changing needs and wants of the potential target market. Making it even more difficult is the problem of accurately determining how much communication is received by the target market and effectiveness in stimulating action.

Before discussing how to arrive at quantitative communication goals to provide media direction, you must have an understanding of some basic media terms: rating point, GRPs (gross rating points), reach, and frequency.

A *rating point* is defined as 1 percent of the universe being measured. A universe could include households, companies, women, men, adults, kids, purchasing agents, etc. in a single market, region, or the total United States. On a total U.S. household basis, a one rating for a commercial or ad means an impression or exposure is made against approximately 900,000 homes nationally (1 percent of 90,000,000 homes). On a single market basis for Chicago, a one rating equates to approximately 31,000 homes (1 percent of 3,100,000 homes).

A *GRP* provides a common term of measurement to determine how much media weight is going into a defined marketplace and to make comparisons among different media. When we buy 100 home GRPs via multiple ad insertions, we are in fact buying the number of homes equal to the total number of homes in that universe. Chicago has approximately 3,100,000 homes with 1 GRP = 31,000 homes and 100 GRPs = 3,100,000 homes.

In actuality, when a schedule of ads and/or commercials is run, some of these homes will be reached more than once, and others not at all. Therefore, some people will see the ad a number of times and others will not see it at all, which leads to the following important media estimate terminology:

> *Reach*—how many different homes/persons we have reached (expressed as an absolute or percentage).

> *Frequency*—how often they have been reached on an average basis.

Reach expresses the number exposed at least once, *frequency* expresses the average number of exposures, while *GRPs*, in the aggregate, represent the total magnitude of a schedule's exposures or a sum of the ratings. When the percent ratings of a specific market segment (example: Women 18 +) are totaled, you have *target audience GRPs*, or, more simply stated, TRPs (target rating points). GRPs, a generic media term, may refer to household GRPs or specific target segment GRPs.

A media schedule that delivers 80 percent reach with a 10 frequency against a specific market equals a total of 800 GRPs. Very simply, then:

$$\text{Percent Reach} \times \text{Frequency} = \text{Total GRPs.}$$

Normally we estimate reach and frequency on a four-week basis, but we can also provide reach and frequency for a weekly promotion, a total schedule, and on an annual basis.

Through research and experience, we have been able to establish standard reach levels for given GRP levels. Using the graph in Exhibit 14.2, you can determine what each medium should generate in reach or GRPs, and you can also determine the frequency. If your local market media plan calls for 300 GRPs in *radio* to support a two-week promotion, it would build an approximate 50 reach and an average frequency of 6 (300 / 50 = 6). Or, if you determined a monthly *magazine* reach of 50 was required, then your GRPs would equal 125 and your frequency is 2.5 (125 / 50 = 2.5). Exhibit 14.2 provides an overall GRP summary for television, radio, and magazine. For more accurate GRP data specific to your market, check with the appropriate media representatives.

To arrive at a *rough approximation* of reach and frequency data for each medium (other than television and radio), you can compute your own GRP data for magazines, newspaper, outdoor, and direct mail. However, for more precise data, you should contact your specific media representative. For your rough calculations use the following formulas.

> Magazine: Use percent coverage for reach (circulation / total market households or total readers / target persons); number of insertions for frequency.

Exhibit 14.2   Relationship of Reach, Frequency, and GRPs

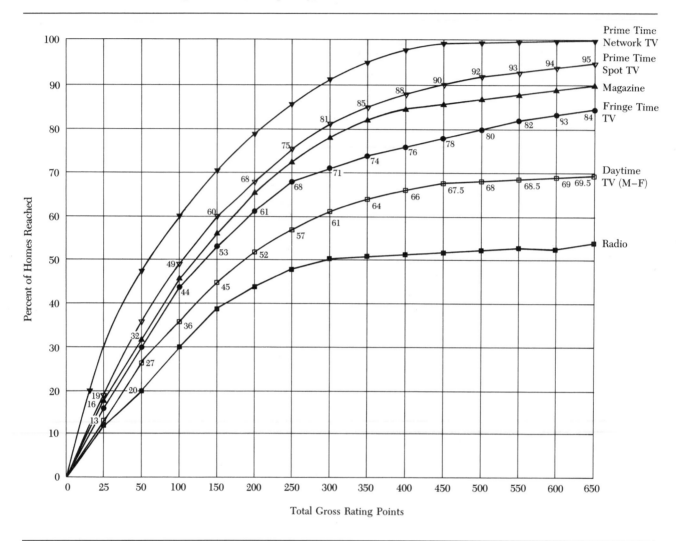

Source: Michael L. Rothschild, *Advertising, From Fundamentals to Strategies*, Lexington, Massachusetts, D.C. Heath and Company, 1987.

Newspaper: Use percent coverage for reach (circulation / total market households or total readers / target persons); number of insertions for frequency.

Outdoor: For a standard four-week showing estimate:

50 showing = 85 reach and 15 frequency

100 showing = 88 reach and 29 frequency

Direct Mail: Use percent coverage for reach (number mailed / total market target households or target persons); number of mailings for frequency.

Once you have estimated reach and frequency for a single medium, you may want to combine media weights with another medium. Although not an exact method (but good enough for approximation), you can use the grid in Exhibit 14.3 to arrive at combined weight levels across media. For example, 300 GRPs of radio and 800 GRPs of magazines are planned (1,100 GRPs total); and yield reaches of 50 and 80, respectively. Then, using the grid, the planner can see that the combined reach is approximately 86 (86 is at the intersection of row 50 and column 80); therefore,

Exhibit 14.3   Accumulated Reach Levels Across Media

All Media Combinations
(Homes and Individuals)

Reach		5	10	15	20	25	30	35	40	45	50	55	60	65	70	75	80	85	90
	5	10	14	19	24	28	33	38	43	47	52	57	62	66	71	76	81	85	90
	10	14	19	23	27	32	36	40	45	50	54	59	63	68	72	77	81	86	91
	15	19	23	27	31	35	39	43	48	52	56	61	65	69	73	78	82	86	91
	20	24	27	31	35	38	42	46	50	55	59	63	67	71	75	79	83	87	91
	25	28	32	35	38	41	44	48	53	57	61	64	68	72	76	79	83	87	92
	30	33	36	39	42	44	47	51	55	59	63	66	70	73	77	80	84	88	92
	35	38	40	43	46	48	51	53	58	62	65	68	71	75	78	81	84	88	92
	40	43	45	48	50	53	55	58	60	64	67	70	73	76	79	82	85	88	92
	45	47	50	52	55	57	59	62	64	66	69	72	75	77	80	83	86	89	93
	50	52	54	56	59	61	63	65	67	69	71	74	76	79	81	84	86	89	93
	55	57	59	61	63	64	66	68	70	72	74	76	78	80	82	85	87	90	93
	60	62	63	65	67	68	70	71	73	75	76	78	80	82	84	86	88	90	94
	65	66	68	69	71	72	73	75	76	77	79	80	82	83	85	86	88	91	94
	70	71	72	73	75	76	77	78	79	80	81	82	84	85	86	87	89	91	94
	75	76	77	78	79	79	80	81	82	83	84	85	86	86	87	88	89	91	95
	80	81	81	82	83	83	84	84	85	86	86	87	88	88	89	89	90	92	95
	85	85	86	86	87	87	88	88	88	89	89	90	90	91	91	91	92	92	95
	90	90	91	91	91	92	92	92	92	93	93	93	94	94	94	95	95	95	95
	95	95	95	96	96	96	96	96	96	97	97	97	97	97	97	98	98	98	98

Source: Michael L. Rothschild, *Advertising, From Fundamentals to Strategies,* Lexington, Massachusetts, D.C. Heath and Company, 1987.

average frequency for the combined 1,100 GRPs must be 12.8 (1,100 / 86 = 12.8). Although neither the graph nor the grid is perfectly accurate, each gives a good approximation for planning purposes.

How to Arrive at Quantitative Media Goals Now that you have an understanding of media measurement, we can review different methods of arriving at a communication weight level goal(s).

Macro Methods of Determining Media Weight Goals Two macro, or market derived, methods can be used in determining the media weight goals for your product. One uses advertising as a percent of sales method based on industry averages, and the second uses a comparison of share of media to share of market sales. Both are market based, while a third micro method is based on moving a specific target market to action. All three have their merits. You might apply a combination of methods, or decide to use one method that best fits your current planning situation. The important point is that you have an understanding of how these different methods are employed to determine the media weight for your product.

The *advertising as a percentage of sales method* begins with a review of the percent of sales allocated to advertising by the product category/industry in which you are competing. You could then use a similar percentage of your projected sales for your media budget after reducing this dollar budget by 10 to 15 percent to cover the cost of production to develop the ads and/or commercials. For example:

Percent advertising of sales for category	3%
Product's projected sales	$1,000,000
Ad budget (3% × $1MM)	$ 30,000
Ad production of 10 percent (10% of $30M ad budget)	$ 3,000
Available media budget ($30M − $3M)	$ 27,000

Now that you have a dollar budget as a basis, you must next use this budget to determine a media weight goal.

To arrive at a rough GRP weight level for your product, contact your media representative to arrive at a very approximate cost per rating point (CPP) by medium. For example,

Cost of average insertion or broadcast spot / Average rating = CPP

Or,

Average radio :60 commercial spot cost of $36 / Average rating of 2 = $18 CPP

You can then divide the total media budget by the CPP for each medium to arrive at an approximate idea of how much media weight you can afford by each potential medium. For example,

$27,000 / $18 CPP = 1,500 GRPs.

Although the above example is for a consumer medium, you could use a similar approach for business-to-business media using an average cost per point for each medium such as trade publications and direct mail.

The advertising as percent of sales media weight goal approach is not very sophisticated, but it does challenge you to maximize the dollars in your media budget. However, keep in mind that because this approach is so broad in application, it does not take into consideration your current marketing situation or the competitive marketing environment. Therefore, advertsing as a percent of sales should, in most situations, be a starting point and is only one method of arriving at the optimum media weight goal.

Another method in determining your media weight goal is the share comparison of media activity to sales—the *Share of Media versus Share of Market* method. This method compares your product's share of media voice (SOV) (in GRP media weight or media dollar expenditures as a percentage of total media advertising in your category or marketplace) to your product's share of market sales (SOM).

	SOV		SOM	
Organization	$M	Percent	$MM	Percent
A	$370	48%	$94.1	39.1%
B	230	29	70.0	29.1
C	69	9	38.6	16.1
D	105	14	38.0	15.7
Total	$774	100%	$240.7	100.0%

If you are using media dollar expenditures, take the media spending for each competitor including your own product from the business review and compare it to the corresponding shares of market. Is your share of media spending above or below that of the competition? Is your share of media spending above or below that of your product's share of market? Based on the direction of your marketing strategies and this SOV to SOM comparison, you can determine media weight goals.

As a very rough guide and only a starting point in using the SOV to SOM media weight determination, consider the following:

Share of voice should approximate share of market.

Usually the greater the share of market, the greater the share of voice.

If you want to increase your share of market, you most often should increase share of voice.

If your share of voice is below your share of market year after year, your sales share will eventually decrease if everything in the competitive market environment and your marketing mix remain constant.

In using this method, keep in mind that there is no guarantee there always will be a direct cause and effect between an increase/decrease of SOV to match a similar increase/decrease in SOM. However, while there is not always perfect correlation, there is a directional cause and effect relationship between SOV and SOM. Broad based studies and the authors' media experience with clients have also shown this cause and effect relationship during recessionary periods when there is a shrinking of the market and a decrease in total market sales for an industry. Companies, on the whole, that maintain or increase their media weight during recessionary periods realize an increase in share of sales and better profits than those companies that reduce ad budgets and corresponding media weights.

Micro Target Market Method Having reviewed media weight levels from a more marketwide or macro standpoint, it is also helpful to approach the setting of media weight goals on a specific target market or micro basis. With this approach you attempt to determine what percent of the target market must be reached and how often. You want to reach this target with the frequency necessary to build product awareness and understanding that will lead to a positive attitude toward the product and eventual purchase. In essence, you are attempting to determine the amount of GRP media weight necessary to *effectively reach* or communicate with a large enough portion of your target market to understand your message for the required sales.

A good place to start in determining the desired reach and frequency is to review your advertising objectives in terms of the percent of target market you projected must have unaided awareness of your product and a predisposed attitude toward your product. Further, based on your marketing objectives, review what percent of the target market you have estimated will try your product, make repeat purchases, and become regular users in order to meet the sales objectives.

It is also wise to review the media weight levels supporting your product over the past year, along with the level of media support for any promotions that may have been run. Based on these past supporting media weight levels, attempt to correlate sales results in order to determine what reach, frequency, and GRP levels are needed for this year's plan to help meet the estimated advertising and promotion objectives.

Depending on the type of product you are selling and its awareness and acceptance by the target market, every situation is different when *setting reach goals*. But as a suggested starting point, based on the authors' experience, you should consider a 60 to 90+ reach of the target market. For a meaningful impact, it is usually necessary to reach well over one half of the target market with your message. This is sometimes difficult to accomplish, particularly with short-term promotions and when the appropriate media vehicles are not readily available.

Once you have estimated your specific reach goal(s) for the year, new product introduction, promotion, event, grand opening, etc., you must now estimate the frequency needed against the target to be reached in order to generate the effective reach necessary to elicit a specific response. In *setting frequency goals* the required frequency to move the desired portion of the target market from product recognition to purchase is really a guestimate. However, a potential range of frequency to make this happen is from a three to ten frequency. To determine whether you need more or less frequency depends upon the following:

More frequency	Less frequency
New product	Established product
New campaign	Established campaign
Complex message	Simple message
Nonuser prospects (trial objective)	User prospects (repeat objective)
High competitive advertising levels	Low competitive advertising levels
Nonloyal user category, especially with short purchase cycle	Stable/loyal user base
Promotion/sales event	

It has been the experience of the authors, specifically with retail clients, that it is usually more successful to reach a smaller percentage of the target market with greater frequency than reach a larger percentage of the target market with minimum frequency. The reason is that it is better to have a smaller audience understand and remember your message than to reach a large audience but not have them thoroughly understand or remember the message.

To help you determine the frequency needed to effectively communicate the message, you can estimate the number of times the individual target person must be reached by determining the necessary frequency for the anticipated response as shown in Exhibit 14.4. To help you, we have included an estimated frequency range for each response. The authors acknowledge that these ranges are very subjective and will vary dramatically with your current marketing situation.

To set a media weight goal simply multiply your estimated reach by the total needed frequency for your total GRP level. For example:

$$\text{Reach } 80 \times \text{Frequency } 9 = \text{GRPs } 720$$

Exhibit 14.4   How to Determine Frequency Goals

Potential Frequency Range	Response	Definition	Judgmental Probability of Producing Response with Advertising Alone
1 to 3	Recognition	Recalls advertising when shown/mentioned product	Least difficult
3 to 6	Unaided awareness	Names product when asked about category	Difficult
4 to 7	Recall	Recalls advertising and identifies product	More difficult
5 to 8	Learning	Associates information about the product with the name	Very difficult
6 to 10	Attitude	Prefers the product, positive attitude	Extremely difficult
1 to 10+	Sales	Purchases	Most difficult

Keep in mind that with this methodology, the frequency of message exposure is based on average frequency. Some people within the target market will be exposed once and others at multiples of the average frequency number.

You probably have surmised from this discussion of setting media weight goals that there is no one hard and fast rule in determining the optimum media weight level for your product, but rather a composite of many factors which you must consider. However, to give you a starting point in *setting your media weight goals*, in Exhibit 14.5 we present some guidelines for you to consider and we hope modify (possibly very dramatically) as you determine the media weight goals for your product. These *very rough* media weight guidelines are based on some quantitative data, but primarily on the personal experience of the authors. Therefore they are very subjective in nature and must be used with extreme caution.

In the package goods area, the 2,500 to 5,000 annual introductory GRP level on the average can generate *aided* brand awareness of 60 to 80 percent and trial rates of up to 20 percent. In the retail environment, the 5,000 to 10,000 GRP level on the average can generate an *unaided* store awareness of 20 to 40 percent and trial rates of up to 20 percent. The trial rate in the retail environment is very dependent on store penetration (or the number of stores you have in the market).

Some examples of media weight goals for a nationally marketed package good would be:

> Provide a minimum of 2,000 GRPs on a national basis for the fiscal year.
>
> Provide a reach of 90 to 95 and a minimum of average frequency of four over major media flight periods.
>
> In the local opportunity markets of Chicago, Los Angeles, and Philadelphia:
>
>> Provide a minimum total (national and local) of 3,000 GRPs annually.
>>
>> Provide a reach of 90 to 95 with a minimum frequency of six for the four-week heavy-up periods.

For a business-to-business manufacturer an example of a media weight goal would be:

> Reach a minimum 80 percent of the target market a minimum of eight times annually.

Qualitative Media Goals The qualitative delivery goals relate to the *impact* of the exposure within the particular medium in which it is run, in terms of the medium

Exhibit 14.5   Media Weight Guidelines

Product/Service Type	Target Audience GRP Weight Levels		
	Minimum Weekly	Seasonal/Event 4 Week Period	Annual
Consumer			
Package goods			
Established	75–150	300– 600	1,000– 3,000
Introductory/Promotional	150–250	600–1,000	1,800– 5,000
Retail/Service			
Established	100–200	400– 800	2,000– 5,000
Introductory/Promotional	175–350	700–1,400	3,000–10,000
Business-to-Business			
Established	24– 50	100– 200	600– 1,600
Introductory/Promotional	50–150	200– 600	1,200– 3,600

providing an optimum environment for the product advertised and the message to be delivered. The media environment must also be consistent with and appropriate to the projected product image. The direction for this goal comes from the product positioning and creative strategy.

The qualitative media goal, while a guide, is also a safeguard. It ensures that the media selected not only provide the necessary impact for the target market, but also enhance the reception of the actual message, not impede it. An advertisement selling the advanced technology of a new car might best be placed in *Car and Driver*, while an advertisement that sells emotional benefits of the new car (such as the feeling of exhilaration one experiences while driving the car) might best be suited for television. A qualitative media goal for a new product that represents a technological break-through might be: "Provide a media environment that is authoritative and credible and has news value." This could eventually translate to placement in "60 Minutes" or local television news.

If your message introduces a chain of new high-fashion women's apparel stores, your communication goal might be: "Provide a media environment that is conducive to the display of quality, high-fashion apparel and relative to a lifestyle of women who purchase this type of clothing." This could eventually translate to the place-ment of an advertisement on the "Dynasty" or "Falcon Crest" television shows, where the wardrobes are watched with as much interest as the plot. This same goal could also translate to a *glitz* ad in the fall fashion edition of an upscale city publication.

Optional Media Objectives for Your Plan

Media Budget   Ideally it usually is best to use the task method in building a media plan, and thereby arrive at a media budget that is the direct result of the type and amount of media necessary to fulfill the communication goals. This type of media budget is then further refined, based on the cumulative marketing plan budget considerations, to implement all the elements of the market mix. However, if there are specific financial media parameters for the media plan, many times they are included as part of the media objectives.

Some examples of media budget objectives would be:

Maintain total media expenditures at 3½ percent of total projected sales.

Execute an annual media plan at the $300,000 budget level.

Media Test Objectives   It is conceivable that the marketing plan calls for a media test(s). If this is the case, a brief statement of the test objectives should be included in this section. Some examples of media test objectives would be:

Test the impact on sales of increasing the media spending from 2 percent to 4 percent of sales.

Test the impact on sales of adding consumer media to the current use of business publications and direct mail to effectively reach new business-to-business clients.

Test the payout effectiveness of adding broadcast to the previously all print media plan.

Step 3

Prepare the Media Strategy

Under media strategy you should include:

- A brief summary of the *media mix*, or the different media to be used—magazines, direct mail, radio, etc.
- *The specific use of each medium*. This is a tactical description of how each of the

specific media is to be used, such as magazine types, ad size, broadcast programming/daypart type, and length of commercials.
■ A description of the *scheduling* of the media in terms of when each medium is used and at what levels.

This strategy section is really the heart of the actual media planning process. It is an evolving and very fluid process because you will be evaluating media elements for each of the strategy points. You will also be combining different media elements, and evaluating these combination alternatives based on a quantitative basis (delivery and efficiency), as well as a qualitative basis in terms of which media environment will best communicate the message. As part of the media strategy section, you will also want to include a rationale once you have decided on each of the specific strategies.

Keep in mind that you might revise the media strategies as the marketing plan evolves because of possible revisions of the sales objectives, marketing strategies, promotional program, budget, etc. Nevertheless, if changes to the media strategies are required, they are relatively easy to implement if you understand and have actually gone through this disciplined media planning process.

Media Mix Strategy

Description and Value Comparison Before you write a media mix strategy, you must first review and evaluate which media will best fulfill the media objectives. This evaluation should compare the individual medium on both a quantitative and qualitative basis.

To begin your evaluation process, do a quick initial screen of the different media, determining which have a possibility of use in a media plan that will meet the objectives. It is a good idea to do this quick screen of *all* media to ensure that you do not automatically rule out a medium based on your preconceived notions or without determining if it could meet the objectives.

As a quick media review and handy reference guide, Exhibit 14.6 provides a general description, and a comparison of media values based on quantitative data and the authors' experience. If you require more indepth background information on each medium, you can review an advertising or media text or check with the appropriate media representatives.

Arriving at the Right Media Mix In order to arrive at the appropriate mix of media you must screen out the obvious inappropriate media; do a quantitative and qualitative analysis of the potential media candidates, and consider how your media selection will impact on the target market in relationship to the competitive media environment.

Screen Out Inappropriate Media After reviewing the strengths and weaknesses of each medium in terms of their appropriateness for meeting the media objectives, screen out those media that logically could not meet the objectives. If you are marketing a new product to a broad general market that required emotional image advertising, you would not use direct mail; if the product was very technical and required detailed explanation, you would not use outdoor; if you were grand opening one, 1,000 square foot ice cream shop in a suburb of Chicago, you would not use television.

Evaluate Each Medium on a CPM Quantitative Basis After eliminating those media that will very obviously *not* meet the objectives, compare the remaining media on

Exhibit 14.6   Handy Media Guide: General Description and Values of Various Media

Medium	Size/Length		Cost Comparison	
	Units Available	Recommended Size/Unit	Standard Unit	Relative Efficiency*
Television				
Network or spot	:60/:30/:15/:10 (spot :15 not regularly available)	:30	:30	Overall above average
Prime				Most costly
Day				Least costly
Early fringe				Average
Late fringe				Above early fringe
News				Network: Average Spot: Close to prime
Sports				Most costly
Cable	:60/:30/:15/:10	:30		Low national but high spot CPM
Radio				
Network ⎰ AM drive	:60/:30/:10	:30	:30	Very efficient vs. TV
⎰ Midday				
Spot ⎰ PM drive		:60	:60§	Generally efficient vs. TV
⎰ Evening				
Local Newspapers	Various	¼ to ½ page	⅓ page	Average/various
Sunday Supplements	Various	½ to full page	⅔ page four color	Par with many magazines
Magazines Consumer				
News Weeklies	Various	½ to full page	Page four color bleed	Generally more efficient than TV
Men's Field				
Women's Field				
Etc.				

*Represents normal relationships of cost efficiency among media types. Individual variances occur frequently.

†Estimated percent of audience who noticed advertising (the probability of the advertising being noticed by the medium's audience). Percent notice based on: :30s in television, Page 4 color in magazines/supplements, ½ page in newspaper, :30s in network radio, :60s in spot radio, and 30-sheet in outdoor. The 70 percent notice

| **Clutter** | | | |
Percent Advertising/ Total Time or Space	**Noticing Value†**	**Reach/Target Audience Pinpointing**	**Communication Values**
		Somewhat precise	*Pros:* Audiovisual impact, most intrusive, demands less active involvement relative to print, immediate impact, quick reach and good frequency, relatively
16% to 23%‡	65	Broad total audience	homogenous national coverage, broad
27	45	Housewives, kids	homogenous local coverage as well as
27	45	Housewives/kids	beyond metro areas.
27	55	Adults	*Cons:* Limited to commercial length
27	60	Adults, somewhat older	constraints, one exposure per expenditure.
27	45	Men Most precise of TV	
17 to 20 per hour	35	Fairly precise in terms of age/sex	*Pros:* Good frequency medium, demands less active involvement, good localized
20 to 30 per hour	35	demographics only and for ethnic targets	spot coverage for city/metro area. *Cons:* Audio impact only, low ratings, limited to commercial length time constraints, one exposure per expenditure, reach builds slower than TV and newspaper.
70	55	Broad total audience	*Pros:* Immediate impact, very high reach potential, coupons get redeemed more quickly, very timely. *Cons:* Low readers per copy, very little pass along, very short life span, limited in production quality.
60 to 65	55	Broad total audience	*Pros:* Immediate impact, very high reach potential, good coupon carrier, better production quality than newspaper. *Cons:* Low readers per copy, very little pass along, very short life span, not as flexible in timing as newspaper.
40 to 60	50	Very precise in terms of many demographics	*Pros:* No time constraints per message, potential for multiple exposures per expenditure, indepth product description potential, generally upscale demography, pass along readership, coupon/promotion delivery vehicle, good production quality. *Cons:* Visual impact only, requires active involvement, less immediate impact, lower reach and local market coverage than TV, radio, and newspaper.

continued

value for direct mail is based on the estimated percentage that open the direct mail piece. (Noticing values for television are for spot TV.) For further explanation of noticing values, review discussion under the heading, "Arriving at the Right Media Mix."

‡Nonnetwork television station affiliates.

Exhibit 14.6—*continued*

| | Size/Length | | Cost Comparison | |
Medium	Units Available	Recommended Size/Unit	Standard Unit	Relative Efficiency*
Business-to-Business/Trade Vertical (targeted via specific industries) Horizontal (targeted via job function)	Various	½ to full page	Page b/w	Expensive but less than direct mail
Outdoor/Out of Home	25/50/100 showing	50‖	50 to 100 showing	Most efficient
Direct Mail	Up to 6 ⅛″ × 11 ½″ × ¼″ thick, 1 oz. or less#	Larger than smaller, B/W plus one color	Various	Most expensive

§A :30 on network radio is half the price of a :60. In the case of spot radio, a :30 spot can cost from 70 percent of a :60 to the same price.

‖A 50 showing means approximately 50 percent of the market will pass one of the locations each day.

#Acceptable size and weight with no incremental postage cost.

a quantitative cost per thousand (CPM) basis to determine media efficiency. A CPM is used as a common denominator for media comparison.

To arrive at a CPM for a medium, you can either divide target audience into the medium cost multiplied by 1,000 (Cost / Audience × 1,000 = CPM) or move the decimal point of the audience three places to the left and divide into the medium cost (Cost / Audience/1,000 = CPM). If a network prime time television :30 commercial cost is $88,245 and the number of the target persons reached is 10,415,000, then $88,245 / 10,415 = $8.47 CPM.

You want to evaluate on a CPM basis each of the potential media in your marketplace that you have screened and deemed appropriate for your product. In order to do your CPM efficiency analysis, you will need both audience and cost information. A listing of some sources for generating audience and cost data is included in Exhibit 14.1.

After you have arrived at an average CPM for each potential medium and to more

| Clutter | | | |
Percent Advertising/ Total Time or Space	Noticing Value†	Reach/Target Audience Pinpointing	Communication Values
40 to 60	65	Precise by industry or job function	*Pros:* In-depth product description potential, reaches relatively small but targeted audience, ads and editorial are highly read, coupon carrier, low cost per inquiry. *Cons:* Visual impact only.
None to some (varies by area)	30	Imprecise	*Pros:* Good for product/package identification, good reach, high frequency, good directional vehicle, local geographic concentration. *Cons:* Visual impact only, limited copy development potential, very high total monthly cost for anything approaching national coverage.
All ad/no editorial	70	Most precise	*Pros:* Extensive copy development potential, very selective, easy to track response, excellent coupon carrier, flexible in terms of timing and types of inclusions per mailing. *Cons:* Visual impact only, easy to discard.

easily compare medium CPMs, you might want to rank order each medium from the lowest to highest CPM. The chart in Exhibit 14.7 provides an example of a national media CPM comparison.

After you have ranked your computed CPM, you might want to weight the gross audience by the probability of the advertising being *noticed by the medium's audience*. This is an important consideration, because the number of target market persons *receiving* the media communication as reported by audience research services and the media vehicles (station, newspaper, magazine, etc.) is usually much higher than the *actual number seeing and/or hearing* the advertising message. Based on a computation of media data and the experience of the authors, a rough estimate of the *noticing value* for the various media is included in Exhibit 14.6, Handy Media Guide. It must be mentioned, however, these estimates of noticing values do include much subjectivity. Further, the research data that provides some objective substance for these estimates is continually changing.

Keeping this in mind, you can apply these noticing values to each medium's gross audience to arrive at a lesser (and hopefully a more realistic) adjusted audience from which you can derive an *adjusted CPM*:

Prime time audience	10,415,000
Noticing value	× .65
Adjusted prime time audience	6,769,750
Average unit cost	$88,245
Adjusted prime time CPM	$13.04

Accordingly, you can then rerank the media CPMs based on the noticing value after adjustments are made as indicated in Exhibit 14.7.

Having reviewed the ranked media CPMs, you can begin to eliminate those media with high CPMs. However, you cannot automatically assume that those with the lowest CPM should be included in your media mix. You must also consider the qualitative factors of each medium and the competition's use of the media. In the final analysis, it is not always the lowest CPM but the lowest cost per sale (CPS). What may appear to be too costly based on a pure CPM evaluation might be the most effective medium in terms of selling goods. In the much more narrowly defined business-to-business marketplace, the use of mass consumer media such as television with its higher gross cost and CPM has proven successful for such companies as Federal Express (overnight mail) and IBM (small business computers).

Exhibit 14.7   Media Mix Cost Comparisons

Medium/Unit Size	Average Unit Cost	Average Rating W25–54	Women 25 to 54 (000)	CPM	Rank	Noticing Value	Adjusted CPM	Rank
Network Television (:30s)								
Daytime								
All	$ 16,060	4.4	3,598	$ 4.46	8	45	$ 9.92	9
ABC	17,540	4.9	3,890	4.51	9		10.02	10
CBS/NBC	11,784	3.4	2,840	4.19	6		9.22	7
Drama	20,540	5.2	3.977	5.16	12		11.48	11
Game shows	7,920	2.5	2,557	3.10	3		6.88	3
Prime time								
All	88,245	11.1	10,415	8.47	16	65	13.04	14
Early morning								
All	12,615	2.9	2,841	4.44	7	35	12.69	13
Early evening news								
All	49,910	6.2	7,669	6.51	13	45	14.46	15
Late night								
ABC Nightline	31,800	3.0	3,125	10.18	18	65	15.66	18
CBS I and II	18,090	2.7	2,273	7.96	15	65	12.24	12
NBC Tonight Letterman	29,920	3.2	3,125	9.57	17	65	14.73	16
Combo fringe	7,583	2.2	980	7.74	14	50	15.48	17
Network Radio (:30s)								
6A-7P scatter plan	1,280	.8	852	1.50	1	35	4.29	2
Magazines (½ Page, 4/C)								
Women's service	30,677	24.4	17,991	1.71	2	50	3.41	1
Newspapers								
Sunday comics (⅓ Page, 4/C)	291,948	60.3	57,192	5.10	11	55	9.28	8
Sunday supplements (½ Page, 4/C)								
Parade	144,700	33.0	30,300	4.78	10	55	8.68	6
USA Weekend	52,924	13.8	12,783	4.14	5		7.53	5
Sunday magazine network	109,069	30.9	27,838	3.92	4		7.12	4

Note: Costs, ratings, and women (000) are not necessarily current or representative data, but CPMs and rankings are accurate as demonstrative ratios.

Evaluation on a Qualitative Basis Having done your quantitative analysis of the media, you must still consider the qualitative factors of each medium. To help you do this, some questions will help you determine those characteristics unique to your product, service, or store that you need to take into account when assessing each medium's ability to *enhance* the advertising message.

- What is required of the creative execution: demonstration, package registration, appetite appeal, technical explanation, consumer offer?
- What is required of the medium as related to the creative execution: sight, sound, and/or motion?
- How is the environment of the medium important to communicating the advertising message: news value, editorial compatibility (e.g., food preparation, home improvement)?
- To what extent is the audience interested in the product category/brand: very, somewhat, mildly?
- How important is immediacy (speed of audience accumulation) to the advertising objective: very, somewhat, mildly?

Competitive Media Mix Considerations You must consider the competition's use of the media mix. What is their media mix selection? When do they use each medium? At what levels? How do they use each medium in relation to the others? If a competitor with a considerably larger media budget dominates the medium that would have been your first choice, you might decide to concentrate all your media dollars in your second choice where you can dominate and where will you not have your media effort diluted.

The point should be made here that with or without competition, it is usually better to concentrate your media dollars in a few media to achieve continual reach and high frequency than to dilute your media dollars over many different media, thereby fragmenting your media effort. However, the more competition you have in the media, the more it becomes necessary for you to do a good job in one medium before placing weight in another. Make sure that each additional medium added to the media mix is used with weight levels that will have competitive impact and generate effective reach. In business-to-business media, you are usually better off concentrating your media in the top two or three publications by industry or job classification; doing so, you have the potential to generate a 75+ reach with the necessary frequency to have competitive impact, while maximizing your media dollars.

Media Mix Strategy Examples After you've evaluated the media alternatives from quantitative, qualitative, and competitive points of view, you must now write your media mix strategy. Below are some examples for a national package goods client:

> Use a combination of network television for national coverage and spot television in the designated high opportunity markets of Chicago, Los Angeles, and Philadelphia.
>
> Use women's service magazines for selective reach against the primary target market and to carry cents-off coupons.

Some examples for a business-to-business crafts manufacturer are:

> Use national trade publications across a minimum of two top craft magazines to broaden reach potential of both primary and secondary target audiences.
>
> Take advantage of all available extras from trade publications when placing orders to increase awareness and obtain new dealers: new product references, direct response cards, and for publication mailing lists.
>
> Use frequency mailings to merchandise new products to large/key accounts.

Specific Usage of Each Medium

Within this media strategy section, define the specific tactical usage of each medium to be employed, based again on the media objectives. Include the following medium specifics where they apply.

Television and Radio—Daypart TV—Day, Fringe, Prime Time, News, Sports. Daypart Radio—AM Drive, Mid-Day, PM Drive, Night—Program types. Length of commercial.

Magazine—List magazine type (news weeklies, sports, etc.) and/or specific magazines by name, ad size, position, black and white, one-, two-, three-, or four-color.

Newspaper—Daily, weekly, and shopper (nonpaid), ad size, section of paper, black and white, one-, two-, three-, and four-color, day of the week.

Outdoor—Level of showing (25/50/100), special location or directional requirements, size if not 30 sheet, list other specifics—painted, rotary, etc.

Direct Mail—Size (height/width), number of pages, quantity, black and white/color specifics.

Medium Usage Strategy Examples Some examples of media vehicle strategy/tactic statements for a package-goods food client would be:

Use full-page, four-color ads in

Women's service magazines—*Women's Day, Family Circle, Ladies Home Journal*, and *Good Housekeeping*.
General interest magazines—*People* and *TV Guide*.
Regional/lifestyle magazines—*Sunset* and *Southern Living*.

For a regional retailer some examples would be:

Use a :30 television daypart mix of 30 percent daytime, 30 percent general fringe, 20 percent prime time, and 20 percent late news.

Use ⅓ page newspaper ads for continuity and ½ to full page ads to support major promotions on Thursdays in the main news section.

Some examples for business-to-business would be:

Use four-color, full page ads in *Food Processing* and use black and white, ½ page ads in *Food Engineering*.

Use black and white plus one-color, 6 by 11 inch postcard for frequency against the 1,000 key accounts.

Scheduling Strategy

Along with the selection of the optimum medium, media vehicle, and ad size/commercial length, you must also determine when the media should run. While the seasonality media objective provides guidelines for when to advertise throughout the year, the scheduling strategy provides specific direction of how the media is to be run.

Scheduling Approaches There are a number of different strategic approaches to scheduling.

Continuity schedules are just that, continuous and run at a relatively fixed, even level to help sustain nonseasonal/nonpromotion sales.

Heavy-up schedules incorporate incremental media weight to support periods of higher market activity, new product or campaign introductions, grand openings, and promotions.

Pulsing schedules run in a continuous on/off pattern, such as the media runs two weeks, then is off two weeks, on two weeks, off two weeks, etc. The on/off pattern is repeated on a regular basis. The pulsing schedule provides more media support when advertising, which helps cut through the media noise level in the market, making the advertising stand out from that of the competition.

Flighting in scheduling is generally three to six weeks of continuous advertising followed by hiatus periods or periods of no advertising. Flighting is used for short-term promotions and events, product introductions, and during periods of high seasonal sales.

Front loading is the running of heavier weight levels with the commencement of a media schedule when you kick off: seasonal advertising, new advertising campaigns, new product introductions/grand openings, promotions, and trade show announcements.

Scheduling Strategy Examples Once you have written your scheduling strategies, make sure you also include a rationale as well. Some examples of scheduling strategies for a package-goods product are:

Schedule a higher level of prime time television during the new creative introductory period.

Schedule prime time television in high impact flights.

Maintain strong levels of daytime television throughout all flights.

For business-to-business advertisers some scheduling strategies are:

Schedule continuity magazine advertising to run alternating months.

Schedule direct mail drops in months when magazine ads do not run.

Combine magazine ads and direct mail in each of the two months prior to the spring trade show.

Media Testing Strategies

If your media objectives call for a media test, then you want to include a media test strategy. This media test strategy should include a strategy statement on media mix, media vehicles/tactics, and scheduling, along with a listing of test markets, and how the test is to be evaluated.

However, keep in mind when testing media that you must include control markets for comparison. These control markets would be very similar to the makeup of your test markets and represent your normal base media schedules. Make sure you test only one media variable at a time so that you can read or evaluate the effectiveness of the media change being tested. Because media testing is a rather involved process, you should refer to a text that provides information on the testing of media.

Step 4

Development of the Final Media Plan with Calendar and Budget

Prepare and Review Alternative Media Plans

Having already set media objectives and strategies, you should by now have solidified your media thinking. You are now ready to rough out in calendar form a graphic representation of at least two potential media plans. Exhibit 14.8 presents a calendar for a hospital media plan. A blank planning calendar is provided in Appendix C. You should prepare alternative plans in terms of different media included, usage of each medium, scheduling, total media weight levels, and budgets. Then compare the alternative plans to each other in terms of total weight placed against the target

Exhibit 14.8   Graphic Calendar for a Hospital Media Plan

1991   **MEDIA CALENDAR**

EXAMPLE
GENERAL HOSPITAL
MADISON DMA
OCTOBER 7, 1990

Monday (Bdcst) Dates

Media	January	February	March	April	May	June	July	August	September	October	November	December	TOTAL TARGET RATING POINTS (TRP'S)
	31 7	14 21 28	4 11 18 25	1 8 15 22 29	6 13 20 27	3 10 17 24	1 8 15 22 29	5 12 19 26	2 9 16 23 30	7 14 21 28	4 11 18 25	2 9 16 23	

ADVERTISING PROGRAM — SUSTAINING — EMERGENCY AND OBSTETRICS — NEW SERVICE INTRODUCTION — SUSTAINING

ADULTS 25-54

TELEVISION :30'S MADISON DMA
20% DAY, 50% FRINGE, 30% PRIME
13 WEEKS AT 200 TRP'S PER WEEK
9 WEEKS AT 300 TRP'S PER WEEK
— 200 TRP'S PER WEEK / 300 TRP'S PER WEEK / 200/WEEK — **5300**

RADIO :60'S MADISON METRO
1/3 AM, 1/3 DAY, 1/3 PM
6 WEEKS AT 200 TRP'S PER WEEK
4 STATIONS
20 SPOTS PER STATION PER WEEK
— 200 TRP'S PER WEEK — **1200**

NEWSPAPER - JOURNAL AND TIMES
1/4 PAGE WEEKDAY (B/W)
8 INSERTIONS
— 1 INSERTION PER WEEK — **554**

NEWSPAPER - JOURNAL AND TIMES
1/2 PAGE SUNDAY (B/W)
5 INSERTIONS
— 1 INSERTION PER WEEK — **346**

OUTDOOR : #100 SHOWING
25 LOCATIONS PER #100 SHOWING
— 600-625 TRP'S PER WEEK — **15312**

TOTAL RATING POINTS: 22712

©1989 by Select Micro Systems, Inc.

---

market (reach, frequency, and GRPs). Also, compare corresponding costs to determine which plan meets the media objectives, maximizing the delivery of the message to the target audience at the lowest cost.

Finalize the Media Plan

After reviewing the alternative plans, you still might not be satisfied. Add to and/ or delete from the best plan alternative to meet your media weight and cost requirements. Even if you have a predetermined media budget, you will most likely have to revise your media plan once the first rough draft of the marketing plan is completed. You will revise your media plan in terms of the weight levels, type of media used, and timing in relation to the other elements of the marketing plan. If you do not have a predetermined media budget, you will most likely revise the media plan to arrive at a media budget that will fit into a fixed marketing budget or a marketing budget developed through a task basis.

Exhibit 14.9   Media Calendar Inclusions

Flow Chart	Product/Service/Store name
Headings	Market(s) name
	National
	Regional (describe)
	Group of Markets that receive the same schedule. Example: Tier I, Tier II, etc.
	(List markets on calendar or attach a list of markets by tier if there are too many
	markets for inclusion on the calendar.)
	Individual market name
	Time period of plan
	Date prepared
	Program/Season (across top—optional)
All Media	Target audience
	Total GRPs/TRPs
	Cost(s) of medium and grand total (optional)
Television	Daypart mix
	GRPs/TRPs per week and total weeks and weight
	Length of spot
Radio	Daypart mix
	Number of spots and GRPs/TRPs per week and total weeks and weight
	Length of spot
	Number of spots per station (optional)
Magazine	Name of publication(s) (attach list of magazines if extensive)
	Size of ad/color
Newspaper	Name of newspaper(s) (attach list of newspapers if extensive)
	Size of ad/color
	Edition
Direct Mail	Number of mailings
	Quantity per mailing
Outdoor	Showing
	Number of boards

Prepare a Complete Media Calendar

Once you have finalized the media plan, make sure you have a complete media calendar in your media section. A good calendar is complete by itself. If your marketing plan dictates a different media plan for each market or grouping of markets, or if you have test markets, make sure each is represented on your calendar. Or you can include a calendar for each market or grouping of markets. Depending on the specifics of your media plan, Exhibit 14.9 shows items that should be considered for inclusion in your media calendar.

Prepare a Media Budget Summary

Along with a finalized media flow chart calendar, also include a media budget that you can exhibit in a number of different ways depending on the needs of your marketing plan. Two media budget examples are presented. One details spending for each medium by quarter (see Exhibit 14.10). If you want to present more spending detail, you can break out your dollars for each medium by month using a similar budget format. If you want to show both weight levels and spending, you can detail GRPs/TRPs and dollars for each quarter or month using a similar format.

If you have included a number of different products or markets in the marketing plan that require specific media support, you should also include a media budget that details media spending by product/market and medium. This example is shown in Exhibit 14.11. (Worksheets for both formats are presented in Appendix C.) It is best to show your media budget summary in the media section and then include media totals as part of the total marketing plan budget which is included at the end of the marketing plan document (discussed in Chapter 17).

As in the media objectives and media strategies sections, you should include under this media graphic plan and budget section a rationale for the final media plan. This rationale should include a brief discussion of the alternate plans considered and why this final plan fulfills the needs of the total marketing program. Alternative plans and budgets discarded can be included in a marketing plan appendix.

Final Check of the Media Plan

As a final check of the media plan, ask yourself the following questions:

- Are the media objectives and strategies consistent with the marketing objectives and strategies; particularly those relating to target audience(s), geographic allocations, seasonality/scheduling, weight levels, and the product positioning?
- Is the media plan complementary and synergistic with advertising objectives, creative strategies, and execution?

Exhibit 14.10   Media Budget: Spending by Medium and Quarter

Product: Hot Dogs
Year: 1992
Date: 10/1/91

Medium	1st Quarter ($000)	2nd Quarter ($000)	3rd Quarter ($000)	4th Quarter ($000)	Total ($000)	Percent
1. Television	$5,250.1	$2,361.0	$3,648.1	$4,430.1	$15,689.3	51.4%
2. Newspaper	2,341.0	1,060.7	1,678.0	1,876.4	6,956.1	22.8
3. Magazine	1,960.2	900.2	1,005.8	1,246.7	5,112.9	16.8
4. Direct Mail	1,102.3	534.2	542.7	580.4	2,759.6	9.0
Total	$10,653.6	$4,856.1	$6,874.6	$8,133.6	$30,517.9	
Percent	34.9%	15.9%	22.5%	26.7%		100%

Exhibit 14.11   Media Budget: Spending by Market and Medium

Product: Apparel
Year: 1992
Date: 11/1/91

Market	Newspapers $M	Newspapers Percent	Television $M	Television Percent	Yellow Pages $M	Yellow Pages Percent	Spending by Market $M	Spending by Market Percent
A. Buffalo	$113.4	12.3%	$50.5	14.9%	$1.1	7.0%	$165.0	13.0%
Des Moines	106.6	11.6	19.7	5.8	1.9	12.1	128.2	10.1
B. Ft Wayne	49.7	5.4	18.8	5.5	0.9	5.7	69.4	5.5
Grand Rapids	46.6	5.1	36.6	10.8	1.1	7.0	84.3	6.6
C. Kansas City	114.0	12.5	51.5	15.2	2.9	18.5	168.4	13.2
D. Lincoln	50.4	5.5	14.9	4.4	1.2	7.7	66.5	5.2
Madison	55.6	6.1	19.8	5.8	0.8	5.1	76.2	6.0
E. Minneapolis	258.9	28.2	82.8	24.4	2.8	17.8	344.5	27.1
Omaha	62.7	6.8	21.8	6.5	2.2	14.0	86.7	6.8
F. Spokane	59.9	6.5	22.8	6.7	0.8	5.1	83.5	6.5
Spending by Medium	$917.	72.1%	$339.2	26.7%	$15.7	1.2%	$1,272.7	100%

- Is the media plan complementary and synergistic with promotion plans?
- Does this media plan demonstrate significant improvements over the previous year's plan?
- Does the plan provide a competitive advantage?
- What are the principal vulnerabilities of the plan, and how can they be addressed?
- Have alternative media plans been evaluated, and do these alternatives represent meaningful strategic differences?
- Have extra steps been taken to enhance the overall impact of the plan—tactical innovations, merchandising support, etc.?
- Are all media strategies and tactics actionable, and stated specifically enough to facilitate execution?
- Does the media plan provide for a realistic financial commitment and flexibility? Do the financial media commitments extend for an entire year? Are they noncancellable?
- Does the plan include test proposals that can contribute important knowledge and are actionable?
- Does this media plan make common sense, and meet with your real world experience?

DOS AND DON'TS

DO

- Remember to ask yourself the who, where, when, and how questions to determine media objectives before you select and schedule the media.
- Make sure you strive for a basic understanding of the reach, frequency, and weight levels necesary to *sell* your product.
- Make sure the media you select not only fully reach the target audience effectively and efficiently, but also enhance the message and are appropriate in terms of affordable advertising production cost.
- Remember our golden media rule: More than less and sooner than later.
- Attempt to dominate your medium of first choice before adding another medium to the mix.
- Use cost per thousand in evaluating media, but remember, the end result is cost per sale.
- Quantify the media before you use it and evaluate for its effectiveness after it runs.
- Concentrate on generating enough frequency to fully communicate the message and sell the product.
- When you have a small share of market and a limited media budget, the key term is media focus. Focus media by demographics, geography, time, and/or medium.
- Remember: If you are a retailer with very low per square foot occupancy cost versus the competition, you most likely will need greater media weight to attract customers.
- If you have a product with intangible benefits and that requires imagery, it most likely needs heavier media weight than other more tangible type products.
- Maximize your media investment with smart scheduling.
- Remember: The shorter the promotion period, the heavier the media schedule.
- Use heavier media weight in larger markets where the noise level is greater.
- The smaller the target market, the greater the need for awareness among this target to generate meaningful response.
- There is a greater need of unaided awareness for retailers who are *not* located in large traffic generating malls. A high level of unaided awareness is necessary among the target market to consider this type of retailer as a choice before the actual shopping experience.

- The more competition within a category, the greater the need to use heavier media weights to differentiate your product from the competition.
- If at all possible, determine your media budget by need, not by what you have in terms of budgeted dollars.
- Once you place your media schedule, make sure it runs and you receive what you paid for.

Don't

- If possible, don't use only advertising media as a percent of sales to determine the media budget.
- Don't underspend in your media plan, particularly for new product introductions, grand openings, test products, and promotions.
- Don't rely on preconceived ideas regarding media selection, but thoroughly review alternative media before making a final decision.
- Just because you have a quality product does not mean it will sell itself. In fact, the higher the quality, typically the greater the need for media weight to build awareness for the quality product's features.
- Don't fragment media dollars over many media, thereby diluting your effort.
- If you can't evaluate media with available data, don't guess which media is best . . . test!
- Don't exclude a medium from your plan without objective consideration and analysis.
- Don't let high gross medium costs scare you off—check out the CPM and CPS.
- Don't use guesswork to develop a media plan—use discipline.
- Don't expect the competition to stand still while you execute an aggressive media plan. Think as if you were the competition and then prepare a contingency media plan for both the short- and long-term.

MERCHANDISING

N ow that you have developed advertising and promotion plans and decided how to deliver their message through your media plan, it is time to focus on how nonmedia communication can enhance the effectiveness of your overall marketing program. Don't overlook the sales generation potential of this very basic, but effective marketing tool.

Start by reviewing the marketing strategies which apply to merchandising and the related problems and opportunities. Then when you are developing your merchandising objectives and strategies, remember that your merchandising program can effectively support and complement your more broadscale marketing and communication efforts.

Merchandising is a tangible communication link between your product and the consumer. Therefore, you need to make sure that this marketing tool is used in a manner which is consistent with the positioning and will complement the other marketing mix tools.

**From This Chapter
You Will Learn**

The definition of merchandising.

The issues affecting your merchandising plan.

How to develop your merchandising objectives and strategies.

OVERVIEW

Definition

We define merchandising as the method used to reinforce advertising messages and communicate product information and promotions through nonmass communication vehicles. Merchandising is a way to make a visual or written statement about your company through a different environment than paid media with or without one-on-one personal communication. Merchandising includes brochures, sell sheets, product displays, video presentations, banners, posters, shelf talkers, table tents, or any other tools that can be used to communicate product attributes, positioning, pricing, or promotion information through nonmedia vehicles.

Issues Affecting Merchandising

Merchandising Delivery Methods

Merchandising communication can be delivered through the following methods:

Personal Sales Presentation: Often brochures, sell sheets, and other forms of merchandising are used to enhance a personal sales visit. The material can guide the sales visit, provide visual and factual support of the sales presentation, and serve as a leave behind for the customer or prospect to reference.

Point-of-Purchase: In many product categories, over two-thirds of the actual purchase decisions are actually made at the point of purchase. For this reason, merchandising is a useful tool at the point of purchase to help affect purchase decisions that are made in-store. Merchandising materials can also be utilized at the point of purchase in the form of shelf talkers, table tents in restaurants, product displays, banners, etc. Merchandising at the point of purchase allows the marketer to make an impact on the purchaser above and beyond what can be expected of a product's packaging.

Events: Merchandising is utilized through special events or company functions where contact with the target market occurs through sales meetings, conventions, mass participation events, concerts, etc. Banners, product displays, or fliers are commonly used at mass participation events to communicate brand name, and product benefits to consumers.

Geography

Your merchandising plan should address where your merchandising programs will be executed. Will they be national, regional, local, or even in selected stores within a market?

Timing

The timing of your merchandising programs is also important. Therefore, the timing of the merchandising execution in relation to the other marketing mix elements must be decided. For example, your plan may require a brochure to be delivered prior to sales visits or after the advertising campaign kick off. Or, you may want a retail store's featured inventory displayed for the duration of an advertising media blitz.

Merchandising's Purpose

Also address what the merchandising is being used to accomplish. You need to describe what marketing tool merchandising will be assisting. Will you be merchandising product attributes, a new or lower price, a promotion, an advertising message, a personal sell-in presentation, etc.? In summary, you must decide upon the communication focus of the merchandising prior to writing this merchandising segment of the marketing plan.

HOW TO DEVELOP A MERCHANDISING PLAN

Step 1

Establish Merchandising Objectives

Your merchandising objectives should include:

- The number of merchandising pieces delivered or displayed at specific target location(s).
- The geography.

- The timing.
- Merchandising's purpose: the communication focus of the merchandising.

The following merchandising objectives might be established to help achieve your marketing strategies:

> Achieve placement of the new product display, communicating the product's benefits, in 40 percent of the grocery stores carrying the product line nationwide in the month of September.
>
> Obtain placement of price promotional tents June through August in 50 percent of the current accounts in the top ten markets.
>
> Display four product banners at each event during the concert series in all markets.

Step 2

Establish Merchandising Strategies

Your merchandising strategies should detail how to achieve your objectives in the following areas:

- The delivery and display method that should be used.
- How to achieve placement of the merchandising elements.
- Description of creative parameters for development of the merchandising materials.

Examples of merchandising strategies include:

> Use the personal sales force to deliver the brochure during sales presentations.
>
> Obtain placement of the shelf talkers by offering a competitive discount on each case in return for participation in the shelf talker program.
>
> Obtain placement of the brand identification banners by the sales force. Employ a weekly monitoring system to assure that the banners remain in place for the four-week period.
>
> The shelf talkers should incorporate visible brand identification and highlight the rules of the sweepstakes. An entry pad should be included.

A worksheet for you to use in developing your merchandising objectives and strategies is provided in Appendix C.

DOS AND DON'TS

Do

- Review your marketing strategies and your problems and opportunities prior to developing your merchandising plan.
- Think of more than one way to use merchandising. There are multiple uses and there should be multiple merchandising executions in your plan.
- Tie in existing creative from advertising, promotion, and publicity to your merchandising. An overall look provides for a unified communication effort and allows one marketing mix tool to reinforce the other.
- Find out from the field what merchandising tools are needed to help them increase their selling effectiveness.
- Make sure the merchandising materials sent to the field are properly utilized. All too often, there is a great deal of time and effort put into producing merchandising materials only to have them receive limited attention or not to be used at all.
- Make sure the merchandising materials that you develop are designed to fit into the retailer's store/shelf format.

Don't

- Don't ignore the importance of execution and persistence as the keys to a successful merchandising program.
- Don't think of merchandising at the last minute. Strategically incorporate this powerful tool into your mix.
- Merchandising materials are expensive. Don't be wasteful, make sure they get used.
- Don't expect your merchandising materials to be readily accepted by the trade. Develop a well thought out program that will assure acceptance.

PUBLICITY

his is the last marketing mix tool to include in your marketing plan. In most cases publicity will play a key but less important role in your marketing plan than many of the other marketing tools.

As with all the other marketing tools, before writing this plan segment, review the problems and opportunities section for specific input and the pertinent marketing strategies for direction.

From This Chapter You Will Learn

The definition of publicity.

The issues affecting your publicity plan.

How to develop your publicity objectives and strategies.

OVERVIEW

Definition

In this book, we will define publicity as *nonpaid media communication* which helps build target market awareness and positively affects attitudes for your product or firm. Publicity provides your firm or product with a benefit not found in any other marketing mix tool. Since publicity utilizes noncommercial communication through independent news media, it adds a dimension of legitimacy that can't be found in advertising.

Obtaining publicity for your firm or product can be difficult with no guarantees on placement or what is ultimately communicated, since publicity is nonpaid and to a large degree noncontrollable. But there are some things you can do to help generate publicity for your firm. These are discussed in the issues section of this chapter.

Before incorporating a publicity segment in your marketing plan, you should ask yourself three questions:

- Do you need and want the added dimension of legitimacy to your overall communications effort?
- Do you need additional media weight without media dollar investment knowing that there is no certainty to the amount (if any) and type of publicity you will receive?
- Are you willing to make the investment in time either through your company staff or an outside agency to garnish publicity knowing its up and downside? Will this investment be worth it?

Also, keep in mind that publicity is only *one* part of public relations. Public relations is very encompassing and deals with creating goodwill for an organization and affecting long-term public opinion issues. If you need in-depth information on public relations, refer to a text exclusively devoted to this subject.

Issues Affecting Publicity

Publicity Planning

Publicity doesn't just happen. In most instances, positive publicity is the result of a written, well thought out plan and a hands on executed program. Included in the publicity section of the marketing plan should be target market, objectives, and strategies. In most cases there are two target markets—the media which needs to be made aware of the news story, and the target market to whom you want to communicate. Before planning your annual publicity program make sure you review the relevant problems, opportunities, and marketing strategies. In addition, make sure that you thoroughly understand the interests of your *product's* target market and those of the *media* target market. Further, make sure before you prepare your publicity plan you have clearly delineated in your mind what you want to accomplish with this marketing tool.

Publicity Is Contingent on What Is Newsworthy

A major task in generating publicity is to attract the attention and interest of newspeople so that eventually your story can be communicated to the target market.

To obtain publicity you must have an angle of interest (hook) for the general public above and beyond the selfish interest of promoting your company. The press has no desire to turn its editorial copy into advertising. The press *does* have a need to provide newsworthy stories of interest to the public.

An estimated 80 percent of news releases are thrown away by newspeople because they are not deemed worthwhile to the medium's audience. Publicity potential was one reason we developed a Downtown Beach Party event for the Coors Young Adult department. The unusual twist of creating a beach party with a million pounds of sand in the middle of a downtown area, as a major charity fundraiser, enabled us to develop extensive television, newspaper, and radio publicity for Coors beer.

In addition to having a good hook, you also must get the attention of the media. To obtain publicity for Coors, charity volunteers in beachwear visited the media with press kits and buckets of sand. Follow-up telephone calls were then made to set up times for the press to photograph the sand dumping prior to the party and for beach tours the day of the party. Exhibit 16.1 is one example of the type of press releases used for this event.

Publicity Should Generate Added Awareness for Your Company, Product Name, and Key Product Attributes

Make sure that the publicity you receive creates positive awareness for your firm and its products. Also, if possible, try to tie your product to a newsworthy happening or event that is consistent with the product's positioning or will highlight its product attributes. A ski retailer sponsoring a sanctioned ski race gives a message that the ski shop is committed to serious skiing. And a ski manufacturer who sponsors the winning skier in the race has the implied endorsement of the champion and is communicating a great deal about the performance of its skis.

If you are sponsoring an event, try to have visual identification in the form of banners, hats, T-shirts, etc., visible the day of the event. Don't forget to get your company's identification on all potential spokespeople.

Exhibit 16.1   Press Release

DOWNTOWN MINNEAPOLIS BEACH PARTY
For the Benefit of the March Foundation
June 20, 1989
FOR IMMEDIATE RELEASE
For More Information Contact:
Margaret Haven
608–256–6357

Minneapolis City Hall's front yard, Fifth Street from Third to Fourth Avenues, will be converted into a block long beach on Saturday, June 29 for the first annual "Downtown Minneapolis Beach Party."

From noon until 6 p.m., Twin Cities residents can party on a manmade beach composed of 42 tons of sand dumped on Fifth Street during a fund raising party for The March Foundation. Live music, food and beverage vendors, and beach activities will also be scattered across the Hennepin County Government Center. Admission to the party is $1 or a bucket of sand.

Activities will include live music, featuring three local bands sponsored by KMLI radio, volleyball, tetherball, body building and tan line contests, and a sand sculpture contest beginning at 12:30 p.m. Prizes will be awarded to the most creative sand sculpture design for winners in three age groups: 6-12, 13-17, and 18 and up.

Event sponsors estimate about 10,000 sun worshippers will forgo the usual weekend sunbathing on Lake Calhoun and other area lakes for the downtown Minneapolis Beach Party. The event is cosponsored by Minneapolis radio station KMLI FM, the Adolph Coors Company of Golden, Colorado, and the local Coors distributor.

The night before party organizers will dump more than a million pounds of sand, raise volleyball nets, and erect lifeguard stands around the County Government Center fountain.

"These parties have been a huge success in other cities," said the local Coors Divisional Sales Manager. "Some of our beach parties have generated up to $50,000 for local charities."

The $1 entrance fee and proceeds from the sale of refreshments will go to The March Foundation. In addition, "The Lift" of Fridley, Minnesota, has donated a sailboard which will be raffled off at the Beach Party.

Types of Potential Articles or News Stories

Several types of articles and stories will generate publicity, if newsworthy.

Straight News Release Announcement of newsworthy events that would happen whether reported or not (opening new offices, new services, etc.) are of potential interest to the general public or specific groups. Workshops for businesspeople or customers, celebrity appearances, etc. are manufactured newsworthy events that are staged at least partially for publicity value. A straight news release of a newsworthy announcement can be sent to such company controlled media as a newsletter or mailing.

Feature Stories While the straight news release is a simple announcement of a future or current event, the feature article explores a subject of interest to the public and can occur at most any time. Ask yourself, "What do I know that the general public would like to, or should know?" Then develop meaningful news articles.

A successful how-to feature article must be genuinely instructive, providing a benefit to the reader. The benefit to the firm comes in subtly establishing the firm as a leader with particular expertise.

Concept Articles These are articles describing the basic concept of your business and why people should take advantage of the offering. An accounting firm might develop a concept article on why businesses should make use of a full-service accounting firm. The concept article stresses the importance of doing things in a particular way and the benefits to be derived from doing it in that manner. However, the reader cannot escape the unstated message that the people who wrote the article, or are quoted in it, are the experts in the field.

Opinion Piece Where controversy exists, so does the opportunity to reinforce a leadership image by taking a stand and communicating that stand. This can be as brief as a well written letter to the editor, or as detailed as a point of view article in local dailies, commentary in television news programs, testimony before legislative committees, etc. Opinion pieces also position the author and author's company as experts in the field. And, long term, the media may come to rely on you for input concerning other issues relevant to your field. In this manner you can become the official spokesperson for your industry, helping your company to be viewed as a leader in the field.

Public Service Advertising/Announcements (PSAs)

PSAs are advertisements run free of charge by the media. Although public service advertising is not a true form of publicity because you do control message content, it is very much like publicity because you do *not* control where, when, or how much the message will run in the media. The time or space for these ads is donated to nonprofit organizations, government agencies, and other groups judged worthy by the broadcast, print, and outdoor media.

The number of available PSAs is often a function of supply and demand for the medium's time or space. Television and radio stations, and to a lesser degree outdoor companies, usually provide more PSA support than newspapers and magazines. The broadcast media have a set number of commercial minutes to fill each hour and if the time is not purchased, they will often run public service announcements. The chance of getting PSA time is often greatest during the postholiday period of January and February, when demand for broadcast time and outdoor advertising is at a minimum. Summer months can also be a good PSA time, particularly for television.

It should be mentioned that it is difficult to generate print PSAs. Your efforts will be much better spent focusing on placement of broadcast and outdoor PSAs.

The Timing of Your Publicity Efforts Is Important

Whether it is a pure publicity activity or PSA program, the timing of placement is critical. When is the consuming target in the mode to purchase? When is the specific media in need of newsworthy information? The weekends are usually slow news times for the broadcast media and good time to place a story with a television and radio station.

HOW TO DEVELOP A PUBLICITY PLAN

Step 1

Establish Your Publicity Objectives

Your publicity objectives should be specific, measurable, and relate to a specific time period similar to your marketing, advertising, and promotion objectives. However, since publicity is not a paid, controlled message, it does not usually focus on affecting a target market behavior but rather on making the target market aware of the product or company in a positive light. Your publicity objectives should address the following:

- The specific purpose of the publicity effort (i.e., announce a grand opening, gain additional exposure for a new product, generate PSA support, etc.).
- The specific target market (medium and audience).
- The time period and marketplace.
- The expected level of exposure, by medium, to be generated from the publicity effort:

    An example of a publicity objective would be:

    In the next year, achieve maximum exposure among sewers for the grand opening events through the television, radio, and newspaper media in each of the 20 DMA markets.

    Obtain coverage from a minimum of two television stations and a minimum of three radio stations.

    Obtain coverage from a minimum of one newspaper before and after the event.

Step 2
Establish Your Publicity Strategies

Publicity strategies describe how to achieve the media coverage delineated in the publicity objectives. Address the following in formulating your strategies:

- Placement and type of news releases or stories.
- Coverage via interviews and/or news conferences with television, radio, newspaper and magazine editor representatives.
- Participation in talk shows and local interest programs such as *PM* magazine.
- Visibility at conventions, seminars, and public events.
- Public service announcements (if you are a nonprofit organization or can develop a joint effort with a nonprofit organization).

In developing your publicity strategies, also consider the following:

Make sure the news media is thoroughly aware of the event or product's news. For example, you may write news releases and deliver them in a memorable way. The Coors Downtown Beach Party news releases were delivered by local personnel equipped with flippers, scuba masks, and surfboards.

Detail a specific follow-up procedure to make certain the news releases weren't forgotten or lost, and most importantly, will be used in some manner.

Develop ways to tie the media into the publicity event itself. Or obtain a third party to help legitimize your requests for publicity support. For example, provide cosponsorship packages to media and charities in return for publicity. The media and charity cosponsors become cosponsors on all paid, printed advertising in return for predetermined publicity requirements both prior to and during the event.

Provide a unique twist to interest the media in providing publicity. This can be communicated in a news release or by phone to the media to pique their interest. Or, provide a chance for an exclusive interview in return for media coverage. This technique worked very well for our Famous Footwear client. Major news media were offered the chance to interview All-Pro Football Player Al Toon of the New York Jets in return for publicity surrounding the opening of a new Famous Footwear store.

Where possible, include memorable but appropriate product identification.

The following is an example of publicity strategies that could be developed to achieve a hypothetical publicity objective. Assume you are developing publicity strategies for the following publicity objective:

Achieve maximum radio and newspaper exposure in each market among young adults 18 to 24 for the five concerts to be staged in the next year, in five to be determined DMA markets.

At a minimum, obtain coverage from two of the top five young adult radio stations.

At a minimum, obtain coverage from a major daily before and after the event.

Potential publicity strategies would be:

Prepare four different news releases, each with a different newsworthy slant on the event to be delivered via mail and personally before and after the event.

Stress the various benefits to the charity in the news release, particularly how important the event is in regard to the charity's yearly fundraising.

Have the local press interview the concert performers and the local charity spokesperson incorporating company identification at the interview site.

A worksheet to use in developing your publicity objectives and strategies is provided in Appendix C.

DOS AND DON'TS

Do

- Plan your publicity effort. It doesn't just happen. Be as detailed as possible. Thoroughly review your target market and their needs prior to developing the publicity plan.
- Approach publicity knowing its limitations but also understanding the potential it provides.
- Make a specific effort to get the attention of the key media newspeople and editorial reporters.
- Be willing to persevere and be persistent with the key media people in order to achieve results.
- Provide the media with a meaningful benefit for featuring your firm, product, or event.
  A unique and/or timely story for their audience.
  A chance to cosponsor a program/promotion that is of interest to the local community.
- Work through or with another organization such as a charity or service group to provide credibility with the media and assistance in staging and publicizing the event.
- When possible include a photograph or illustration with your news release, as this sometimes increases the chance of getting your story covered (as eye catching or unique as possible).
- Provide a contact name and phone number to media representatives for further questions.
- Record and evaluate the publicity received to determine if the objectives were met and to improve your future publicity programs.
- Generating meaningful publicity is hard work. Do it right or not at all.

Don't

- Don't look at publicity as a substitution for advertising. You can't control the content or the amount of exposure. Look at publicity as an extra or bonus.
- Don't assess potential stories from a company perspective, but rather from a news editor's position. The media has a responsibility to stay objective and fulfill the needs of their audience.

- Don't confuse publicity with public relations. The first is to generate media exposure for your product. The second is more encompassing and deals with the long-term image of your product.
- Don't assume all media vehicles are the same. Take time to know the media vehicle and the kind of stories its people are interested in.
- Don't write your firm or product's whole life story in a press release. Give only the basic facts in two to three pages of triple spaced copy.
- Don't expect publicity efforts employed on a sporadic, hit and miss basis to be effective. Use it in planned, continuous manner.
- Don't overcommercialize your message. Try to provide needed information. If you are too self-serving, it will be difficult to obtain publicity.
- Don't generate publicity without considering its impact on your overall positioning.

MARKETING BUDGET,

PAYBACK ANALYSIS,

AND MARKETING CALENDAR

N ow that you have completed the objectives and strategies for each tool of your marketing plan, you need to prepare a budget, project a payback from the results of your marketing effort, and develop a marketing calendar. This process involves three separate steps.

- Develop a *budget* to provide estimated costs associated with each marketing tool used in the marketing plan.
- Utilize a *payback analysis* to determine if the results of your marketing plan will produce adequate revenues to meet sales and profit goals. If the payback indicates that your plan will not allow you to meet sales and profit goals, you may need to revise your budget and/or your marketing plan objectives and subsequent strategies and executions.
- Once you have reconciled your budget and payback analysis, a *marketing calendar* should be developed to provide a summary of all marketing executions in one visual presentation.

From This Chapter You Will Learn

How to utilize three basic budgeting methods: percent of sales, task, and competitive.

How to develop a payback analysis.

How to develop an integrated marketing calendar for your marketing plan.

BUDGETING OVERVIEW

Based upon our experience, no matter what budgeting approach is employed, it seems there are never enough marketing dollars. For this reason, the marketer needs to determine priorities for the plan, along with corresponding executional costs for the various marketing activities. Then, based on the priorities and associated costs, pare back the activities to meet the predetermined budget level striking a balance between what needs to be accomplished and what you can realistically afford. Ideally, you will be able to develop your own budget which is both realistic from a total spending standpoint and yet will provide the necessary resources to support a successful marketing plan.

HOW TO DEVELOP YOUR BUDGET

Step 1
Percent of Sales

The first step in developing a budget for your marketing plan is to review the amount spent on advertising/media, promotion, and total marketing by other firms in your industry. Usually, an industry standard exists which will provide the average percent of sales that will account for the advertising/media budget, the promotion budget and sometimes even the total marketing budget.

The major disadvantage with this method is that it creates a situation where sales determine marketing expenditures. However, the whole idea behind a disciplined campaign development is the belief that marketing affects sales. With the percent of sales method, when sales decline and there are problems to be solved, there is less money available to solve them.

The method makes most sense if used as a way to determine a starting point. This is how we recommend you use this method—as a first step in developing your budget. Additionally, if your firm has no real history with the effects of marketing and advertising, then the percent of sales method will act as a way to allocate expenditures that should be fairly consistent with industry standards. You can find the industry advertising to sales ratios for the standard industrial classifications (SIC) codes within a published report by Schonfeld and Associates. *Advertising Age* also publishes the advertising to sales ratio of the top 100 advertisers each year. Another source is *Fairchild Fact Files,* a publication which provides information on individual consumer industries. Annual reports and 10–Ks are another excellent source for this information.

Step 2
Task Method

The second step in developing a budget is to utilize the task method. This method attempts to develop a budget that will adequately support the marketing mix activity in your plan to achieve the sales and marketing objectives. To arrive at the total dollar budget, you must estimate the costs for each marketing tool execution involved in the plan. The assumption is that through a disciplined planning process, challenging yet realistic sales objectives were established, along with a marketing plan to meet those objectives. Thus, the budget will allow the objectives to be met in an efficient manner. An aggressive marketing plan will result in a more aggressive budget utilizing this method. However there is no *real* test of affordability or profitability which is why a payout analysis is presented in the payout section of this chapter.

Step 3
Competitive Method

The final step for consideration is to attempt estimating the sales and marketing budgets of the leading competitive firms. Then compare these estimates to your sales and marketing budget. This method might allow your firm to match or beat specific competitive expenditures, helping to assure that you remain competitive in the marketplace. The advantage of this method is it provides the potential for an immediate response to competitive actions. The disadvantages are that it is difficult to estimate competitors' budgets and it does not take into consideration the inherent potential of your firm based upon data developed from the business review. Utilizing this method alone, you may be restricting the actual potential of your firm based upon your competitors' lack of insight and marketing ability.

USING A COMBINATION OF THE THREE STEPS TO FINALIZE YOUR SUPPORT

If the data are available, we recommend using a combination of all three steps in finalizing your marketing budget. First use the *percent of sales method* to provide a guideline or rough ballpark budget figure based upon your product's historical spending and that of the marketplace. Used properly, the percent of sales number will help provide insight into whether you might be starting too low or too high based upon the experiences of other similar companies in your industry.

Next, use the *task method*. This will provide you with a budget that will be your best chance to achieve the stated objectives in your own marketing plan. The task method is not as biased nor is it limiting in that the budget is derived based solely upon what is required to provide for the success of your individual marketing plan. Product history and industry averages play a lesser role in this budgeting process. However, if the task method budget varies substantially from the percent of sales method budget, you need to review the reasons why your plan requires either substantially more or less expenditures than the industry average. If for example you are introducing a new product, you may be required to spend at greater levels than the industry average to obtain initial trial of the new product while still maintaining sales of your existing lines.

Finally, consider using the *competitive budgeting method* as a device to help you respond to competitive pressures in the marketplace. If your company is consistently spending less than a major competitor and it is losing market share while this competitor is gaining market share, then perhaps you might develop a budget that allows you to be more competitive from a spending standpoint. There is not much any marketer can do, no matter how sophisticated, if continually and dramatically outspent by the competition.

HOW TO DEVELOP YOUR BUDGET FORMAT

In preparing your budget you should begin with a rationale which outlines what the budget is designed to accomplish. The rationale covers:

- Restatement of the sales goals
- Marketing objectives
- Geography parameters
- Plan time frame

Following the rationale is a breakout of planned expenses by line item under each expense category. The budget line item categories include all applicable marketing mix tools along with any other miscellaneous marketing expense items such as research. The example shown in Exhibit 17.1 can serve as a prototype for your budgeting process. The only difference between this budget and one you may develop

Exhibit 17.1   Heartland 1991 Marketing Plan Budget

Rationale

The budget for the fiscal year is designed to:

1. Provide support necessary to meet the aggressive sales goal of increasing store for store sales 15 percent over the previous year.

2. Provide support necessary to meet the systemwide marketing objectives of:

   Increase existing customer purchasing rates from 1.2 to 2 purchases per year.

   Initiate new trial, increasing the customer base 20 percent above current levels of 5,000 active customers per store.

Marketing Mix Tool (Nov 5, 1990)	$M	Percent of Total Budget
Media		
Television (6 markets)	$350.0	31.8%
900 TRP's :30's		
900 TRP's :10's		
Newspaper (12 markets)	202.0	18.3
30, 1/3 page insertions		
Direct mail (12 markets/24 stores)	120.0	10.9
10,000 per store per drop		
Postage (4 drops per year)		
Media total	$672.0	61.0%
Production		
Television	$100.0	9.1
2:30 and 3:10 spots (to be used for two years)		
Newspaper	18.0	1.6
Type, photography/illustration for 30 ads		
Direct mail	100.0	9.1
Four direct mail drops, 240M pieces per drop		
Photography, type, printing		
Production total	$218.0	19.8%
Promotion		
Redemption cost	$120.0	10.9
Redemption cost of $5 off coupon in two of the four mailings.		
Estimated response of 5 percent		
5 percent × 480,000 mailing = 24,000		
24,000 × $5 = $120,000		
Media		
Media costs calculated in media section		
Production		
Product costs calculated in production section		
Promotion total	$120.0	10.9%
Merchandising		
Store signage	$30.0	2.7
20 signs per store per month to support planned media promotions and		
in-store promotions		
Point of purchase displays	10.0	0.9
Two pop displays per store to support the April and December		
promotions		
Merchandising total	$40.0	3.6%
Selling Costs		
Sales incentive programs	$20.0	1.8
Sales total	$20.0	1.8%
Research Costs		
Market research	$32.0	2.9
Market wide $20.0		
In-store $12.0		
Research total	$32.0	2.9%
Total budget estimate	$1,102.0	100.0%
Total sales estimate	$24,000.0	
Marketing budget as a percent of sales		4.6 percent

continued

Exhibit 17.1 — *continued*

Marketing Mix Tool	$M	Percent of Sales
Total Budget Compared to Industry Average and Previous Year		
Marketing as a percent of sales per plan:	1,102	4.6
Marketing as a percent of sales per industry average:		4.0
Index company budget to industry average: 115*		
Index company budget to previous year ($1,000M/$1,102M): 110		
Total Planned Budget Compared to Competition†		
Total planned budget for Company:	1,102	4.6
Total estimated budget Competitor A:	2,000	4.5
Total estimated budget Competitor B:	1,000	5.5

*In this example the planned budget would be 15 points above the industry average for marketing as a percent of sales and 10 points above the previous year's plan.

†If the data exists, we recommend that this analysis be accomplished on an individual market basis and a national basis. This will help demonstrate localized geographic spending policies of competitors.

is that your budget may have more line item expense categories. (A worksheet is provided in Appendix C.) If you are going to be developing new products there will be a new product development expense category. If you include publicity in your plan this marketing tool will also have a budget line item.

PAYBACK ANALYSIS OVERVIEW

An important part of any budget is the payback analysis. The payback analysis provides the marketer with a projection of whether the marketing plan or specific marketing programs in the plan will generate revenues in excess of expenses. The payback analysis should review both short-run and long-run projected sales and associated costs to estimate the initial program payback in year one and the projected payback in the second and third year.

Reconciling Your Budget and Payback Analysis

If the payout analysis determines that the marketing plan dollar investment cannot be justified, a rethinking and adjustment of sales objectives and marketing plan objectives, strategies, use of the marketing mix tools, and budget expenditures is needed. After this is accomplished another payout analysis is needed to further determine if the new plan will meet payout expectations.

How to Develop Your Payback Analysis

We recommend using one of two payback methodologies: the contribution to fixed cost or the gross margin to net sales.

Contribution to Fixed Overhead Payback Analysis

Many retailers, service organizations, and sometimes manufacturers use a contribution to fixed cost payback. It focuses on two sets of figures:

Sales and revenues.

All direct marketing costs associated with the sale of the product to the consumer.

Contribution to fixed costs or overhead payback results are determined by first calculating estimated gross sales and then subtracting cost of goods sold to derive a gross profit on sales figure. Next all variable selling expenses directly associated with the sales of the product (selling costs, advertising and media expenditures, etc.) are subtracted from the gross profit figure to provide a contribution to fixed cost figure. This method can be utilized to analyze individual marketing programs or a whole year's plan.

The contribution to fixed cost method is utilized because it accurately demonstrates the results of the marketing executions. Only the revenues and expenses directly attributed to each marketing effort are utilized in the analysis. By doing this, the marketer can judge each marketing program on its own merits and on the basis of whether it will contribute to help cover the company's fixed costs.

The short-term objective is to make sure the marketing programs generate enough sales to adequately cover the direct marketing costs necessary to generate the sales. The longer-term objective is to develop programs that cover both direct marketing costs and fixed overhead resulting in a profit to the firm.

Exhibit 17.2 provides a contribution to fixed cost payback example for a start-up direct mail/response program for an existing firm.

There are few limitations to this methodology for most companies. However, the question of capacity needs to be addressed. If for example you brew beer and you are at full capacity, the marketer would need to make sure that the revenues from *all the marketing programs* together cover both total variable marketing expenses and total fixed overhead. However, unless there is the issue of full capacity, *individual*

Exhibit 17.2   Contribution to Fixed Overhead Payback Analysis for a Direct Response Marketing Program

	Estimated Response		
Projected Mailing to 10,000 Customers	Low 1 Percent	Medium 2.5 Percent	High 5 Percent
Responses	100	250	500
Gross sales ($26 per order)	$2,600	$6,500	$13,000
Less refunds (5 percent of sales)	130	325	650
Less cancellations (2 percent of sales)	52	130	260
Net sales	2,418	6,045	12,090
Less cost of goods sold (40 percent)	967	2,418	4,836
Gross profit	1,451	3,627	7,254
Less selling expense			
Catalog production mailing (@ 20 cents per piece)	2,000	2,000	2,000
List rental	N/C	N/C	N/C
Photography	N/C	N/C	N/C
Type	N/C	N/C	N/C
Boxes, forms, supplies (2 percent of gross)	52	130	260
Order processing ($3.20/order)	320	800	1,600
Return postage	N/C	N/C	N/C
Telephone	10	10	10
Credit card (30 percent credit card sales with 3 percent charge from store's bank)	23	59	117
Total Expenses	$2,405	$2,999	$3,987
Contribution to Fixed Costs	$(954)	$ 626	$3,267

marketing programs should normally be judged only on their ability to cover variable expenses and contribute to fixed overhead. The overhead will be there whether the program is executed or not. *Thus if there is excess capacity,* it is always better to execute an additional program which covers the variable costs associated with the program and will contribute some additional revenue toward covering some of the fixed costs.

The payback analysis shown in Exhibit 17.3 is for a retail chain considering the implementation of its yearly marketing plan. (A worksheet is provided in Appendix C.) The analysis determines if projected sales will cover marketing expenditures allowing for a contribution to fixed costs and overhead.

Gross Margin to Net Sales Payback Analysis

With package goods marketers, payback calculations are sometimes analyzed slightly differently than for retailers. The gross margin often is defined as covering advertising, promotion and profit and is referred to as gross margin to net sales or sometimes as advertising, promotion, and profit (AP&P). For example, if there is a 40 percent gross margin, 40 percent of all sales would cover advertising and promotion costs (consumer and trade), and provide the profit. Furthermore, 60 percent of the sales would cover all allocated fixed costs (plant, equipment, etc.) as well as the variable selling costs (selling costs, salaries, raw material needed to produce product, etc.).

The example shown in Exhibit 17.4 utilizes the gross margin to net sales payback methodology. We are assuming a 40 percent margin on a new product. The payback analysis is projected for three years in order to determine both the short-term and the longer-term profitability for the new product. In this example the product is projected to payback sometime early in year three. (A worksheet is provided in Appendix C.)

Exhibit 17.3   Contribution to Fixed Overhead Payback Analysis for a Retail Marketing Plan

Assumptions

The plan will result in a 10 percent store-for-store increase in sales over last year.

Cost of goods sold will average 50 percent throughout the year.

Nine stores	$M	$M
Sales	$7,920.0	
Less cost of goods sold	3,960.0	
Gross profit		$3,960.0
Less:		
Media	$ 316.8	
Production costs	31.7	
Promotion costs	50.0	
Merchandising	30.0	
Selling	25.0	
Research	20.0	
Public relations/miscellaneous	5.0	
Total marketing mix tools		478.5
Contribution to fixed costs		$3,481.5
Fixed costs		3,081.5
Profit before taxes		$ 400.0

**Exhibit 17.4   Gross Margin to Net Sales Payback
Analysis for a New Package
Goods Product**

Assumptions:

$100MM product category, with growth rate of 10 percent per year.

Three competing brands in the category and miscellaneous private labels.

Introduction of new product at an expected margin of 40 percent.

	Year 1 Projections	Year 2 Projections	Year 3 Projections
Net sales	$10.0MM	$12.0MM	$13.0MM
Gross margin (40%)	4.0	4.8	5.2
Less promotion	3.0	2.5	1.5
Less advertising	2.0	1.5	1.5
Profit/(loss)	(1.0)	0.8	2.2

Use Your Finance Department for Help

If you are using the contribution method, you should review your financial operating statements to determine the amount needed to cover fixed costs. Or, your finance department can provide you with further details specific to your company, which will allow you to arrive at the sales needed to cover fixed costs and provide a profit for your company.

Furthermore, if you are using the net sales method, your finance department should be able to again provide you with an accurate margin figure as defined in this chapter.

MARKETING CALENDAR OVERVIEW

After the marketing plan budget and payback have been completed, it is time to summarize the plan on a single page. This summary should be in the form of a marketing calendar. When completed, the marketing calendar will serve as a visual summary of the marketing plan for the specific designated period or more likely, the coming year.

A marketing calendar should contain the following elements:

- Headings including product/service/store name, time period, date prepared, a geographic reference (national, regional, group of markets or tier) or individual market name.
- A visual summary of the marketing program week by week outlining all marketing tool executions, and including all other marketing related activities such as research.
- A visual summary of media weight levels by week.
- Prepare a separate marketing calendar if there are substantial geographic differences and also for test markets.

Exhibit 17.5 shows a prototype for you to follow when developing your own marketing calendar. A retail chain plan is used for the example. A blank calendar is provided in Appendix C.

Exhibit 17.5   Marketing Calendar for a Retail Chain

HEARTLAND	1991 NATIONAL MARKETING CALENDAR	DECEMBER 1, 1990

Monday (Bdcst) Dates

Media	January	February	March	April	May	June	July	August	September	October	November	December

MARKETING PROGRAMS:

Mainline Promotions — MAINLINE / MAINLINE / MAINLINE

Clearance Sale — CLEARANCE / CLEARANCE

Half Price Sale — HALF PRICE

Anniversary Sale — ANNIVERSARY

Price/Item and Thanksgiving Sale — THANKSGIVING

Holiday Sale — HOLIDAY

MEDIA ACTIVITIES:

Television
7 weeks of 200 GRPs
50% :10s & 50% :30s — TELEVISION

Newspaper
12 1/3-Page Ads — 1/3-PAGE NEWSPAPER ADS
12 1/4-Page Ads — 1/4-PAGE NEWSPAPER ADS

Direct Mail
4 Mailings
10,000 Per Store, Per Mailing — DIRECT MAIL

NON-MEDIA ACTIVITIES:
Point of Purchase Displays
In-Store Signage
In-Store Seminars
Promotion POP
Research
Market and In-Store
In-Store Price Promotion
Red Tag Sale
In-Store Volume Discount
Promotion & Gift Wrapping

©1989 by Select Micro Systems, Inc.

DOS AND DON'TS

Do

- Develop *budgets* utilizing the task, percent of sales and competitive budgeting techniques.
- Be prepared to change your *budgets* and/or your marketing plan after the *payback analysis* is completed if you are either over your predetermined budget or you determine your plan is not paying back at the expected rate.
- Visually show your entire year's marketing program on a single page *calendar*.

Don't

- Don't substantially reduce your *budget* without rethinking your sales objectives and marketing activities.
- Don't prepare a payback analysis that gives the results you are looking for. If your plan will not generate sufficient sales to cover expenses, change your plan.
- Don't forget to continually update your marketing budget and calendar whenever changes are made in your marketing plan.

EVALUATION

A fter completing your marketing plan you need to evaluate the results. An evaluation methodology should be established to assure ongoing evaluation of the marketing plan executions. This information will provide invaluable feedback from which to make modifications during the year. It will also provide a database from which to make strategic decisions that have impact on the following year's plan.

From This Chapter You Will Learn

How to evaluate your marketing plan execution(s) using two alternative methods: comparative and sales trend methodology and pre- and postresearch.

OVERVIEW

Upon completion of specific marketing activities such as an individual advertising campaign, a promotion, a pricing change, a media test, or a year-long plan, there should be an evaluation of the results.

Comparative and Sales Trend Method

This sales evaluation method analyzes current sales with the previous year's sales *prior* to, *during*, and *after* any given marketing execution. Sales are analyzed prior to the promotion period to determine if there was a downward, upward, or flat sales trend compared to the previous year's sales. Sales are also compared in this same manner to last year's both during and after the execution period. In analyzing the *preperiod*, the *execution period*, and the *postperiod* separately, added insight is provided on the affect of the individual test or marketing execution. Sales might have been trending down prior to the marketing execution. Even a small increase during the marketing execution period would mean that the marketing execution might have helped reverse a negative trend. Then, in analyzing sales after the marketing execution period, the marketer can begin to determine if the marketing execution had any long-term effect on sales. If the marketing execution was designed to gain new users or trial of the product, the sales results in the months after the execution will help determine if repeat purchase or continuity of purchase was achieved.

There are two types of sales trending methodologies: sales trending analysis with control markets and without control markets.

Sales Trending Analysis with Control Markets

This methodology utilizes control markets (markets with no marketing execution or markets receiving a mainline marketing execution) to compare against test markets receiving a new marketing execution or the marketing execution you want to analyze. Control and test markets should be similar in terms of sales volume, sales trending, distribution levels, penetration/marketing coverage, size, demographic profile, and other market and media characteristics. Also, there should be a minimum of two test and two control markets to guard against any anomalies.

In summary, control markets allow for a benchmark on whether the specific marketing execution was responsible for sales increases in the test markets. If the analysis demonstrates that sales and profits in test markets which received advertising were substantially above control markets which received no advertising, then the decision should be made to consider rolling out advertising to other markets.

Sales Trending Analysis without Control Markets

Whenever possible, we recommend using the sales trending analysis with control markets. However, for many businesses, control markets are not available because the business is located solely in one market or in a minimal number of markets. In other situations, the marketer needs to analyze results of a marketing execution that was implemented across all markets. In these situations, a sales trending analysis without control markets is used. Sales are analyzed before, during, and after the execution to determine if the period during the marketing execution received greater total sales and greater percentage sales increases or decreases over last year. Without control markets, the marketer can't be sure that the sales results are totally a function of the marketing execution. The results could be the effect of other market factors which caused marketwide sales increases or decreases for not only your company, but the competition as well. However, even without control markets, the sales trending analysis provides general insight into the success or failure of individual marketing executions.

Sometimes test market performance is compared to national or total company sales. In this case, the national or company total is used as a benchmark. The method is not as accurate as test versus control market evaluation, but it does provide a basis for comparison.

Pre- and Postresearch

Pre- and postmarket primary research is implemented both before and after the execution of the plan. Most pre- and postresearch involves awareness, attitude, and behavior tracking studies. These studies monitor the movement of awareness, attitude, and behavior variables both before and after the marketing execution.

While increased sales is a very valuable indicator of the success of a marketing execution, it is not the only one. Many times while sales remain relatively flat, there is a significant movement in awareness and attitudes. These shifts signal the probability of future increases in sales. As has been proven time and time again, with increase in awareness there is a good probability that there will be an increased level of purchases.

Pre- and postresearch can also serve as a diagnostic tool to help explain *why* sales went up or down. Research can uncover changes in consumer awareness of your product, attitudes about your product, changing purchase behavior patterns, or competitive strengths and weaknesses as reasons for increases or decreases in sales. Thus, the research evaluation method has the capability of providing more in-depth information than the sales trending method.

In summary, research allows the marketer to evaluate the success or failure of marketing and communication programs. Research can help you determine whether

Exhibit 18.1   Advertising Awareness/Attitude Indices

	No Advertising Control Markets			Advertising Test Markets			Net Gain
	Pre	Post	Difference	Pre	Post	Difference	
Advertising awareness	(100)	(105)	+5	(100)	(152)	+52	+47
Better source of energy information	(100)	(82)	−18	(100)	(135)	+35	+53
More concerned about energy conservation	(100)	(84)	−16	(100)	(127)	+27	+43
More concerned with the environment	(100)	(100)	—	(100)	(115)	+15	+15

you met your advertising objectives of "increasing awareness from 50 percent to 60 percent" and "improving the quality ratings of your product." In addition, research can help evaluate the success of other such marketing objectives as "increasing the sales ratio (percent of customers shopping who make a purchase) from 30 percent to 40 percent." Above all, research is an evaluation tool which lets you determine why your sales goals were or were not achieved.

The example in Exhibit 18.1 demonstrates the ability of pre- and postresearch to evaluate the results of an advertising program. In this example a utility was evaluating the effectiveness of its campaign to persuade consumers that it was a better source of energy information and more concerned about energy conservation and environmental issues. The numbers have been indexed for confidentiality. The results clearly provided the utility with insights into the effectiveness of the campaign.

HOW TO DEVELOP THE EVALUATION PROCESS

The growth rate of improvement sales trending model demonstrates how to measure your marketing activities. A retail example is used; however, a similar procedure could be established for any business type.

The only changes needed to make the model applicable to any business would be in the evaluation categories. These would be made consistent with the business. A manufacturer would use product sales and units sold. A retailer could use such measurements as visits, transactions, dollars per transaction, units sold and product sales. And a service firm would use sales and people served.

You should plan to use a similar method for your evaluation system. A worksheet is provided in Appendix C. However, wherever appropriate we suggest that the pre- and postresearch evaluation method also be utilized and that the research be executed by a professional research firm.

Growth Rate of Improvement Sales Trending Model Example

The following provides an example of an evaluation objective and strategies along with an execution format for the growth rate of improvement sales trending evaluation process.

Evaluation Objective

Develop a data feedback methodology to monitor and determine results of marketing test strategies and executions.

Exhibit 18.2   Test versus Control Market Dollar Sales Analysis: Test Period 2/24 to 3/30 (Weekly per Store Average)

	Last Year Dollars (000)	This Year Dollars (000)	Percent Change Dollars
Preperiod 1/20-2/23			
Test market—Detroit (2 Stores)	$121.0	$185.1	+53%
Control market—Indianapolis (2 Stores)	118.0	159.3	+35
Test Period 2/24-2/30			
Test market—Detroit (2 Stores)	29.0	53.4	+84
Control market—Indianapolis (2 Stores)	26.0	25.7	-1

	Preperiod Percent Change	Test Period Percent Change	Percent Point Gain/Loss
Growth Rate Improvement (GRI)			
Test market—Detroit (2 Stores)	+53%	+84%	+31%
Control market—Indianapolis (2 Stores)	+35	-1	-36
Net percent point difference	+18%	+85%	+67%

Incremental Sales: GRI: +67 percent × Test Period Sales $53,400 = Net Weekly Gain $35,778.

Note: The same method would be used for visits and/or transactions if the data are available.

Evaluation Strategies

Implement a disciplined data feedback system in order to quickly and easily evaluate sales activity for marketing planning and execution.

Utilize the growth rate of improvement (GRI) method.

Execution

Each *test market* is compared against a *control market* of similar type and number of stores and per store sales averages. The test markets receive the test activity and the control markets receive the regularly scheduled marketing activity. If you don't have control markets, the test market can be compared against your national system or all other markets.

Step 1

A *preperiod* is analyzed to determine sales trending prior to the test period.

Step 2

For the *test period*, the period during which the marketing program is executed, data are analyzed to determine sales trending.

Step 3

For the *postperiod*, the period immediately following a test period, data are analyzed to determine sales trending.

Step 4

Finally a *growth rate of improvement* is analyzed by determining the difference between visits, transactions, and sales dollars per store in the preperiod, the test

Exhibit 18.3   Test versus National Dollar Sales Analysis: Test Period 2/24 to 3/30 (Weekly per Store Average)

	Last Year Dollars (000)	This Year Dollars (000)	Percent Change Dollars
Pre Period: 1/20-2/23			
Test market—Detroit (2 Stores)	$121.0	$185.1	+53%
National system average	120.0	144.0	+20
Test Period: 2/24-3/30			
Test market—Detroit (2 Stores)	29.0	53.4	+84
National system average	27.0	31.6	+17

	Preperiod Percent Change	Test Period Percent Change	Percent Point Gain/Loss
Growth Rate Improvement (GRI)			
Test market—Detroit (2 Stores)	+53%	+84%	+31%
National system average	+20	+17	−3
Net Percent Point Difference	+33%	+67%	+34%

Incremental Sales: GRI: +34 percent × Test Period Sales $53,400 = Net Weekly Gain $18,156.

Note: The same method would be used for visits and/or transactions if the data are available.

period, and the postperiod. The data enables the marketer to determine incremental visits, transactions, and sales during the test period for each market and to evaluate the rate of success.

Whenever feasible you should utilize the growth rate improvement method to compare the preperiod to the test period, test period to postperiod, and the preperiod to the postperiod. The *preperiod is compared to the test* to determine if the test altered expected behavior. If the preperiod showed sales were flat and the test period demonstrated a marked increase in sales, a determination would be made that the marketing program executed during the test period was effective. The *test period is compared to the post* to determine if the marketing execution had a lasting affect and to gain knowledge on how much if any sales drop off after the test period. Finally, a very important long-term analysis is the *preperiod comparison to the postperiod*. This comparison shows if the marketing execution had a positive affect on sales *after* the test as compared to sales trending before the marketing execution or test period.

Examples of Preperiod to Test Period Comparisons

Two examples demonstrate a preperiod comparison to test period. Exhibit 18.2 compares a test market to a control market and Exhibit 18.3 compares a test market to the national system average.

DOS and DON'TS

Do

■ *Evaluate* the key elements of your marketing plan to determine their success.
■ Use what you learned from the *evaluation* process in your plan for next year.

Don't

- Don't just *evaluate* your total year's results. Whenever possible, evaluate each promotion, each campaign, and the effectiveness of each of your marketing tools. Then apply what you have learned.
- Don't implement a marketing execution without an agreed upon, up front *evaluation* methodology.

CONCLUSION

ow that you have an understanding of how to prepare a marketing plan, you can draw on the idea starters in Appendix A to help you actually develop and implement a successful marketing plan.

Once the marketing plan is written and approved . . . use it . . . constantly!

Use your marketing plan:

- As a continual guide providing ongoing direction for your company's marketing program.
- As a reference to answer questions.
- As a quantitative resource with which to make decisions based on fact, not on gut feeling.
- For perspective and focus when you get carried away in the minutiae of day-to-day execution.
- As a reminder of what you set out to accomplish for the current year and for future years.
- As a basis for evaluation.

Make sure all key staff members have read the marketing plan and understand it so they can carry out their specific marketing responsibilities and work together toward the same goals in a coordinated, effective, and efficient manner. To make sure the marketing plan is implemented in a timely manner, prepare an action timetable that lists each marketing activity to be executed along with person responsible and completion date.

It is a good idea to update the appropriate sections of *just* the marketing plan (not the marketing background section) on a quarterly basis to respond to the continually changing marketplace. Attempt to have in place at the end of each quarter an annual marketing plan that covers 12 months in advance of the quarter in which you are working. Change only those elements of the marketing plan that must respond to a change in the marketplace and require very advanced planning, such as promotion planning that affects inventory/production needs, real estate/facility considerations, and distribution requirements.

With this continually evolving 12-month advance planning, not only are you prepared for both the present and the future, but you will also save time when you again need to prepare your complete, formalized, traditional one-year plan. This formalized annual marketing plan should include the disciplined marketing planning process, which means preparing the marketing background data, incorporating updated and new information as well as the findings from your marketing plan evaluation. Accordingly, you should, on a continual basis throughout the year, collect pertinent market, competitive, and company data, and jot down ideas for the next year's plan while implementing the current year's plan. Based on the updated business review and the new list of specific problems and opportunities, you will then prepare a new annual marketing plan to be updated quarterly on a 12-month evolving basis.

In summary, remember the marketing plan is your real competitive advantage in an increasingly combative marketplace. It is the ultimate secret weapon in winning business battles. If your marketing plan is prepared with discipline and properly implemented, you can't lose!

CHARGE!!

IDEA STARTERS BY
MARKETING SITUATION

O n the following pages across the top you will find eleven column headings, each one corresponding to a different marketing situation you may encounter as you prepare and execute this marketing plan. On the left you will find idea starters grouped under each marketing mix tool. To use this idea grid, simply choose the marketing situation in which you find your product and the marketing mix tool with which you are currently working, selecting the best ideas for the specific situation. For example, if you are looking for promotion ideas to help open a new store, check under the marketing situation column head New Product/ Store Intro/Grand Opening in the Promotion section of idea starters from over 25 different ideas.

Idea Starters by Marketing Situation

Idea Starters for Each Marketing Mix Tool	Marketing Situations				
	Flat/Continual Decline in Sales	Increase Small User Base	Poor Repeat/ Limited Loyalty	Need to Build Amount Purchased	New/Greater Competition
Product/Service/Store					
Offer in more convenient, smaller/ larger sizes	X	X	X	X	
Make store easier to shop				X	
Test new department/product extensions	X	X			X
Provide follow-up repair/maintenance program			X		X
Reformulate/update product/retail concept	X	X	X		X
Add new products to line	X	X	X		X
New product for emerging market for specific need/ use	X	X			X
Test new shops/boutique/services within store	X	X	X	X	X
Provide home delivery/shop at home service	X	X	X		X
Provide product/service at home or on location	X	X	X		X
Offer money-back guarantee			X	X	X
Develop new products with existing products/materials or equipment/ technology	X	X			X
Develop more/varied uses for your product	X	X		X	
Develop private store brand/label and sell at value			X		X
Develop a different product by price segment in same category		X		X	X
Develop product for special uses/time of year (i.e., McDonald's Shamrock Shakes)		X			X
Develop special trial sizes	X	X			X
Do primary research for the product/ retail concept with potential target market/current customer	X	X	X		X
Branding/Packaging					
Change name to reflect repositioning of store	X	X			
Brand for direct association with target market					
Brand for creditability		X	X		
Brand by price category (i.e., Budget Rent-A-Car)					X
Brand for suggestion of quality or function					
Brand for communication of benefit					
Update packaging/signage for changing target market		X			
Package multiple units of same item together			X	X	X
Package different products together (i.e., shampoo with conditioner)		X		X	X
Include handy feature on package (i.e., spout, carry handle, etc.)		X			X
Include usage information inside or on package (i.e., recipe, additional uses, etc.)		X	X	X	X

	Marketing Situations				
Low Awareness	Need to Improve/ Change Image	New Product/ Store Intro/ Grand Opening	Seasonal Sales Problem/Opportunity	Need Support From Intermediate Markets/Channels	Regional/Local Market/Store Problem
		X			
			X		X
	X				
		X			X
		X			X
	X	X			
	X	X			X
		X			
		X			
	X	X			
	X	X			
		X	X		
	X				
		X	X		X
		X			X
X	X			X	X
	X	X			
X	X	X			
	X	X			
X	X	X			
X	X	X			
		X			
		X			

continued

Idea Starters by Marketing Situation—*continued*

Idea Starters for Each Marketing Mix Tool	Marketing Situations				
	Flat/Continual Decline in Sales	Increase Small User Base	Poor Repeat/ Limited Loyalty	Need to Build Amount Purchased	New/Greater Competition
Branding/Packaging—continued					
Include contest on package		X	X		X
Redesign package or store to serve secondary benefit		X	X	X	
Develop package for disposability, and/or increase shelf life		X	X		X
Develop permanent reader board inside and outside store that changes daily		X		X	
Package for visual sampling of product (see product through package window)		X			X
Build in additional feature for after use (i.e., package container becomes drinking glass)		X	X		X
Make package easy to stock for trade			X		X
Make package and display piece one in the same/dependent on each other		X		X	X
Research brand/package alternatives					X
Pricing					
Set up customer panel that monitors competitive pricing					X
Employ volume discount program				X	X
Vary price points by seasonality and market differences					
Price to skim (introduce at high price, then reduce price to broaden consumer base)					
Price at lower level to steal share	X	X			X
Match price to intended perceived quality of product (i.e., high price to support premium image)			X		
Penetration pricing—introduce at low price and hold		X		X	X
Cream pricing—introduce at high price and hold					
Employ flexible pricing, negotiate with each customer from highest to lowest price				X	X
Price based on replacement cost, not what was paid for product		X			X
Product line pricing (maintain similar price range for all products in line)					
Test higher/lower prices in various markets	X	X	X	X	X
Fit product to price ranges		X		X	X
Price all merchandise at one price		X			X
Parity price but regularly feature lower price specials for lower price perception	X	X			X
Distribution/Store Penetration					
Fully distribute product/penetrate each market before rolling out to other markets		X			X
Employ new channel—sell product in new/different retail outlets; retail through direct mail	X	X			X

	Marketing Situations				
Low Awareness	Need to Improve/ Change Image	New Product/ Store Intro/ Grand Opening	Seasonal Sales Problem/Opportunity	Need Support From Intermediate Markets/Channels	Regional/Local Market/Store Problem
		X			
		X		X*	
X			X		
	X	X			
	X				
		X		X	
				X	
	X	X			
				X	X
			X		X
		X	X		X
		X			X
	X	X			
		X			
	X	X			
					X
				X	
		X		X	
				X	X
		X			
	X				X
	X				
X				X	
		X		X	X

continued

Idea Starters by Marketing Situation—*continued*

Idea Starters for Each Marketing Mix Tool	Marketing Situations				
	Flat/Continual Decline in Sales	Increase Small User Base	Poor Repeat/ Limited Loyalty	Need to Build Amount Purchased	New/Greater Competition
Distribution/Store Penetration—continued					
Use exclusive/selective distribution					
Use extensive mass market distribution	X	X			X
Establish minimum distribution levels prior to use of other marketing activities (i.e., advertising)					
Continually monitor distribution/out-of-stock versus competition to understand performance	X		X		X
Letter/printed piece/sample/premium to purchasing agent, trade, etc.			X	X	
Concentrate store penetration in markets with high product usage and low media cost		X			X
Develop limited service satellite outlets in outlying areas to feed main facility		X	X		X
Intensive distribution employing trade discounts					X
Send sample of product to home of buyer/purchasing agent or spouse					
Optimum distribution/inventory for new product introduction/grand opening		X			
Offer merchandise on consignment or guarantee return		X			X
Provide co-op advertising program		X			X
Personal Selling/Operations					
Institute/strengthen sales commission programs	X	X	X	X	
Institute highly visible peer recognition program with reward	X	X		X	
Research and then fulfill vocation and avocation needs of staff—graduated dollar incentive program; free vacation/prizes for winning sales contest	X			X	
Change method of selling product, (i.e., direct versus manufacturer's representative)	X			X	X
Continuous sales training/seminars	X			X	
Sponsor all company events (convention, banquet, dinner, sales meeting, etc.)	X			X	X
Institute on-going feedback program from field on promotion, selling, merchandising, product, inventory, etc.		X	X	X	
Initiate ongoing internal competition among sales staff/districts/stores		X		X	X
Incentives/prizes for number of sales contacts and selling ratio	X	X	X		

	Marketing Situations				
Low Awareness	Need to Improve/ Change Image	New Product/ Store Intro/ Grand Opening	Seasonal Sales Problem/Opportunity	Need Support From Intermediate Markets/Channels	Regional/Local Market/Store Problem
	X	X		X	X
		X		*	X
		X			X
				X	X
X		X			X
X					X
				X	X
		X		X	X
		X		X	
		X		X	X
X		X	X	X	X
			X	X	X
			X	X	
				X	
				X	X
				X	X
		X		X	X
		X		X	X
		X	X	X	X
				X	X

continued

Idea Starters by Marketing Situation—*continued*

Idea Starters for Each Marketing Mix Tool	Marketing Situations				
	Flat/Continual Decline in Sales	Increase Small User Base	Poor Repeat/ Limited Loyalty	Need to Build Amount Purchased	New/Greater Competition
Promotion					
Half-price sale (buy one, get second at half price)	X	X		X	X
Sampling—free product/gift/service; on pack/in mail		X			
Free goods with purchase	X	X	X		
Media carried coupon	X	X	X	X	X
Salesperson carried coupon	X	X		X	X
Bounce-back coupon	X		X	X	X
Multiple coupon for greater redemption	X	X	X	X	X
Instant coupon redeemed when product purchased	X	X			X
Gambler's sale (everyone receives discount but discount amount is left to chance)	X	X	X		X
Cross-ruff package couponing by similar demographic targets	X	X			X
Stage "Let's Make Deal" auction on selected/sale merchandise	X		X	X	
Tie-in offer with noncompetitor in-store, on pack, in ad		X			X
Offer free/lower cost financing	X	X		X	X
Trial sizes	X	X			X
Low price as loss leaders	X	X			X
Use trial-to-loyalty continuity program	X	X	X		X
Free product with series of purchases via punch card	X		X	X	
Sweepstakes that require some show of product knowledge to enter					
Value packs	X	X		X	X
Premiums	X	X	X	X	X
In-store/department couponing	X		X	X	
In-store demonstration with sampling		X			
Free samples to the trade/buyers at office and home					
Discounts for special groups (seniors, students etc.)	X	X	X		X
Sweepstakes—on/in pack; in-store; in ad		X	X	X	X
Game with many/all instant winners and few big winners	X	X	X		X
Continuous specials on specific days/ hours	X	X	X	X	X
Use a grand opening of one store to sell all market stores for month(s)	X	X			X
Tie promotions to timely local, regional, and national events					
Free goods/discount for referring friend	X	X			X
"2 for 1" special	X	X			X
Provide a free service to bring customers to outlet	X	X			X
In/on pack coupon	X	X	X	X	X
In-store/other retailer cross-ruff couponing	X			X	X
Graduated open or coupon sale (i.e., 10 percent off one item, 20 percent off two, etc.)	X			X	X

	Marketing Situations				
Low Awareness	Need to Improve/ Change Image	New Product/ Store Intro/ Grand Opening	Seasonal Sales Problem/Opportunity	Need Support From Intermediate Markets/Channels	Regional/Local Market/Store Problem
		X	X		
X	X	X		X	
		X	X	X	
X		X	X	X	X
		X	X	X	X
		X	X		X
		X		X	X
		X	X		X
			X	X	X
			X		X
X	X		X		X
					X
					X
					X
X		X			X
		X			
X	X	X		X	
		X	X	X	X
		X	X	X	X
		X		X	X
X	X	X	X	X	
			X	X	
			X		
X		X	X		X
X			X		X
			X		
		X	X		X
		X			X
				X	X
					X

continued

Idea Starters by Marketing Situation—*continued*

Idea Starters for Each Marketing Mix Tool	Marketing Situations				
	Flat/Continual Decline in Sales	Increase Small User Base	Poor Repeat/ Limited Loyalty	Need to Build Amount Purchased	New/Greater Competition
Promotion—continued					
Premiums—free with purchase; self-liquidating; continuity (i.e., set of glasses)	X	X	X	X	X
Bonus pack (i.e., 20 percent extra product at no extra cost)	X	X	X	X	X
Refunds—mail-in for cash/coupons; rebates	X	X	X	X	X
Stamps			X		X
Volume discounts—reduced price; free item with multiple purchases (punch card); free case with multiple purchases	X		X	X	X
Make coupon as large as the page it is printed on		X			X
Free appealing gift to first 50 to 500 customers	X	X	X		X
Establish customer club (i.e., free coffee breakfast club)			X		
Coupon turn-about—promote acceptance of competitors' coupons	X	X	X		X
Pre/post clearance sales/specials	X	X	X		X
Develop value added specials by packaging items together at special price		X	X	X	X
Contest		X			
In-store display allowance		X			X
Discount allowance for product feature in retailer ad		X			X
Free new product with purchase of an established product	X	X			X
Premiums/prizes with contest for trade based on their knowledge of your product					X
Have charity sell product/dollar savings certificates	X	X			
Stage election/contest for naming the best local, regional, and national sports team		X			
Celebrate customer's birthday with free goods/specials			X		
Sell gift/dollar certificates (generates positive slippage)	X	X	X		
Free gift with purchase of dollar certificates	X	X	X		
Dollars-off purchase with donation to charity (i.e., bring used coat for needy, receive dollar discount)	X	X			
Double coupon—instant and bounce back coupons for immediate and subsequent purchase	X	X	X		X
Cross-ruff coupon from high to low volume and complimentary brands	X	X	X	X	
Retailers solicit co-op promotion support and tie-in with manufacturers and industry groups					

	Marketing Situations				
Low Awareness	Need to Improve/ Change Image	New Product/ Store Intro/ Grand Opening	Seasonal Sales Problem/Opportunity	Need Support From Intermediate Markets/Channels	Regional/Local Market/Store Problem
		X	X	X	X
				X	
				X	
			X	X	
X		X			
		X			X
	X				X
					X
			X		
		X	X		
X	X	X		X	X
X		X		X	X
X				X	
		X		X	
	X		X		X
X	X		X		
	X				
			X		
			X		
	X		X		X
X	X	X			X

continued

Idea Starters by Marketing Situation—*continued*

Idea Starters for Each Marketing Mix Tool	Marketing Situations				
	Flat/Continual Decline in Sales	Increase Small User Base	Poor Repeat/ Limited Loyalty	Need to Build Amount Purchased	New/Greater Competition
Advertising Message					
Stress product's quality/inherent drama/uniqueness		X	X		X
Stress brand name			X		X
Emphasize profitability of product to trade					
Feature consumer advertising to trade that will be supporting the product					
Use problem/solution approach when building market		X			
Use band wagon (everyone is doing it) approach		X	X		
Testimonial by authority/celebrity figure					
Comparative product/pricing	X	X			X
Feature alternative product uses	X	X	X	X	X
Use music for mood, entertainment, emotion, continuity, attention					
Use emotion to create difference for personalized commodity type product like beer, cigarettes					X
Educational/editorial type advertising to help build/preempt the market		X		X	
Use company spokesperson					X
Use animation for greater interest/ entertainment value					
For :30s use two integrated :15s/three :10s for different messages					X
Provide key decision information to encourage purchase		X			
Borrowed interest/familiarity for imagery and/or memorability with established music, sound, phrase					
Make sure audio and video in TV sync together for most effective communication					
Make sure you have adequate name identification—early and late product identification in broadcast commercials					
When logical and possible, "new"/ "grand opening" and "free" are powerful words to use in your advertising	X	X			X
Advertising Media					
Increase media weight	X	X			X
Use heavy television	X	X			
Use direct mail in store's trading area	X	X			
Use direct mail against competition's customer trading area					X
Build and use direct mail customer list for all heavy users	X		X		X
Test direct mail to new target markets	X	X			
Use multiple, smaller ads in same issue of newspaper/magazine					
For target market impact, test medium never used before	X	X			X

		Marketing Situations			
Low Awareness	Need to Improve/Change Image	New Product/Store Intro/Grand Opening	Seasonal Sales Problem/Opportunity	Need Support From Intermediate Markets/Channels	Regional/Local Market/Store Problem
	X	X			
X		X			X
		X		X	
		X		X	
X					
	X	X			
X	X				
X					
X	X				
X	X				
X	X	X			X
X	X	X			X
X		X			
X	X	X			
X	X	X			
X	X				
X	X				
X	X	X		X	X
X	X	X			X
X	X	X			X
X	X	X			X
			X	X	X
		X			
X		X			
X	X	X			X

continued

Idea Starters by Marketing Situation—*continued*

Idea Starters for Each Marketing Mix Tool	Marketing Situations				
	Flat/Continual Decline in Sales	Increase Small User Base	Poor Repeat/Limited Loyalty	Need to Build Amount Purchased	New/Greater Competition
Advertising Media—continued					
Use cable TV for specially targeted groups by usage, demographics and geography		X	X		
Roadblock same time period/news on all TV stations					
Target outdoor/transit around store, in concentrated area, near company buying office, competition		X			X
If available and efficient, use :10s/:15s for additional frequency					X
Provide radio station tie-in promotion in return for free spots					
Sponsor high rated/memorable television special once/twice a year if budget is limited					
Local/suburban newspapers to target selected areas	X	X			X
Stage periodic media blitz in TV/radio with spots every hour on all TV/top radio stations	X	X			X
Use :10/small space ads as teasers with frequency for product intro, grand opening, promotion					
Follow-up direct mail with telemarketing for increased response	X	X	X	X	
Negotiate free radio bonus spots, remote broadcast, etc. when purchasing radio spots from stations					
Use heavy radio schedule for high frequency	X				
Sponsor community events, local sports events (high school)			X		
Place multiple spots within the same program for immediate message reinforcement					
Use broadcast medium/large print ads to attract new customers/build the market	X	X			
Use unique coupon insert in print medium (i.e., bag, cut-out game, toy, etc.)	X	X			
Frequency trade mailings to office and home					
Free-standing insert (FSI) in newspaper (good coupon carrier)		X			X
Ethnic media to expand the user base	X	X			
Develop trade-out agreement with broadcast station exchanging advertising time for your product/service					
Use colored comics to reach whole family (adults, teens, kids) for cost of black and white		X			
Use direct mail/outdoor around new store in large multiple store market					
Manufacturers develop disciplined, aggressive media co-op program for dealers/retailers for added, efficient media weight					

		Marketing Situations			
Low Awareness	Need to Improve/ Change Image	New Product/ Store Intro/ Grand Opening	Seasonal Sales Problem/ Opportunity	Need Support From Intermediate Markets/Channels	Regional/Local Market/Store Problem
X		X			X
X		X			
X		X		X	X
X		X			X
X		X			X
X	X	X			
X	X	X			X
X	X	X			X
X	X	X			
					X
X	X				X
X	X	X			X
	X				X
X		X			
X		X			
X		X			
		X		X	X
X		X		X	
X	X	X			X
X		X			X
X					
X		X			X
X		X		X	

continued

Idea Starters by Marketing Situation—*continued*

Idea Starters for Each Marketing Mix Tool	Marketing Situations				
	Flat/Continual Decline in Sales	Increase Small User Base	Poor Repeat/ Limited Loyalty	Need to Build Amount Purchased	New/Greater Competition
Merchandising					
Use cross-ruff display to sell other products/departments	X	X		X	
Use buttons to suggestive sell				X	
Do tie-in display with noncompetitor		X		X	
Announce timely specials in store via P.A. system				X	
Feature new/add-on products at checkout				X	
Use same window signs to sell inside as well as outside store				X	
Tie-in all trade and in-store display materials to advertising					
Flyer/handouts in high traffic areas, on neighborhood bulletin boards					X
Communicate guarantee of product/ lowest price in store to enhance sale	X	X	X	X	X
Kids play area in store		X	X	X	
Decorate store with unique mobiles/ balloons				X	
Distribute coupons in store	X	X	X		X
Aisle, point-of-purchase (P.O.P.) displays to sell/sample product/ distribute coupons		X		X	
Use in-store advertising for point-of-sale (P.O.S.) awareness (i.e., grocery cart, video reader board)		X		X	
Provide demonstrations/lessons on how to use product and expand its uses (i.e., use of fabrics for home decorating, not just for sewing clothes)	X	X	X	X	
Make display compatible with product and target market (i.e., in-store shoot a basket display for athletic shoes)			X		X
When purchasing radio, newspaper, and magazines ask for free merchandising such as on-air contest and/or product merchandising to the intermediate/ consumer markets					
Have a grand open house to draw people and expose all areas of stores	X	X		X	
Bag stuffers with useful and changing message including specials	X	X	X		
Use TV monitor or large screen for in-store information, sales, entertainment			X	X	
Use store as deposit center for charity drive		X			
Use store as meeting place for groups/ clubs			X		
Answer store phone with special message			X		
Customer newsletter with timely information, promotion announcements, cross-ruff/discount coupons			X	X	X

	Marketing Situations				
Low Awareness	Need to Improve/ Change Image	New Product/ Store Intro/ Grand Opening	Seasonal Sales Problem/ Opportunity	Need Support From Intermediate Markets/Channels	Regional/Local Market/Store Problem
	X	X			X
		X			X
X					
	X	X			
X	X	X		X	
X	X				
	X	X			
X	X	X			
		X			X
		X			X
X		X		X	X
		X			
	X	X	X		X
X		X		X	X
X	X		X		X
	X	X		X	X
	X				
X	X				
	X				
	X		X		
X	X				X

continued

Idea Starters by Marketing Situation—*continued*

Idea Starters for Each Marketing Mix Tool	Marketing Situations				
	Flat/Continual Decline in Sales	Increase Small User Base	Poor Repeat/ Limited Loyalty	Need to Build Amount Purchased	New/Greater Competition
Merchandising—continued					
Shelf talkers whenever possible		X			X
Put information of product on video cassette for review by purchasing agent at convenient time in home or office					
Use shopping bag as walking billboard/reminder			X		
Merchandise future sales	X		X		X
Place product information/coupons at point of purchase		X		X	X
Publicity					
Tie-in with radio/TV station and charity to sponsor event		X			
Contribution to charity for every product sold		X	X	X	
Tie-in with charity and secure free PSAs from broadcast stations		X			
Request PSA support from media public affairs director, salesperson, and station manager		X			
Sponsor community events (i.e., fairs, community interest programs, etc.)					
Market by market visits by company representative with local news media people		X			
Charity tie-ins on special day(s) and gift giving times of year		X			
Provide game contest with prizes and coupons for spectator participation at sporting events, concerts, etc.		X			
Sponsor celebrity market tour/in-store appearance					
Feature representatives for various companies in retail outlet			X		
Provide news media with periodic stories on high interest topics relative to product/store/company					
Volunteer program for community activities (i.e., team physician for high school sports)					
Tie publicity events to introduction/ grand opening					
Send/deliver news release to news/ editorial staff with free product/ premium and/or in unique manner					

	Marketing Situations					
	Low Awareness	Need to Improve/ Change Image	New Product/ Store Intro/ Grand Opening	Seasonal Sales Problem/ Opportunity	Need Support From Intermediate Markets/Channels	Regional/Local Market/Store Problem
	X		X			X
			X		X	
	X	X		X		
			X		X	X
	X	X	X			X
		X		X		X
	X	X	X			X
	X	X		X		X
	X	X				X
	X	X	X			X
	X	X		X		
	X	X				X
	X	X	X			X
			X			X
	X	X	X	X		X
		X				X
	X	X	X			X
	X	X	X			X

WORKSHEETS FOR
THE BUSINESS REVIEW

T he following worksheets correspond to the steps in Chapter 2 of the Business Review. The purpose of the charts is to provide the marketer with a guide on how to assimilate data in order to answer the questions listed in each step of the Business Review. Note that there are ten business review steps and eight chart sections. Due to the nature of material covered in Steps 1 and 5 there are no corresponding charts.

Note that some of the worksheets do *not* appear in Chapter 2. These worksheets are prefaced with an introductory description.

Also included at the bottom of each chart is material to use as reference on where to find the information necessary to complete the chart.

Worksheets for Chapter 3, Problems and Opportunities, are also included in this Appendix.

Step 2

Review of the Consumer Target Market

WORKSHEET

Demographic Profile by Volume

Demographic Descriptor	Percent of Total Population (Total Population Number)	Percent of Total Purchases (Total Dollar/ Unit Volume)
Age		
Under 18		
18 to 24		
25 to 34		
35 to 44		
45 to 54		
55+		
Sex		
Male		
Female		
Household Income		
$15,000 and Under		
$15,001 to $24,000		
$24,001 to $30,000		
$30,001 to $40,000		
$40,001 to $50,000		
$50,001+		
Education		
Did not graduate high school		
Graduated high school		
Some college		
Graduated college		
Occupation		
White-collar		
Blue-collar		
Farmer		
Employment		
Full-time		
Part-time		
Unemployed		
Family Size		
1		
2		
3 to 4		
5 to 6		
7+		
Geography		
Urban		
Suburban		
Rural		
Home		
Own home		
Rent		

continued

Demographic Profile by Volume—*continued*

Where to Find This Information

SMRB (Simmons Market Research Bureau)

MRI (Mediamark Resarch, Inc.)

Fairchild Fact Files.

Census data/county business patterns.

Industry trade publication research departments.

Industry research studies (supplied through trade associations).

WORKSHEET

Demographic Profile by Concentration

Demographic Descriptor	Percent of Category that Purchases Product Nationally (%)*	Concentration Index: Category/Total
Age		
Under 18		
18 to 24		
25 to 34		
35 to 44		
45 to 54		
55+		
Sex		
Male		
Female		
Household Income		
$15,000 and Under		
$15,001 to $24,000		
$24,001 to $30,000		
$30,001 to $40,000		
$40,001 to $50,000		
$50,001+		
Education		
Did not graduate high school		
Graduated high school		
Some college		
Graduated college		
Occupation		
White-collar		
Blue-collar		
Farmer		
Family Size		
1		
2		
3 to 4		
5 to 6		
7+		

continued

Demographic Profile by Concentration—*continued*

Demographic Descriptor	Percent of Category that Purchases Product Nationally (%)*	Concentration Index: Category/Total
Geography		
Urban		
Suburban		
Rural		
Home		
Own home		
Rent		
Employment		
Full-time		
Part-time		
Unemployed		

*Provide percent of *total* population that purchases product nationally in the parentheses.

Where to Find This Information

SMRB (Simmons Market Research Bureau)

MRI (Mediamark Research, Inc.)

Fairchild Fact Files.

Census Bureau/county business patterns.

Industry trade publications/research surveys from trade associations.

Your company records.

WORKSHEET

Demographic Description of Company Purchasers Compared to Category Purchasers

Demographic Descriptor	Percent Purchasers of Product Nationally ( )*	Percent Purchasers of Company Product ( )*	Index: Company to National Purchasers
Age			
Under 18			
18 to 24			
25 to 34			
35 to 44			
45 to 54			
55+			
Sex			
Male			
Female			
Household Income			
$15,000 and Under			
$15,001 to $24,000			
$24,001 to $30,000			
$30,001 to $40,000			
$40,001 to $50,000			
$50,001+			

continued

Demographic Description of Company Purchasers
Compared to Category Purchasers—*continued*

Demographic Descriptor	Percent Purchasers of Product Nationally ( )*	Percent Purchasers of Company Product ( )*	Index: Company to National Purchasers
Education			
Did not graduate high school			
Graduated high school			
Some college			
Graduated college			
Occupation			
White-collar			
Blue-collar			
Farmer			
Employment			
Full-time			
Part-time			
Unemployed			
Family Size			
1			
2			
3 to 4			
5 to 6			
7+			
Geography			
Urban			
Suburban			
Rural			
Home			
Own home			
Rent			

*Provide total dollar volume in parentheses.

Where to Find This Information

SMRB (Simmons Market Research Bureau)

MRI (Mediamark Research, Inc.)

Your company records.

Primary research.

WORKSHEET

Heavy User Demographic Descriptors Compared to All User Demographics Descriptors

	Heavy User Demographic Profile	Total Demographic Profile
Age		
Sex		
Household income		
Education		
Employment		
Family size		
Geography		
Home ownership		

Lifestyle Description of the Heavy User Compared to the Average User

Where to Find This Information

SMRB (Simmons Market Research Bureau)

MRI (Mediamark Research, Inc.)

Your company records.

Primary research.

Step 3

Review of Business-to-Business Target Market

WORKSHEET

National Distribution of Businesses by Size within SIC Category

This chart demonstrates the total number of businesses that *exist nationally* and categorizes those businesses by SIC category. It also delineates the number of busi-

SIC	Total Establishments	
	Number	Percent of Total Census
Agriculture/Forestry/Fisheries		
Mining		
Construction		
Manufacturing		
Transportation		
Public Utilities		
Wholesale Trade		
Retail Trade		
Finance/Insurance/Real Estate Services		
Public Administration		
Percent		
Total Census		

Where to Find This Information

County Business Patterns, U.S. Department of Commerce, Bureau of the Census.

WORKSHEET

Company Distribution of Customers by Size within SIC Category

This chart demonstrates the total number of customers *a firm has* and categorizes those businesses by SIC category. The SIC categories could be further broken out if necessary (e.g., sporting good retailers versus the overall category of retailers). It

SIC	Company Customers	
	Number	Percent of Total Customers
Agriculture/Forestry/Fisheries		
Mining		
Construction		
Manufacturing		
Transportation		
Public Utilities		
Wholesale Trade		
Retail Trade		
Finance/Insurance/Real Estate Services		
Public Administration		
Percent		
Total Customers		

Where to Find This Information

Company data.

nesses by SIC within the six parameters certain employment and dollar volume of the business.

Percent of Establishments by Employment Size Class						Percent of Establishments by Dollar Volume ($MM)					
1 to 4	5 to 9	10 to 19	20 to 49	50 to 99	100+	000 to 1	2 to 9	10 to 49	50 to 99	100 to 499	500+

Dun's Marketing Service, a company of the Dun & Bradstreet Corporation.

also delineates the number of businesses by SIC within the size parameters of number of employees and dollar volume of the business. This chart can then be compared with the previous one to determine company penetration of each SIC category.

Percent of Establishments by Employment Size Class						Percent of Establishments by Dollar Volume ($MM)					
1 to 4	5 to 9	10 to 19	20 to 49	50 to 99	100+	000 to 1	2 to 9	10 to 49	50 to 99	100 to 499	500+

WORKSHEET

Revenue Distribution of Clients by SIC Category

SIC	Number of Customers	Total Company Sales per SIC Category	Average $ per Client ($M)	Index to Average (Average $ per Client/Average All Categories)	Index to Average (Total Sales per SIC Category/Average $ per Client All Categories)
Agriculture/Forestry/ Fisheries					
Mining					
Construction					
Manufacturing					
Transportation					
Public Utilities					
Wholesale Trade					
Retail Trade					
Finance/Insurance/ Real Estate Services					
Public Administration					
Total					
Average All Categories					

Where to Find This Information

Trade publications.

Company records.

WORKSHEET

Product Category Purchases by Outlet Type

Outlet Type	Where Consumers Purchase	Percent of Total Outlets

Where to Find This Information

Trade publications

Industry sources

WORKSHEET

National Distribution of Businesses by Size by State by SIC

This chart demonstrates the total number of businesses that *exist by state* and categorizes those businesses by SIC category. This provides a clear demand picture on a statewide basis, or even county by county if necessary, enabling analysis of

SIC	Total Establishments	
	Number	Percent of Total Census
Agriculture/Forestry/Fisheries		
Mining		
Construction		
Manufacturing		
Transportation		
Public Utilities		
Wholesale Trade		
Retail Trade		
Finance/Insurance/Real Estate Services		
Public Administration		
Percent		
Total Census		

Where to Find This Information

County business patterns, U.S. Department of Commerce, Bureau of the Census.

WORKSHEET

Company Distribution of Customers by Size by State by SIC

This chart allows for a comparison of *company business* with the total potential business in the marketplace. Through utilizing the previous chart, the marketer can

SIC	Company Customers	
	Number	Percent of Total Customers
Agriculture/Forestry/Fisheries		
Mining		
Construction		
Manufacturing		
Transportation		
Public Utilities		
Wholesale Trade		
Retail Trade		
Finance/Insurance/Real Estate Services		
Public Administration		
Percent		
Total Customers		

Where to Find This Information

Company data.

demand potential within more narrowly defined geographic trading areas. A chart for each state would be constructed.

Percent of Establishments by Employment Size Class						Percent of Establishments by Dollar Volume ($MM)					
1 to 4	5 to 9	10 to 19	20 to 49	50 to 99	100+	000 to 1	2 to 9	10 to 49	50 to 99	100 to 499	500+

Dun's Marketing Service, a company of the Dun and Bradstreet Corporation.

determine penetration of clients and focus emphasis against areas of high potential. A chart for each state would be constructed.

Percent of Establishments by Employment Size Class						Percent of Establishments by Dollar Volume ($MM)					
1 to 4	5 to 9	10 to 19	20 to 49	50 to 99	100+	000 to 1	2 to 9	10 to 49	50 to 99	100 to 499	500+

Step 4
Sales Analysis

WORKSHEET

Sales Growth Analysis of Company Branch or Product Categories Relative to Industry Trends

The purpose of this chart is twofold—first, to track growth of total company sales relative to total industry sales, and second, to track growth of company product categories as compared to industry product categories. There are specific product categories under both the industry and company totals.

	1986		1987		1988		1989		1990		1990 Percent of Category	Percent Change 1986-1990
	Units	$	Units	$	Units	$	Units	$	Units	$		
Industry Total												
Brand Category A												
Brand Category B												
Company Total												
Brand A												
Brand B												

Where to Find This Information

U.S. Bureau of the Census, current industrial reports.

Fairchild Fact Files.

Trade research.

Trade publications.

Sales and Marketing Management Survey of Buying Power.

U.S. Bureau of the Census, current industrial reports.

Company data.

Annual reports/10–K reports from public companies.

WORKSHEET

Industry Sales Compared to Company Sales

Year	Total Industry Sales M	Change	Total Company Sales M	Change	Your Company's Market Share
1986	$	%	$	%	%
1987					
1988					
1989					
1990					

Estimated Sales by Competitor	Sales 1986	Market Share	Sales 1987	Market Share	Sales 1988	Market Share	Sales 1989	Market Share	Sales 1990	Market Share
Competitor A		%		%		%		%		%
Competitor B										
Competitor C										
Total Market Sales										

Where to Find This Information

Industry research reports.

Trade publications.

Fairchild Fact Files/Government Census Reports.

Annual reports/10-K reports from public companies.

Company data.

WORKSHEET

Store-for-Store Sales

Market	Sales Volume (M)	Change from Previous Year	Number of Stores	Per Store Average (M)	Change from Previous Year	Per Store Average Indexed to System average ($ M)
City A						
City B						
City C						
City D						
City E						

Note: Make sure your year-to-year analysis of per store averages includes comparable stores that have been open for the full year.

Where to Find This Information

Company data.

WORKSHEET

Sales Seasonality by Month

Month	Company Percentage of Sales	Company Index to Average ( )	Industry Percentage of Sales	Industry Index to Average ( )
January				
February				
March				
April				
May				
June				
July				
August				
September				
October				
November				
December				

Where to Find This Information

Fairchild Fact Files.

Company data.

WORKSHEET

Brand Seasonality by Month

	Base*	November		December		Etc.
		Percent of Total Dollars	Index to Total Year	Percent of Total Dollars	Index to Total Year	
Company Brand X	%			%		
Company Brand Y						
Company Brand Z						

*Base equals total figures for the year.

Where to Find This Information

Company data.

Step 6

Purchase Rates/ Buying Habits

WORKSHEET

National Category Development Index (CDI)

DMA	Percent of U.S. Population	Percent of Product Dollar Volume	Category Development Index: CDI (Volume/Population)	Population Number (000)	Dollar Volume of Product Category Nationally ($000)	Per Capita Consumption
City 1	%	%			$	$
City 2						
City 3						
City 4						

Where to Find This Information

Sales & Marketing Management Survey of Buying Power

WORKSHEET

Company Brand Development Index (BDI)

DMA	Percent of U.S. Population	Percent of Dollar Volume	Brand Development Index: BDI (Volume/Population)	Population Number (000)	Dollar Volume Company (000)	Per Capita Consumption
City 1	%	%			$	$
City 2						
City 3						
City 4						

Where to Find This Information

Company data

WORKSHEET

Trading Areas by Store

Zip Codes Surrounding Store	Percent of Customers Over 1 Week Period
	%

Where to Find This Information

Company store survey.

Company mailing lists.

WORKSHEET

Brand Loyalty

Brand	All	Sole	Loyalty Index	Sole and Primary	Loyalty Index	All Users
	%	%		%		%

Where to Find This Information

SMRB (Simmons Market Research Bureau)

MRI (Mediamark Research, Inc.)

Primary research.

WORKSHEET

Purchasing Rates/Buying Habits

This chart provides examples of what can be achieved through this type of primary research. A "heavy purchasers" and "all purchasers" category is provided for each question.

Number of _____ (whatever the product category) purchased in one year.
   Heavy purchasers _____
   Purchasers _____

Number of stores usually visited to find what you want per purchase.
   Heavy purchasers _____
   Purchasers _____

Amount purchased per visit (dollars and units).
   Heavy users _____
   Users _____

Visits to *your store* per month/year.
   Heavy purchasers _____
   Purchasers _____

Visits to *all stores* per month/year.
   Heavy purchasers _____
   Purchasers _____

Purchases at *your store* per month/year.
   Heavy purchasers _____
   Purchasers _____

Purchases at all stores per month/year.
   Heavy purchasers _____
   Purchasers _____

continued

Purchasing Rates/Buying Habits—*continued*

Average purchase ratio in percent of people who purchase versus those who do not with each visit to the store.

Heavy users _____

Users _____

Where to Find This Information

In-store survey.

WORKSHEET

Trial/Retrial

Brand	Percent Ever Used	Percent Used Last 6 Months	Loyalty Measure: Percent Used Past 6 Months/Percent Ever Used
Company X			
A			
B			
Competition			
C			
D			
E			
F			

Where to Find This Information

Market survey.

Step 7

Distribution

WORKSHEET

Purchases by Outlet Type (5 Year Trend)

Distribution Outlet Type	Total Sales				Points Change 1986 to 1990	
	1986		1990			
	Units	Dollars	Units	Dollars	Units	Dollars
	%	%	%	%	%	%

Where to Find This Information

Fairchild Fact Files.

Trade Publications.

WORKSHEET

Store Penetration Analysis I

	Number of Stores	Sales Last Year (M)	Estimated Number TV HH's (M)	Sales per HH
Group 1 Markets (Weaker Markets)				
A				
B				
C				
D				
E				
F				
Subtotal				
Group 2 Markets (Stronger Markets)				
G				
H				
I				
J				
K				
L				
Subtotal				
Totals/Averages Groups 1 and 2				
Average per store sales Groups 1 and 2 $				

Where to Find This Information

In-house sources/company data.

SDRS

Nielsen Test Market Profiles

Current Advertising Plans		Future Advertising Plans			
5 percent of Sales (M)	Target Market Media Weight Level	Average Sales per HH	Number of Stores Needed	_____ Percent of Sales (M)	Target Market Media Weight Level

WORKSHEET

Store Penetration Analysis II

	Number of Stores	Existing Stores per 100M* HHs	Total Sales Last Year (M)	Advertising Budget: _____ Percent of Sales	Estimated 1 Week Cost	Estimated Number Weeks	Penetration of 1 Store per 100M HHs		
							Minimum 1/100M HHs	$	New Estimated Number Weeks
A									
B									
C									
D									
E									
F									
G									
H									
I									
J									
K									
L									
All Stores									

*Or whatever you determine to be the optimum.

Where to Find This Information

In-house sources/company data.

SRDS

Nielsen Test Market Profiles

WORKSHEET

Market Coverage Chart

	Coverage for Your Product	Percent of Total Product Business in Market % ACV	Percent of Shelf Space Given Your Product in Store	Percent Shelf Space for Main Competitors in Product Category	
				Competitor 1	Competitor 2
Outlet A		%	%	%	%
Outlet B					
Outlet C					
Outlet D					
Outlet E					
Outlet F					
Outlet G					
Outlet H					
Outlet I					

Note: An identical chart would be created for each key market.

Where to Find This Information

Store checks/interviews with store managers.

Nielsen.

SAMI.

Step 8

Pricing

WORKSHEET

Price of Your Company's Product Relative to the Competition During Key Selling Periods

	Price 1st Quarter	Price 2nd Quarter	Price 3rd Quarter	Price 4th Quarter
Your Company				
Competitor A				
Competitor B				
Competitor C				
Competitor D				

Where to Find This Information

Company data.

WORKSHEET

Distribution of Sales by Price Point (5 Year Trend)

	Price Range Product Category		Price Range Company's Product	
	Percent of Sales	Percent of Items	Percent of Sales	Percent of Items
1990				
$____ to $____				
$____ to $____				
$____ to $____				
$____ to $____				
$____ to $____				
$____ to $____				
1989				
$____ to $____				
$____ to $____				
$____ to $____				
$____ to $____				
$____ to $____				
$____ to $____				
1988				
$____ to $____				
$____ to $____				
$____ to $____				
$____ to $____				
$____ to $____				
$____ to $____				
1987 etc.				
1986 etc.				

Where to Find This Information

Fairchild Fact Files.

Company data.

Trade publications.

Step 9

Historical Marketing Review of Your Company versus the Competition

WORKSHEET

Annual Competitive Spending Analysis

Competitor	Total Dollar Expenditures	Share of Spending— Total Expenditures	Change from Last Year	Television			Newspaper		
				Total Dollar Expenditures	Percent	Change from Last Year	Total Dollar Expenditures	Percent	Change from Last Year
	$	%	%	$	%	%	$	%	%

Note: The above information should also be obtained on a *quarterly basis* to track seasonality of spending. If available, total dollars for each category should also be obtained.

Where to Find This Information

Media representatives from television stations, newspapers, radio stations, outdoor companies.

LNA (Leading National Advertisers) for national companies.

PIB.

RADAR.

Media Records.

BAR.

Magazine			Radio			Outdoor		
Total Dollar Expenditures	Percent	Change from Last Year	Total Dollar Expenditures	Percent	Change from Last Year	Total Dollar Expenditures	Percent	Change from Last Year
$	%	%	$	%	%	$	%	%

WORKSHEET

Competitive Analysis

Your Company	Competitor A	Competitor B	Competitor C	Competitor D
Market Share/Sales				
Current				
Growth/Decline Past 5 years				
Target Market				
Primary				
Secondary				
Marketing Objectives/Strategies				
Positioning				
Product/Branding/Packaging				
Strengths				
Weaknesses				
Pricing Strategies/Pricing Structure				
Distribution/Store Penetration/Market Coverage Strategy				
Geographic Sales Territory				
Store/Outlet locations and description of locations (e.g., for retailers strip center, mall, etc.)				
Personal Selling Strategies				
Promotion Strategies				
Advertising Message				
Media Strategies and Expenditures				
TV				
Radio				
Newspaper				
Outdoor				
Direct mail				
Other				
Customer Service Policies				
Merchandising Strategies				
Publicity Strategies				
Testing/Marketing R&D Strategies				
Summary of Strengths and Weaknesses				

Where to Find This Information

Your company's past experiences.

Primary research.

Fairchild Fact Files.

continued

Competitive Analysis—*continued*

Trade publications.

Industry 10-K reports.

Media representatives.

Field sales reps.

Radio TV Reports.

Step 10

Demand Analysis

WORKSHEET

Demand Potential

1. **Target Market**
   DMA population
   Target market

2. **Geographic Territory**
   Target market in store trading area

3. **Consumption Constraints**

4. **Average Purchases per Year per Customer**

5. **Total Purchases per Year in Category**

6. **Average Price**

7. **Total Dollar Purchases per Year**

8. **Your Company's Share of Purchases**
   Estimated market share of _____

9. **Additional Factors**

Final Demand Expectations for Your Company

Where to Find This Information

Business Review.

FORMAT

Problems and Opportunities

Corporate Philosophy/Description of the Company

Problems

Opportunities

Target Market

Problems

Opportunities

Sales Analysis

Problems

Opportunities

Product Awareness and Attributes

Problems

continued

Problems and Opportunities—*continued*

Product Awareness and Attributes—*continued*

Opportunities

Purchase Rates/Buying Habits

Problems

Opportunities

Distribution

Problems

Opportunities

Pricing

Problems

Opportunities

continued

Problems and Opportunities—*continued*

Historical Marketing Review of the Competition versus Your Company

Problems

Opportunities

Demand Analysis

Problems

Opportunities

C

WORKSHEETS AND FORMATS FOR THE MARKETING PLAN

The following worksheets correspond to the preparation of your marketing plan presented in Chapters 4 through 18 of this book. Their purpose is to provide the marketer with a strategic framework for effeciently preparing an effective, well thought out marketing plan. Use these worksheets to identify and compile material for each of the sections as well as to use as formats in completing your marketing plan.

WORKSHEET

Sales Objectives: Macro Method

Market and Share Data

	Market Sales Volume				Company Share Percent of the Market			
	$ ( )	Percent Change Previous Year	Units ( )	Percent Change Previous Year	$	Percent Points Change from Previous Year	Units	Percent Points Change from Previous Year
Previous 5 Years								
1								
2								
3								
4								
5								
Projections Next 3 Years								
1								
2								
3								

Three Year Sales Projection for Company

	Dollars			Units		
Year	Market Sales $ Volume ( )	× Company Share Percent of Market	= Company $ Sales ( )	Market Sales Unit Volume ( )	× Company Unit Share Percent of Market	= Company Unit Sales ( )
1						
2						
3						

WORKSHEET

Sales Objectives: Micro Method

Projection from Top: Sales Forecast for Manufacturing, Service, or Retail Category*

	Company Sales Volume			
	$ ( )	Percent Change Previous Year	Units ( )	Percent Change Previous Year

Previous 5 Years

1
2
3
4
5

Next 3 Years Projections

1
2
3

Note: Complete a worksheet for your company's total sales and a worksheet for each individual product or department.

*Based on your type of business, include in your sales projections dollars and units/transactions/persons served, and take into consideration *new* products, distribution channels, stores or services, and price changes.

Use net dollar sales to trade/intermediate markets.

Projections from Bottom: Sales Forecast by Distribution Channel for Manufacturers*

	Existing			New		
	Number	Dollars (MM)	Units	Number	Dollars (MM)	Units
Direct accounts		$			$	
Wholesalers/ Brokers						
Other						
Total						

Note: Develop projections for each year for a three-year period.

*In your sales projections, take into consideration *new* products, changes in distribution outlets, and price changes. Use net dollar sales to trade/intermediate markets.

continued

Sales Objectives: Micro Methods—*continued*

Projections from Bottom: Sales Forecast
by Store for Retailers*

	Stores	
	$	**Transactions**
Market	( )	( )

Name/Store number

Market total

Note: Develop projections for each year for a three-year period.

*In your sales projections, take into consideration *new* stores, products, and services along with price changes. Service organizations use service office/center in place of stores. Use dollar sales to ultimate purchasers. Service organizations use persons served in place of transactions.

WORKSHEET

Sales Objectives Expense-Plus Method
(Budget Based for One Year)
(Historical Review and Calculation)

Budget Based for One Year

Previous 5 Years	Gross Margin Percent of Sales	Profit Percent of Sales	Expenses	
			Percent of Sales	Dollars ( )
1				
2				
3				
4				
5				

Expected Margin _____ % − Expected Profit _____ % = Operating Expense _____ %.

Budget Expense Dollars $_____/Operating Expense _____ % = Sales Objective $_____.

WORKSHEET

Sales Objectives

Reconciliation of Sales Objectives

	Macro		Micro		Expense Plus		Composite Sales Objectives	
	$	Units	$	Units	$		$	Units
	( )	( )	( )	( )	( )		( )	( )

Short-term
1 Year

Long-term
2 year
3 year

WORKSHEET

Qualitative Adjustment of Quantitative Factors

Qualitative Impacting Factors	+/− Point Change	Percentage Adjustment	×	Composite Sales Objective	=	Adjusted Sales Objective

Total

Final Adjusted Average
(Total of adjusted sales objectives
divided by number of calculated
factors)   _____

Note: 1. List qualitative factors and to what extent they will impact on the previous numerically-arrived-at
sales objectives. Adjust composite sales objective(s) accordingly to arrive at final sales objective(s).
2. Use qualitative adjustments for units, transactions, or persons served, as well as for sales dollars
objectives. However, percentage point adjustment may differ from dollars.

FORMAT

Sales Objectives for Manufacturers

Short-Term (One Year)

1. Increase dollar sales _____ % over previous year, from $_____ to $_____.

2. Increase unit sales _____ % over previous year, from _____ to _____.

Long-Term*

1. Increase dollar sales _____ % from 19_____ to 19_____ , from $_____ to $_____.

2. Increase unit sales _____ % from 19_____ to 19_____ , from _____ to _____.

Rationale

Note: 1. Use this format for total company sales as well as for specific products.
     2. Include profit objectives as well, using a similar format.

*List two and three year sales objectives separately.

FORMAT

Sales Objectives for Retail and Service*

Short-Term (One Year)

1. Increase total sales _____ % and transactions _____ % over previous year, from $_____ to $_____ and from _____ transactions to _____ transactions.

2. Increase comparable store sales _____ % and transactions _____ % over previous year, from $_____ to $_____ and from _____ transactions to _____ transactions.

Long-Term†

1. Increase total sales _____ % and transactions _____ % for 19_____ to 19_____, from $_____ to $_____ and from _____ transactions to _____ transactions.

2. Increase comparable store sales _____ % and transactions _____ % for 19_____ to 19_____, from $_____ to $_____ and from _____ transactions to _____ transactions.

Rationale

Note: 1. Use this format for total company sales as well as for specific retail and service categories. Retailers might also want to use unit objectives as well. Service organizations use dollar and persons/companies served.
2. Include profit objectives as well using a similar format.

†List two and three year sales objectives separately.

FORMAT

**Target Market for Consumer
(Package Goods, Retail, Service)**
_____

Primary Market
_____

Secondary Market (Where Applicable)
_____

Users/Purchasers

Influencers

Trade
_____

Rationale
_____

_____

FORMAT

Target Market for Business-to-Business

Primary*

Secondary* (Where Applicable)

Intermediate

End User

Other

Rationale

*List decision maker(s) with descriptor whenever possible.

FORMAT

Marketing Objectives

Short-Term Objectives

Rationale

Long-Term Objectives

Rationale

FORMAT

Marketing Strategies

Build the Market or Steal Market Share Strategies

Rationale

National, Regional, and Local Marketing Strategies

Rationale

Seasonality Strategies

Rationale

Competitive Strategies

Rationale

continued

Marketing Strategies—*continued*

Target Market Strategies

Rationale

Product Strategies

Rationale

Packaging Strategies

Rationale

Pricing Strategies

Rationale

continued

Marketing Strategies—*continued*

Distribution of Product/Store Penetration Strategies

Rationale

Personal Selling/Operation Strategies

Rationale

Promotion Strategies

Rationale

Spending Strategies

Rationale

continued

Marketing Strategies—*continued*

Advertising Message Strategies

Rationale

Advertising Media Strategies

Rationale

Merchandising Strategies

Rationale

Publicity Strategies

Rationale

continued

Marketing Strategies—*continued*

Marketing R&D (Research and Development) Strategies

Rationale

Primary Research Strategies

Rationale

WORKSHEET

Positioning: Matching Product Differences to the Target Market's Needs/Wants

Key Competition

1

2

3

4

5

Differences from Competitor

Product/Store/Service Attributes/Benefits

New Products/Improvements

Packaging/Store Appearance

Branding/Name/Reputation

Distribution/Penetration

Price

Key Target Market

Characteristics—Needs/Wants

What

Where

When

Why (Benefit)

continued

Positioning: Matching Product Differences—*continued*

Differences from Competitor	Characteristics—Needs/Wants
Advertising (Message/Media)	**How Purchased/Used**
Promotion	**How the Target and Its Needs/Wants Are Changing**
Merchandising	
Personal Selling and Service	
Publicity	

WORKSHEET

Positioning: Mapping Product Importance
by Competitive Ranking

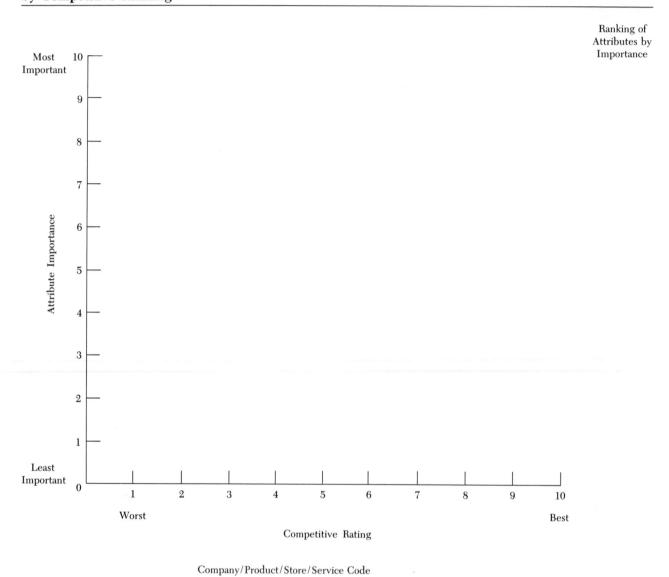

Ranking of
Attributes by
Importance

Company/Product/Store/Service Code

Name   Code

FORMAT

Positioning Strategy

Strategy Statement

Qualifier/Descriptors (Only if Necessary)

Rationale

FORMAT

Product

Product Objectives

Product Strategies

Rationale

FORMAT

Branding/New Name

Branding Objectives

Branding Strategy

Branding Parameters

Brand/Name Alternatives

Rationale

FORMAT

Packaging

Packaging Objectives

Packaging Strategies

Rationale

FORMAT

Price

Price Objectives

Rationale

Price Strategies

Rationale

FORMAT

Distribution

Distribution Objectives

Distribution Strategies

Rationale

FORMAT

Personal Selling/Operation

Selling/Operations Objectives

Selling/Operations Strategies

Rationale

FORMAT

Promotion

Promotion Objectives

Promotion Strategies

Rationale

FORMAT

Promotion Program Execution _____

Program Theme _____

Sales Objective _____

Promotion Objective _____

Promotion Strategies _____

Description _____

Support _____

Rationale _____

_____

WORKSHEET

Calculating Cost of a Coupon Promotion

	High	Medium	Low

Redemption Costs

Value of coupon
Number of coupons distributed
Estimated redemption rate
Number redeemed
Dollar value or offer (number redeemed ×
   value of coupon)

Advertising and Media Costs

Printing of coupons
Mailing cost/envelopes

Total cost of promotion

WORKSHEET

Payback Calculation for Open Promotion

Situation

Promotion:
Time period:
Geography:

Sales

Estimated sales for period without promotion
Estimated gross margin dollars for period without promotion
Estimated sales with promotion
Estimated gross margin dollars with promotion
Estimated net margin dollar increase with promotion

Media and Advertising Cost

Estimated ongoing advertising and media costs with or without promotion*
Total advertising and media costs with promotion
Incremental advertising and media costs due to promotion

Payout

Incremental margin sales
Incremental advertising and media expenditures
Contribution to fixed overhead

*What would have been spent in regular mainline advertising and media.

FORMAT

Advertising Message

Objectives

Awareness

Attitudes

Rationale for Objectives

Advertising Strategy

Promise

Support for this Promise

Tone of the Advertising

Rationale for Strategy

continued

Advertising Message—*continued*

Advertising Execution (If no separate advertising implementation plan is prepared)

Additional/Key Strategy Information

Specific Legal Considerations

Advertising Requirements

FORMAT

Advertising Implementation Plan

Date: _____

Product: _____

Job Title: _____

Prepared By: _____

Job Description: (including requirements/sizes)

Plan Approval

	Name	Approved	Date
1.			
2.			
3.			
4.			

Advertising Strategy:

Due Dates:

Concept	_____	Art/Photography	_____
Copy/Layout/Boards	_____	TV Shoot	_____
Client Ok	_____	Mechanical	_____
Preproduction (Print/TV/AV)	_____	Ship to Printer	_____
		Ship Finished Job	_____
		1st Air Date/Insertion/Use	_____

Budget:

Total Project Cost:

$ _____

Estimate needed from:

☐ Art/Photography

☐ Commercial Production

☐ Multiimage

☐ Print Production

Estimate needed by: _____

continued

Advertising Implementation Plan—*continued*

Guidelines for Writing Implementation Plans

Follow general order of subjects listed, selecting those which apply to the current job. If pertinent information is not available, indicate date it will be available. Attach additional information to this planning form.

Print	Radio/TV/Multiimage	Copy
Quantity	Storyboards	Product/Service
Stock	Medium (Film, Tape, Slides)	Objective/Strategy
Size	Length	Target Market (Attached
Colors	Music	additional information to this
Delivery, Mailing List/		planning form)
Labels		Benefits—Major
Proofs		Benefits—Minor
Printing Process		Exclusives
Preprints and Reprints		Buying Information
Publication Requirements		Appeal
Releases		Emotion
Art/Photography		Limitations
Price Information		Musts (Incl. Legal Requirements)
Logo, Sig. Code/Ad #		Research Info.
		Competitive Info.

Art	Budget Limitations
Layout/Storyboard Stage	Internal Time/$
Art Reference	Outside Suppliers/$ Available
Detail Information	

Name/Department

This copy for: ☐ _____

☐ _____

☐ _____

☐ _____

FORMAT

Media Plan

Media Objectives

Target Audience

Geography

Seasonality

Communication Goals
Quantitative

Qualitative

Budget (Optional)

Media Test Objectives (if applicable)

Rationale for Objectives

continued

Media Plan—*continued*

Media Strategies

Media Mix

Specific Medium Usage

Scheduling

Rationale for Strategies

FORMAT

MEDIA CALENDAR

YEAR: _____

BROADCAST MONTHS (WEEK BEGINNING MONDAY)

Media	January	February	March	April	May	June	July	August	September	October	November	December

FORMAT

Media Budget

Spending by Medium and Quarter

Company/Product/Service:

Year

Date:

Medium	1st Quarter ($)	2nd Quarter ($)	3rd Quarter ($)	4th Quarter ($)
Total	$	$	$	$
Percent	%	%	%	%

Spending by Product/Market and Medium

Company/Product/Service:

Year:

Date:

Product/Market	Medium							
	$( )	Percent	$( )	Percent	$( )	Percent	$( )	Percent
Total Spending by Medium	$	%	$	%	$	%	$	%

Total ($)	Percent %
$ ——————	——————
	100%

Total Spending by Product/Market

$( ) Percent	$( ) Percent	$( ) Percent
$ ———— %	$ ———— %	$ ———— 100%

FORMAT

Merchandising

Merchandising Objectives

Merchandising Strategies

Rationale

FORMAT

Publicity

Objectives

Strategies

Rationale

WORKSHEET

Marketing Budget

	($M)	Percent of Total Budget

Marketing Mix Tool
Media
  Television
  Newspaper
  Radio
  Direct mail
  Outdoor
  Other
  Total
Production
  Television
  Newspaper
  Radio
  Direct mail
  Outdoor
  Other
  Total
Product/Branding/Packaging
  Total
Personal Selling/Operations
  Total
Promotion
  Redemption cost
  Media support
  Production
  Total
Merchandising
  Production
  Total
Publicity
  Total
Research
    Total
Miscellaneous
    Total
Grand Total

Total Budget Compared to Industry Average and Previous Year

Marketing as a percent of sales per plan.
Marketing as a percent of sales per industry average.
Index company budget to industry average.
Index company budget to previous year.

Total Planned Budget Compared to Competition

Total planned budget for company.
Total estimated budget for Competitor A.
Total estimated budget for Competitor B.
Total estimated budget for Competitor C.

WORKSHEET

Contribution to Fixed Overhead

Payback Analysis

Assumptions

Sales
Less cost of goods sold
 Gross profit
Less:
 Media
 Production costs
 Promotion costs
 Merchandising
 Selling
 Research
 Public relations/miscellaneous
  Total marketing mix tools
Contribution to fixed costs
Fixed costs
Profit before taxes

WORKSHEET

Gross Margin to Net Sales

Payback Analysis

Assumptions

	Year 1 Projections	Year 2 Projections	Year 3 Projections
Net sales			
Gross margin			
Less promotion			
Less advertising			
Profit/loss			

FORMAT

YEAR: _____

MARKETING CALENDAR

Media	January	February	March	April	May	June	July	August	September	October	November	December	
MARKETING PROGRAMS:													
MEDIA ACTIVITIES:													
NON-MEDIA ACTIVITIES:													

WORKSHEET

Growth Rate of Improvement Sales Trending Model

Evaluation Objective

Evaluation Strategies

Evaluation Execution

Test Market versus Control Market Dollar Sales Analysis

Test Period _____

Preperiod versus
Test Period _____

	Last Year	This Year	Percent Change
Preperiod			
Test market			
Control market			
Test period			
Test market			
Control market			

Growth Rate Improvement	Preperiod Percent Change	Test Period Percent Change	Point Gain/Loss
Test market			
Control market			
Net percent point difference			

Incremental sales: GRI _____ × Test Period Sales $_____ = Net Weekly Gain $_____.

Test Period versus
Postperiod _____

	Last Year	This Year	Percent Change
Test period			
Test market			
Control market			
Postperiod			
Test market			
Control market			

continued

Growth Rate of Improvement—*continued*

Growth Rate Improvement	Test Period Percent Change	Postperiod Percent Change	Point Gain/Loss

Test market
Control market
   Net percent point difference
Incremental sales: GRI _____ × Test Period Sales $_____ = Net Weekly Gain $_____.

Postperiod versus Preperiod _____

	Last Year	This Year	Percent Change

Postperiod
   Test market
   Control market
Preperiod
   Test market
   Control market

Growth Rate Improvement	Postperiod Percent Change	Preperiod Percent Change	Point Gain/Loss

Test market
Control market
   Net percent point difference
Incremental sales: GRI _____ × Test Period Sales $_____ = Net Weekly Gain $_____.

Test Market versus National System Average Dollar Sales Analysis

Test Period _____

Preperiod versus Test Period _____

	Last Year	This Year	Percent Change

Preperiod
   Test market
   National system average
Test period
   Test market
   National system average

Growth Rate Improvement	Preperiod Percent Change	Test Period Percent Change	Point Gain/Loss

Test market
National system average
   Net percent point difference
Incremental sales: GRI _____ × Test Period Sales $_____ = Net Weekly Gain $_____.

continued

Growth Rate of Improvement—*continued*

Test Period versus Postperiod _____

	Last Year	This Year	Percent Change
Test period			
Test market			
National system average			
Postperiod			
Test market			
National system average			

Growth Rate Improvement	Test period Percent Change	Postperiod Percent Change	Point Gain/Loss
Test market			
National system average			
Net percent point difference			

Incremental sales: GRI _____ × Test Period Sales $_____ = Net Weekly Gain $_____.

Postperiod versus Preperiod _____

	Last Year	This Year	Percent Change
Post period			
Test market			
National system average			
Preperiod			
Test market			
National system average			

Growth Rate Improvement	Postperiod Percent Change	Preperiod Percent Change	Point Gain/Loss
Test market			
National system average			
Net percent point difference			

Incremental sales: GRI _____ × Test Period Sales $_____ = Net Weekly Gain $_____.

Index

About the Authors

Roman G. Hiebing, Jr., is president of The Hiebing Group, a consumer advertising, marketing, and consulting agency that has over the years provided full-service capability to a diverse clientele. These have included consumer goods companies, such as Kimberly-Clark, Coors, and Mercury Marine; retailers, such as McDonald's, Northwest Fabrics, and Famous Footwear; and service companies, such as Wisconsin Power and Light and Meriter Health Services.

Roman received his graduate degree in marketing and advertising from the University of Wisconsin where he wrote his master's thesis, "Territorial Marketing in Restaurant Franchising," a portion of which was published in *Restaurant Business*. The thesis was the basis for the Brat and Brau chain of restaurants he founded in 1969. In addition to his work in the agency and restaurant business, he teaches advertising and marketing in the Schools of Business and Journalism at the University of Wisconsin.

Prior to founding The Hiebing Group, Roman spent seven years with the Leo Burnett Company in Chicago working on such accounts as Kelloggs, United Airlines, Kentucky Fried Chicken, and Pillsbury. After his Chicago agency experience, Roman returned to Madison, Wisconsin, and became president of Stephan & Brady, a $17 million advertising agency that serviced consumer and business-to-business clients, such as Miles Laboratories, Parker Pen, and Grain Processing.

Scott W. Cooper is a partner and an account supervisor of The Hiebing Group, a consumer advertising, marketing, and consulting firm. He supervises the marketing and advertising activities of clients, such as Coors, Famous Footwear, and the First National Bank Group. Prior to his current position, Scott had experience in trade, industrial, and packaged goods marketing from both the client and agency side of the business.

Scott received his B.S. degree in economics from the University of Wisconsin and his M.B.A. from Miami University, Oxford, Ohio. He currently teaches retail and wholesale management in the Business School at the University of Wisconsin.

Scott also founded the Heartland Mail Order Company specializing in craft supplies. Based on this entrepreneur experience, and his client and agency experience, Scott coauthored an article in the May 1984, *Direct Marketing Magazine*, "Improve Company Operations with Quality Control Systems."

TITLES OF INTEREST IN MARKETING,
DIRECT MARKETING, AND SALES PROMOTION

SUCCESSFUL DIRECT MARKETING METHODS, Fourth Edition, by Bob Stone
PROFITABLE DIRECT MARKETING, Second Edition, by Jim Kobs
CREATIVE STRATEGY IN DIRECT MARKETING, by Susan K. Jones
READINGS AND CASES IN DIRECT MARKETING, by Herb Brown and Bruce Buskirk
STRATEGIC DATABASE MARKETING, by Robert R. Jackson and Paul Wang
SUCCESSFUL TELEMARKETING, Second Edition, by Bob Stone and John Wyman
BUSINESS TO BUSINESS DIRECT MARKETING, by Robert Bly
INTEGRATED MARKETING COMMUNICATIONS, by Don E. Schultz, Stanley I. Tannenbaum, and Robert F.
  Lauterborn
NEW DIRECTIONS IN MARKETING, by Aubrey Wilson
GREEN MARKETING, by Jacquelyn Ottman
MARKETING CORPORATE IMAGE: THE COMPANY AS YOUR NUMBER ONE PRODUCT, by James R. Gregory with
  Jack G. Wiechmann
HOW TO CREATE SUCCESSFUL CATALOGS, by Maxwell Sroge
SALES PROMOTION ESSENTIALS, Second Edition, by Don E. Schultz, William A. Robinson and Lisa Petrison
PROMOTIONAL MARKETING: IDEAS AND TECHNIQUES FOR SUCCESS IN SALES PROMOTION, by William A. Robinson
  and Christine Hauri
BEST SALES PROMOTIONS, Sixth Edition, by William A. Robinson
INSIDE THE LEADING MAIL ORDER HOUSES, Third Edition, by Maxwell Sroge
NEW PRODUCT DEVELOPMENT, Second Edition, by George Gruenwald
NEW PRODUCT DEVELOPMENT CHECKLISTS, by George Gruenwald
CLASSIC FAILURES IN PRODUCT MARKETING, by Donald W. Hendon
THE COMPLETE TRAVEL MARKETING HANDBOOK, by Andrew Vladimir
HOW TO TURN CUSTOMER SERVICE INTO CUSTOMER SALES, by Bernard Katz
THE MARKETING PLAN, by Robert K. Skacel
ADVERTISING & MARKETING CHECKLISTS, by Ron Kaatz
SECRETS OF SUCCESSFUL DIRECT MAIL, by Richard V. Benson
U.S. DEPARTMENT OF COMMERCE GUIDE TO EXPORTING
HOW TO GET PEOPLE TO DO THINGS YOUR WAY, by J. Robert Parkinson
THE 1-DAY MARKETING PLAN, by Roman A. Hiebing, Jr. and Scott W. Cooper
HOW TO WRITE A SUCCESSFUL MARKETING PLAN, by Roman G. Hiebing, Jr. and Scott W. Cooper
DEVELOPING, IMPLEMENTING, AND MANAGING EFFECTIVE MARKETING PLANS, by Hal Goetsch
HOW TO EVALUATE AND IMPROVE YOUR MARKETING DEPARTMENT, by Keith Sparling and Gerard Earls
SELLING TO A SEGMENTED MARKET, by Chester A. Swenson
MARKET-ORIENTED PRICING, by Michael Morris and Gene Morris
STATE-OF-THE-ART MARKETING RESEARCH, by A.B. Blankenship and George E. Breen
WAS THERE A PEPSI GENERATION BEFORE PEPSI DISCOVERED IT?, by Stanley C. Hollander and Richard Germain
BUSINESS TO BUSINESS COMMUNICATIONS HANDBOOK, by Fred Messner
SALES LEADS: HOW TO CONVERT EVERY PROSPECT INTO A CUSTOMER, by Robert Donath, James Obermeyer, Carol
  Dixon and Richard Crocker
AMA MARKETING TOOLBOX (SERIES), by David Parmerlee & Allan Sutherlin
AMA COMPLETE GUIDE TO SMALL BUSINESS MARKETING, by Ken Cook
101 TIPS FOR MORE PROFITABLE CATALOGS, by Maxwell Sroge
HOW TO GET THE MOST OUT OF TRADE SHOWS, by Steve Miller
HOW TO GET THE MOST OUT OF SALES MEETINGS, by James Dance
MARKETING TO CHINA, by Xu Bai Yi
STRATEGIC MARKET PLANNING, by Robert J. Hamper and L. Sue Baugh
COMMONSENSE DIRECT MARKETING, Second Edition, by Drayton Bird
NTC'S DICTIONARY OF DIRECT MAIL AND MAILING LIST TERMINOLOGY AND TECHNIQUES, by Nat G. Bodian

For further information or a current catalog, write:
NTC Business Books
a division of *NTC Publishing Group*
4255 West Touhy Avenue
Lincolnwood, Illinois 60646-1975 U.S.A.